T0301642

Working Time

Working Time

Theory and Policy Implications

François Contensou

Professor of Economics, ESSEC, France

Radu Vranceanu

Associate Professor of Economics, ESSEC, France

Edward Elgar
Cheltenham, UK • Northampton, MA, USA

Published by
Edward Elgar Publishing Limited
Glensanda House
Montpellier Parade
Cheltenham
Glos GL50 1UA
UK

Edward Elgar Publishing, Inc.
136 West Street
Suite 202
Northampton
Massachusetts 01060
USA

A catalogue record for this book
is available from the British Library

Library of Congress Cataloguing in Publication Data

Contensou, François, 1944–
    Working time : theory and policy implications / François Contensou,
        Radu Vranceanu
    Includes bibliographical references and index.
    1. Hours of labor. 2. Labor economics. I. Vranceanu, Radu, 1964– II. Title.

HD5106.C645 2000
331'.01—dc21   99–088518

ISBN 978 1 85898 996 9

Printed and bound by CPI Group (UK) Ltd, Croydon, CR0 4YY

Contents

List of Figures

List of Tables

Foreword

The activity of the productive sector of the economy amounts to destroying leisure time and other renewable or non renewable resources to create goods and services. In the now ubiquitous decentralized private economies, the rhythm of the productive machinery, as measured by its requirements in terms of human working time, is not decreed. As a market fact, having direct and overwhelming consequences on output and welfare, a clear understanding of its determination is a first order necessity.

A simple answer has been proposed by the elementary version of the neoclassical school, which boldly considers working time as a regular commodity. In this analysis, working time is explained jointly by the terms in which destroyed leisure time creates goods, depending upon the applied technology, and by consumption/leisure preferences. Free workers must be retained at the working place by wages able to compensate the disutility of work, and stay as long as this compensation is effective; for a given technology, actual working time in a competitive economy would be determined, in last resort, by their individual psychology.

Hard facts, however, are not easily reconciled with simple models. If free markets generally bring out Walrasian equilibrium, in which, owing to flexibility of the wage rate and other prices, all forms of rationing are eliminated, how can we account for unemployment or for the dissatisfaction with actual working time steadily reported by incumbent workers?

In particular, market forces sometimes lead to a paradoxical situation in which overwork by insiders and joblessness are simultaneously to be deplored, unsurprisingly nurturing the development of the work-sharing paradigm. If the productive sector induces a lopsided distribution of tasks in which some individuals work too much and others not at all, why should governments abstain from imposing time limits expected to compel the firms to reshuffle their demand for labor services in favor of the unemployed?

This paradigm, based on an alleged market failure, has gained some political momentum in the countries plagued by substantial unemployment figures, especially where the cultural context indulges government interference in the economy. This explains why the rationale behind working time regulation has shifted in such places from health safeguarding to job sharing considerations.

It must be acknowledged that if calls for capped working time are sometimes stated in naive and oversimplified terms, the tools of received economic theory cannot be readily applied to the challenging question of predicting the reaction of a market economy to such regulation. Economic theory has in fact evolved and refined its concepts at length with some benign neglect for working time issues. Only in recent years, a host of labor economists, to mention only Alison Booth, Pierre Cahuc, Lars Calmfors, Felix FitzRoy, Daniel Hamermesh, Robert Hart or Michael Hoel, have brought a significant contribution into this field of academic literature.

The state of the art explains why this book does not present itself as a frontal attack on the problem of working time mandatory reduction. It aims chiefly at reconsidering labor contract theory with an emphasis on working time determination in a series of different economic or analytical contexts. As a main contribution, utility competition has been extensively applied to static and dynamic analysis of the market for labor services and has proved a convenient way of including both wages and working time in the participation constraint which firms have to accept.

The sensitivity of employment to imposed maximum working time is examined at each step as an application. Our analyses shed their own light on this topic, and emphasize the general conditions under which such a policy may be effective. It turns out that the obtained relationship between working time and employment may be quite complex, even if significant simplifying assumptions are taken for granted with respect to the functioning of the economy. Such a conclusion should temper sanguine optimism in this matter, and a serious diagnosis before embarking on such policies is clearly called for.

It must be noticed that all the results have in fact been obtained in line with the neoclassical paradigm, only improving the terms of its application within its own method. Further research may still be contemplated along these lines: interaction of labor demand and productive equipment, effects of working time on the accumulation and growth process, interaction between effort variables and working time and so on. Other important developments might be derived from more consideration bestowed on externalities. Working time affects more than the individual worker's utility. Leisure time in common within different social groups makes possible specific activities and may also create congestion effects, adding to the complexity of defining optimum states and describing the rules of their decentralization.

The text is organized as follows:

In Chapter 1, the evolution of relevant economic thought is epitomized, starting from the Mercantilists and ending with pioneering neoclassical writers. Chapter 2 describes the basic stylized observable facts pertaining to working time and Chapter 3 proposes a survey of the main policies applied in the domain of working time.

Chapter 4 focuses on the traditional view of the individual labor supply. Refining traditional analyses, Chapter 5 investigates in formal terms the foundations of cost and production functions.

Chapter 6 develops cost minimization models, building on more detailed cost and production structures than standard analysis; Chapter 7 extends the previous problem to heterogeneous workers and emphasizes the role of anti-discrimination rules or incomplete information in the design of optimal labor contracts by the firm. In Chapter 8 the adjustment of firms to legal overtime premium schemes is detailed.

The profit maximizing hypothesis is better fitted to describing the long run adaptation of the economic system. In Chapter 9 working time is analyzed under utility competition in the labor market. More organized labor markets are introduced in Chapter 10 where profit maximization takes place in an economy in which trade unions have a dominant influence on supply side.

The following two chapters are more policy oriented. Chapter 11 brings out the role of complementariness between two types of jobs. Chapter 12 considers the case of an economy made up of two vertically integrated sectors, where a working time constraint is applied to hours in the sector providing a productive service to the second sector.

Dynamic analysis is introduced first in the framework of a flow model of labor market with a matching function as detailed in Chapter 13. Chapter 14 finally sketches the adjustment of working time and employment in the presence of cost of change applying to employment and when market constraints or stylized flexibility agreements supersede the public policy applying to overtime premium rates.

Acknowledgments

We express our gratitude to our families and friends who supported us when carrying out this interesting project and had to put up with the external effects of our untimely overwork. We benefited from highly valuable comments from the participants in the workshops "Economie du Travail" of the Paris 1 and Paris 2 Universities, in the EALE Conferences in Khania (1996), Aarhus (1997) and Regensburg (1999). We are grateful to Pierre Cahuc and Felix FitzRoy for their comments on our own research used in this text, but we claim exclusive responsibility for its shortcomings and imperfections.

In ESSEC, Dean Van Wijk was of constant and warm support and we benefited from the research center facilities. In the library, serendipitous Sophie Chaton-Magnanou proved that obtaining whatever remote or arcane reference is compatible with constant friendliness. Delphine Perrot and Vanessa Ribes provided useful assistance with bibliographical research.

Last but not least, we thank Kirk Thomson for skilfully reviewing our text.

1
Brief history of working time theory

The history of economic thought clearly illustrates the variety of intellectual attitudes to the explanation of working time and to the assessment of its role in the general functioning of the economy. In the three traditionally distinguished stages of the development of economic analysis, authors called Mercantilists, Classics and Neoclassics have in fact offered deeply conflicting versions of labor contracts, in different material and ideological contexts. As far as the first two categories of writers are concerned, working time was always analyzed in close connection with the pervasive notion of the subsistence wage. In the second half of the nineteenth century, Karl Marx, as a dissident Classic, deserves special scrutiny, since working time lies at the heart of the concept of surplus value extraction. In the last decades of the same century, the founders of the Neoclassical School brought in turn a radical change, affecting mainly the tools of economic analysis by means of new concepts designed with unprecedented precision, such as utility functions or production functions. Leaving aside the subsistence concept and placing great emphasis on the workers' consent to work, they fundamentally transformed the theory of wages and the explanation of working time.

1.1 The Mercantilists and the scarcity of labor

It is well known that the so-called mercantilist authors had more diversity than unity, and defining the gist of their thought is possible only at risk of oversimplification. Most of them, however, such as Jean Bodin, Bernard de Mandeville, and more explicitly Josiah Child (in his *Brief Observations Concerning Trade and Interest of Money*, 1668) far from being harbingers of Malthusian preoccupations, seem to be concerned by what they consider to be the scarcity of population and labor services. This demographic preoccupation induces them paradoxically to recommend low wages, strictly commensurate with subsistence levels.

A stylized account of their interpretation of labor markets can be summarized in the following way: workers have such consumption/leisure preferences that they adjust their individual labor supply (the number of hours they want to work) to their objective of obtaining *mere subsistence*. In such circumstances, any increase in the hourly wage rate therefore reduces proportionally this number of hours. William Petty's observation (*Political Arithmetick*, 1690), according to which higher prices of the necessities purchased by the working class (supposed to induce lower real wage rates) generally entail an increased labor supply, explicitly illustrates this view. Combined with a derogatory value judgement on leisure (spare time is wasted in taverns), such an analysis entitles the wise to advise against pay rises, which are doomed to aggravate the scarcity of labor (see also Screpanti and Zamagni, 1993).

Two implicit postulates of this doctrine are worth noticing:

- The assumed preferences of the workers imply what is called a negatively sloped individual (short term) labor supply curve whose elasticity with respect to the hourly wage rate is (-1); a 1% increase in the wage rate would systematically trigger a one per cent reduction of the voluntarily worked hours. This point is compatible with contemporary textbook analysis where a backward bending supply curve is often exhibited as a possible consequence of individual preferences.[1] It is an especially well-suited approximation in situations of exhausting working days, any increase in potential income created by a higher hourly wage rate being dissipated in "buying" rest time.

- The effective working time is not unilaterally determined by the employer; it is at least influenced by the workers' preferences. In contemporary terms, actual working time is close to the worker's supply curve.

This last observation shows that in the opinion of the mercantilist writers, the employers could not control simultaneously wages and working time. Had they been able to fix working time *and* the daily compensation of work, increasing wages would not entail losses in available labor services and the mercantilist recommendation could not be understood. Setting working

---

[1] It will be shown in Chapter 4 that such supply behavior may be viewed as a limit case derived from well-behaved neoclassical utility functions.

time and wages within certain bounds was possible in a feudal society and is always possible when the employer is, at least locally a monopsony, buying labor services from isolated workers with no alternative income. The fact that the workers' preferences are reflected by actual working times, implies a minimum level of competition between employers on the labor market. When the firms are profit maximizers, workers' mobility among non-perfectly colluding employers explains that their preferences do matter in the observable labor conditions.

1.2   The Classics and Marx

1.2.1   Smith and Marx on working time

The unchallenged authority of Adam Smith, from the publication of his masterpiece *An Inquiry into the Nature and Causes of the Wealth of Nations* in 1776, to the dawn of the neoclassical school and later, has not contributed to fostering the interest of economists in the determination of working time. It is worth noticing that in his immensely influential text, encompassing so many different economic and social topics, working time receives little attention and mostly indirect.

A striking feature of Smith's account of labor relations however, is his intimate conviction that collusion among employers is a natural state of affairs, admitting few exceptions, for instance when there is excess demand on the goods market. Consequently, the balance of negotiating powers is considerably biased to the detriment of workers, unable, for want of resources, to sustain any lasting conflict. The role of the state in this view consists mainly in sustaining this unequal situation and protecting the property rights of the better-off.

In spite of this dismal representation of the workers' fate, Smith considers that wages tend to rise (above the subsistence level) when the economy is growing and to fall when it is in a steady state, but he draws no definite conclusion about individual working time in general.

If Adam Smith abstained from building clear explanations of working time, in many other respects he set the stage for the far reaching analyses of Karl Marx, simultaneously his follower and his contradictor. Marx is the only significant classical writer in economics, who explicitly devoted an entire chapter of his work to the determination of daily working time. Below, we consider exclusively the ideas expressed in *Das Kapital*, Chapter 10, "The Working Day", disregarding any form of posthumous Marxian economics (Marx, 1867).

Marx's ambition consists in demonstrating that the civil liberties and political equality obtained in Western Europe after eliminating the remnants of feudal bonds are illusions obscuring the reality of persistent slavery in the economic side of life. For this purpose, he brings hard facts into the picture, resorting mainly to excerpts from reports by physicians or British Factory Inspectors appointed by Parliament and he upholds an exclusive interpretation of them.

1.2.2 Reported facts and their interpretation in Marx's approach

Among the facts mentioned by Marx in a detailed and serious inquiry is the appalling condition of workers, including a strikingly abusive daily working time. Many employers appear to impose upon men, women and children a daily burden often grossly incompatible with human health and the very preservation of the labor force. The British Parliament had reacted to this situation by imposing the increasingly binding rules of the Factory Acts (1833, 1850, 1864), intended to curb the capitalists' greed for what was to be called surplus value and to limit the inordinate extension of the working day.

Marx also infers additional information about workers' preferences from a survey conducted in 1848 by Leonard Horner, a competent factory inspector, at a moment when working time for adult males was still unregulated. According to this report, 70% of the men wanted a reduction of their working time to 10 hours (from 12), the others wanted to work 11 hours, but only a negligible minority wanted to maintain the existing 12 hours day.

The most striking aspect of Marx's analysis is the clear and explicit assumption that there is a market for "labor power" but not a market for labor services. This means that an employer, having paid for the subsistence of the worker is entitled to use this power as long as he wants. Hence, there is a fundamental conflict between workers and employers. It is worth noticing that subsistence is to be understood as a one dimensional concept, being defined as a minimum standard of the consumption of goods and there is no such thing as a subsistence level of rest time. Since workers need food and other minimum necessities in the very short run, whereas the effects of overwork on health may not be immediately felt, the individual employer is constrained by the former subsistence dimension and not by the latter. At the individual level, each employer tends therefore to increase working time and the "exploitation rate", which explains the harsh conditions imposed upon workers, sometimes leading to the attrition of their labor power. As a class, the capitalists want the working class to keep its working capacity. This collective objective, conflicting with their individual interests is achieved through the limiting terms of the Factory Acts.[2]

---

[2] According to Marx, the famous law is in fact comparable to regulations preventing the farmers from applying too intensive techniques, profitable in the short run, but detrimental to the future fertility of land.

In spite of the proclaimed intentions of the author, it is not so easy to determine the precise explanation of observed working time suggested in this famous chapter, since two different theories are actually invoked in this text.

On the one hand, if we accept the argument that the British Parliament is the repository of power of the capitalist class, the Factory Acts are nothing but a roundabout way for this group to reach what is called, in modern games theory, a cooperative sustainable equilibrium, incompatible with pure competition and in which the second dimension of the subsistence constraint is given due consideration. In this interpretation, the working class is absent economically and politically from working time determination and actual working time is mainly explained by the terms of the law.

On the other hand, in the same text, working time is considered as the central stake of class struggle.

> Hence is it that in the history of capitalist production, the determination of what is a working-day, presents itself as the result of a struggle, a struggle between collective capital, i.e., the class of capitalists and collective labor, i.e., the working class. (Marx, 1867, p.235)

Actual working time should therefore be explained by the balance of power between capitalists and workers. This balance of power changes according to circumstances and in particular throughout the economic cycle. In periods of glut on the goods market, unemployment increases and still strengthens the negotiating position of employers. In consequence, working time should change counter-cyclically. Such an interpretation implies an economic role of the working class in more or less decentralized negotiations, cyclical changes in the length of the working day not being ruled by laws.

1.2.3 Other facts and alternative interpretations

We have seen that Marx reported the main results of Horner's inquiry in Lancashire, in which a majority of workers called for a shorter working day. But recorded answers to Horner's questions also explicitly indicated that these people were ready to accept simultaneously a proportional decrease of the daily wage bill.[3] Such an attitude is not easy to reconcile either with the strict subsistence doctrine, or with the basic assumption that employers buy working power and not labor services. Can the above mentioned mill workers really wish to earn, in the proposed ten hours (two hours less than the real duration), an income representing less than subsistence?

---

[3] Of course, no survey is necessary to show that workers would prefer to work less for a constant daily compensation.

Some other interesting facts – also omitted by Marx – were reported in the same inquiry, giving a more complete picture of preferences and labor market competition. Ewin G. West (1983, p.275), having retrieved the original survey, directly quotes Leonard Horner:

> It has however been again and again stated to me by mill-owners, that those who wish to work their factories more than ten hours a day have no difficulty in finding adult males to enable them to do so; that at all times, when a mill was working longer hours than its neighbors, it was always sure to draw to it the best hands; and that at this time most mill-owners who cannot, from the nature of their manufacture work without young persons and women, and therefore not more than ten hours a day, are loosing some of their best workers among the adult males, by their going to mills where they can get higher wages by working twelve hours.

If we are to believe this last excerpt, it is clear that the market exists for labor services and not for labor power, a longer working time having an explicit cost for the employer and involving increased earnings for the employee. Workers' mobility exists, at least in some instances, and, when there is rivalry among their potential employers, they are able to express in some way their consumption/leisure preferences.

1.2.4 The exploitation paradox

Marx defines the exploitation rate by dividing the day into two theoretical intervals: in the first interval t_1, the worker produces the counterpart of his own subsistence. In the following interval t_2, he produces surplus value captured by the employer. The exploitation rate e is defined by $e = t_2/t_1$. In this analysis, he follows the lines already drawn by his contemporary classical economists. In particular, Nassau Senior argued against the Factory Acts, saying that profits, being reaped in the last hours of a working day, a reduction of working time could curtail them to the point of driving capital away from trade.

If the employer pays for the labor power only and can extend working time at no internal cost, he will tend to do so. But if competition in the labor market compels employers to pay a fixed hourly wage rate instead of a fixed daily subsistence level, exploitation should take a very different form. Disdainfully compared to a store of energy, the worker could yield less and less power as time elapses. Due to exertion, worker's efficiency diminishes over time. Thus, fresh workers in the first hours of activity may work faster and produce fewer rejects than tired workers in the last hours of the day, at the same hourly cost. In such circumstances, the employer's interest would consist in shortening the working day to be able to keep the highest possible working pace. To minimize wage costs per unit of output, he would try to buy only the most productive labor services obtained from fresh workers. In other words, for any given output the firm would tend to substitute late hours with early hours provided by new workers supposed to be available in the "reserve army" of the unemployed. The constraint of providing the worker with subsistence creates, however, a lower limit to this reduction. In such a case, the conflict over working time would be exactly opposite to the one described in Marx's analysis, the workers demanding a sufficient number of hours.

Marx's argument against the classical economists is that they failed to show that the general situation created by unfettered capitalism turns workers into slaves, behind the scene of civil and political emancipation. It seems clear that slavery in his text is not proven, but assumed from the outset. This is a consequence of Marx's notion of a labor power market in which what is traded is the right to put people to work for an undefined time interval. The persons you can arbitrarily compel to work for shorter or longer periods without any form of compensation are nothing but slaves. From such premises, proving exploitation is straightforward. In Marx's vision, capitalism is a special case of a slave system in which the slaves are not owned but rented for the price of subsistence. Consequently, the attrition of the productive forces of the workers is no loss for the individual capitalist, and the State has to interfere and supply a moderating constraint, in fact the working time dimension of subsistence. This constraint enables the system to follow a course deemed sustainable by the capitalist class, but bound to self-destruction according to Marx's final predictions.

1.3   Early neoclassical views

1.3.1   Léon Walras and the consistency of private decentralized economies

Neoclassical thought introduced radical changes in economic analysis with direct consequences for the theory of labor markets and wages. The foundation of the new school, once called "marginalist", is traditionally attributed to Stanley W. Jevons, Carl Menger and Léon Walras, but, in fact, it follows earlier steps taken by Hermann Heinrich Gossen in 1854.[4]

In the neoclassical paradigm, great emphasis is placed on individual choices as a consequence of individual liberties in the sphere of economics. The most consistent and synthetic model of this time is that of Walras

---

[4]His fundamental text is *Entwicklung der Gesetze des menschlichen Verkehrs und der daraus fließenden Regeln für menschilches Handeln*. See Blaug (1985, Chapter 8) and Screpanti and Zamagni (1993) for a detailed account of this remarkable period of economic thought.

(*Eléments d'économie politique pure*, 1874). Walrasian economics, resting on the notion of the General Equilibrium System, have played a major role in shaping the subsequent development of economic theory. The central economic problem in this stream of thought consists in assessing the capacity of decentralized private economies to generate a relative price system signaling the marginal cost of commodities and bringing about a so-called "Walrasian equilibrium". This last notion refers to a state of the economy in which all the transactions planned by the individual agents are mutually compatible, given the resources and the available productive techniques. It is an ideal state in which any form of rationing has been eliminated by the system of relative prices. Each form of supply motivated by a positive price is matched by an equivalent demand. The existence of a General Equilibrium is therefore a test of the consistency of competitive decentralized economies. It can be said that the Walrasian General Equilibrium System is a formalized version of the celebrated Adam Smith's "invisible hand" parable.

As far as labor markets are concerned, Walrasian static equilibrium implies full employment, all the hours supplied by workers being exactly demanded by firms. It is worth noticing that this should imply external equilibrium (every person wanting to work finds a job for the market wage) and internal equilibrium (every incumbent employee works exactly the number of hours he or she wants). In fact, Walras is not explicit about labor market equilibrium. His abstract approach tends to include labor services in a broader concept of factors of production and his book does not contain any detailed analysis of labor supply behavior, able to match what can be found in Stanley Jevons' treatise *The Theory of Political Economy*, first published in 1871.

Resorting to the concept of utility functions, the latter author was able to formalize elegantly the individual behavior with respect to work. His model does not explicitly aim at working time determination but is closely associated with this question.

1.3.2 Jevons' utility and disutility analysis

It may seem surprising that such a familiar notion as work needs a formal definition. Jevons defines work as "any painful exertion of mind or body undergone partly or wholly with a view to future good" (Jevons, 1871, p.168). An activity cannot be considered as work without an element of pain or negative utility calling for compensation.

According to him, it is possible to explain the activity of a worker in considering the balance between the utility derived from the produce of work and the disutility of the productive energy spent. A diagrammatic approach is proposed by the author (Figure 1.1 reproduces the original graph).

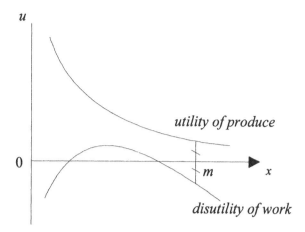

FIGURE 1.1. Optimal working time

The output x being measured on the horizontal axis, an upper curve indicates the incremental utility derived from the output from labor, assumed to be monotonously decreasing. A lower curve indicates the increments of utility derived from labor itself. It is assumed that this marginal utility is first (for small values of the activity index) negative, may cross the horizontal axis, but diminishes again for higher activity levels. The worker increases satisfaction until the output reaches a point m where disutility of incremental activity exactly offsets utility of the incremental production.

Point m may illustrate the choice of an independent producer or of a hired worker as well. In this latter case, the upper curve indicates the marginal utility of earned wages.

The suggested model explicitly determines optimum output and implicitly explains working time; noting the utility of output by $u = u(x)$, the disutility of labor as a function of elapsed time t by $L = L(t)$, and introducing a production function $x = x(t)$, the optimal working time is defined by:

$$\frac{du}{dx}\frac{dx}{dt} = \frac{dL}{dt} \qquad (1.1)$$

this equality corresponding to the first order condition in the problem of maximizing $u\{x(t)\} - L(t)$.

The author has sketched the comparative statics of his model. An increased wage rate may induce the workers to supply fewer hours if the upper curve shifts in such a way that point m moves leftward. This explains the most current behavior of regular workers. If some professionals (successful lawyers or physicians) tend to work more when they are in increased demand, it is because they can afford in such circumstances to select the most interesting cases or because working itself is not felt so negatively: "In some characters and in some occupations, in short, success of labor only excites to new exertions, the work itself being of an interesting and stimulating nature" (Jevons, 1871, p.182). This sort of occupation however should not be called "work", after the very definition suggested by the author.

After Jevons' contribution, the new analytical apparatus changed the terms of debates about the determination of labor supply. Long term labor supply being mainly influenced by demographic facts, short term labor supply was assimilated to the choice of the number of hours people wanted to work. A further step was taken by influential writers like Alfred Marshall (1920) and Francis Edgeworth (1925) supporting the view that effective duration of work was directly explained by this supply, pointing at the relative freedom of workers to adjust working time by occupational or geographic mutations. The effective daily duration of work was considered to be determined by the supply side, since firms which comply with workers' choice have a competitive advantage in bidding in the labor market. (This argument will be developed in Chapter 6.) The new school was consequently at odds with the demand determined working time in Marx's approach. It must however be kept in mind that economists of that time were not unanimously inclined to accept this vision of the labor contract. Böhm-Bawerk was still upholding a far less idealized interpretation: "Bound by the fetters of the wage contract, or at least of long established vocational habits, we perform the serious economic tasks of our calling, for the most part at least, in a definite number of working hours a day" (Böhm-Bawerk, 1888, p.178). No hint is given to help know who has forged the fetters, with which objectives and under which limitations.

1.3.3 A controversy about the short run supply of labor

The controversy between the American economist Frank Knight and the influential British professor Lionel Robbins illustrates the early neoclassical considerations pertaining to the short run supply curve.[5]

Knight's (1921) analysis was built in utility terms; he claimed that any increase of the wage rate was bound to reduce the number of hours workers were ready to supply:

> Suppose that at a higher rate per hour or per piece, a man previously at the perfect equilibrium adjustment works as before and earns a proportionately higher income. When, now, he goes to spend the extra money, he will naturally want to increase his expenditure for many commodities consumed and to take on some new ones. To divide his resources in such a way as to preserve equal importance of equal expenditure in all fields he must evidently lay out part of his new funds for increased

---

[5] See Douglas (1934) for a detailed comment on this controversy.

leisure; i.e. buy back some of his working time or spend some of his money by the process of not earning it. (Knight, 1921, p.117–118)

The reader may notice that Knight has taken into consideration only the income effect of the wage increase, while omitting possible consumption/leisure substitutions due to changes in the relative price of the two goods.[6] Knight's unambiguous conclusion was criticized by Lionel Robbins (1930) whose contention rested on the original concept of "demand for income". In this view, the behavior of the worker can be specified through a demand for income diagram. As would be the case for any other commodity, income is demanded according to its unit price. For regular commodities, the unit price commonly used in usual Marshallian graphs is constant. But if the price for one unit of income is the familiar but psychic notion of effort, this price is neither constant (income is obtained by working time of varying disutility), nor observable. What is observable is the "time price" of the income unit. Noting by w the hourly wage rate, the price to pay in working hours for each income unit is $p = 1/w$.

In Figure 1.2, income I is measured on the horizontal axis and the time price on the vertical axis. The demand for income $I(p)$ representing a decreasing function of p is a negatively sloped curve fully reflecting the worker's preferences.

For a given value of the current wage rate w, the time-price p is also determined and induces a worker's equilibrium represented on the demand curve by point E. In this worker's equilibrium, the marginal utility of income is exactly balanced by the marginal disutility of work. The income demanded is I_E, and it is obtained by working a number of hours $h = I_E/w = pI_E$. It is therefore represented by the rectangular shaded area OI_EEp.

The supply of working time is of the form:

$$h^s(p) = pI(p) \qquad (1.2)$$

The question of the sensitivity of the individual supply of working hours h^s with respect to the wage rate is related to the elasticity of the demand for income function. In elasticity terms, $p = 1/w \Rightarrow \eta_p^h = -\eta_w^h$.

From equation (1.2),

$$\frac{dh^s}{dp} = I(p) + p\frac{dI(p)}{dp} = I(p)\left[1 + \eta_p^I\right] \qquad (1.3)$$

---

[6] His conclusion is close to the Mercantilists' prediction founded on the subsistence doctrine and was apparently supported by data from a celebrated inquiry carried out in the French coal mining industry by François Simiand (1907).

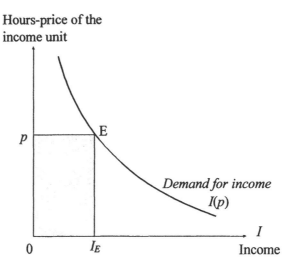

FIGURE 1.2. Demand for income and total hours supply

where η_p^I stands for the elasticity of the demand for income with respect to its unit price $\dfrac{dI}{dp}\dfrac{p}{I}$.

Therefore, $\eta_p^I < (-1) \Rightarrow \eta_p^h < 0$ and $\eta_w^h > 0$. The individual supply elasticity of working time η_w^h is therefore positive if $\eta_p^I < (-1)$, negative if $\eta_p^I > (-1)$.

Lionel Robbins' interpretation is attractive since it is performed in the familiar terms of demand schedules and critical elasticities analogous to the terms involved in the famous King law. It is compatible with different short run labor supply behaviors which were to be more thoroughly explained in terms of indifference curves and income and substitution effects in the subsequent development of neoclassical thought (see Chapter 4).

1.4   Conclusion

As this first chapter sets out to confirm, working time is a permanent topic in economic analysis, closely linked to the notion of worker's welfare, even if this latter concept was initially perceived as a subsistence limit. The successive doctrines related to the elements of labor contract clearly depend on more or less arbitrary selections of axioms in the representation of basic circumstances in which labor relations are formed. The Mercantilists allowed for some form of competition among firms, and scarcity of workers enabled them to impose their preferred working time. This optimum working time rests on specific implicit assumptions in terms of the individual preferences of the workers. The Classics switched to an opposite negotiation context in which a structural excess supply of workers tends to empty the worker's choice and drive down wages to the subsistence level, giving no expression to individual consumption/leisure preferences. Marx attempted to give a general status to his analysis of a special case, in which the market for working hours yields to a market for labor power. The precise condition for the stability of this form of exchange in terms of market structures, individual and collective behavior were not clearly enunciated.

Traditional neoclassical writers introduced a more explicitly axiomatic form of thought and gave more details about their representation of market structures, preferences, productive techniques and individual behavior. The most sanguine of them developed an idealized vision of the economy, in which flexible prices – including wage rates – eliminate all forms of rationing such as joblessness or overwork. Such an optimistic view may be obtained only at the price of overstating the realm of perfect competition, overlooking intrinsic features of labor cost structure and time varying workers' effectiveness, as well as neglecting the role of limited information and of collective bargaining in labor relations.

Modern working time analysis should take into consideration the essential features of contemporary labor markets. After presenting the main observed stylized facts and policies, this text will build on several theoretical analyses in a more general framework.

2
Basic facts

Over the twentieth century, the recorded yearly average number of hours worked per employee has steadily declined in most countries of the industrialized world.

However, since the early eighties, this trend has faded and even reversed in some countries. Whereas working time was rather uniformly distributed among the main industrializing countries in the first decade of the century, the recent evolution in the nineties has introduced more variety, and deviations are tending to increase from one country to another. For instance, although worked hours continue to decline steadily in the Netherlands, they have slightly increased in the United States, Sweden and Finland, and stabilized in France.

A wide range of durations now prevails in observed working time. A working week of 40 hours is still the current norm in most economies of the Western world, but the fraction of employees actually working 40 hours is falling. In many countries, the respective proportions of people working very short and very long hours have increased, contributing to increased domestic variance.

Part-time jobs in particular have become common in many countries. While this development may reflect a choice by employees in some cases, it is also often interpreted as a consequence of the need for more varied and flexible arrangements expressed by employers having to cope with stringent constraints imposed by technology and customers.

At a more subjective level, it must be said that a lot of surveys tend to confirm that many employees are in some sense not satisfied with the actual duration of their work; but the nature of this rationing is not uniform, since some of them wish to work more for the going hourly wage, and others less.

2.1   Trends in working hours

As is well known, in the first factories established in Manchester and in the neighboring towns of Lancashire, at the end of the eighteenth century, working time was extremely long. According to Bienefeld (1972), the representative textile factory used to operate 69 hours per week at the beginning of the nineteenth century, extending its working week to the bewildering score of 72 hours in 1830. By mid-century, textile firms still demanded between 58 to 60 hours (10.5–11 hours of work per day from Monday to Friday and 3–7 hours on Saturday). Such orders of magnitude must be kept in mind when considering the weekly standard of 40 hours recorded today in the greatest part of the developed world.

Maddison (1995) brings into the picture some interesting evidence pertaining to the long term trend (1870-1992) in hours per worker (Table 2.1). For more than a hundred years, the trend in annual hours has been clearly downward sloping, but with large discrepancies between countries. This downward trend was reinforced after the Second World War, with the notable exception of Japan, where working hours reached a peak in 1960.

YEAR	Canada	France	W. Ger.	Italy	Japan	UK	US
1870	2964	2945	2941	2886	2945	2984	2964
1890	2789	2770	2765	2714	2770	2807	2789
1913	2605	2588	2584	2536	2588	2624	2605
1929	2399	2297	2284	2228	2364	2286	2342
1938	2240	1848	2316	1927	2391	2267	2062
1950	1967	1926	2316	1997	2166	1958	1867
1960	1877	1919	2081	...	2318	1913	1795
1973	1788	1771	1804	1612	2042	1688	1717
1987	1673	1543	1607	1528[a]	2020	1557	1608
1992	1656	1542	1563	1490	1876	1491	1589

TABLE 2.1. Annual hours worked per person employed, 1870-1992. Source: Maddison (1995). (a) 1985

It is worth mentioning that in the same interval 1870–1992, estimates of per capita GDP have been multiplied by a factor close to ten (Maddison, 1995). Since the share of wages in output remained rather constant throughout the interval, one may infer that, in the long run, this fall in worked hours has been accompanied by a significant increase in the wage income.

Data for the recent period are provided by the OECD (1998) and are presented in Table 2.2. The sharpest decline in working hours per employee can be observed in Japan, a country which has faced a severe economic crisis since 1991; the government's measures in favor of reduced hours, and the initial high duration of work may provide an explanation for this abrupt variation in hours (more details will be provided in Chapter 3).

	1990	1996	Δ%		1990	1996	Δ%
Canada	1718	1721	+0.2	Japan	2052	1919	−6.5
Finland	1668	1692	+1.4	Korea	2512	2465	−1.9
France	1539	1547	+0.5	Netherlands	1433	1397	−2.5
Germany	1583	1522	−3.9	Spain	1762	1747	−0.9
Ireland	1843	1799	−2.4	UK[b]	1773	1732	−2.3
Italy	1694	1682[a]	−0.7	US	1936	1951	+0.8

TABLE 2.2. Average yearly working time per wage earner, 1990 and 1996. Source: OECD, *Employment Outlook*, 1998. (a) 1984, (b) total employment

The average time is obtained here by dividing all the worked hours in the economy by the total number of employees. The plain variation of this average may therefore conceal different types of change. Most workers are legally employed according to the terms of a labor contract based on a standard or statutory duration of work: they are full-time workers. This statutory duration may come from legislation or from collective bargains at branch level (see the next chapter). Average yearly hours of work of these full-time workers may fall in relation to the downward trend in actual weekly hours, and also as a consequence of an increase in the yearly number of vacation days. In most European countries, vacations increased from 2–3 weeks in the fifties to 4–6 weeks at the beginning of the eighties. In the United States, vacations increase during the same interval from one week to 2.5 weeks (OECD, 1998). In Japan, legal vacations were increased in 1987 from 6 to 10 yearly days, and this normal length increases with work experience. But the specific features of labor relations in this country and existing social norms probably explain why many workers do not exhaust the legal period to which they are entitled.

As a result of an increased demand for internal flexibility and variety of labor resources, part-time labor contracts flourished in most developed countries in the eighties. Under such arrangements, employees may work fewer hours than the statutory benchmark. As shown in Table 2.3, part-time contracts are quite widespread in the late nineties. (Note that most

definitions of part-time contracts changed between 1979 and 1996, thus
data in the respective columns cannot serve for direct comparisons.)

	1979	1996		1979	1996
Canada	13.8	18.9	Japan	15.4	21.8
Finland	6.6	7.9	Netherlands	16.6	36.5
France	8.1	16.0	Sweden	23.6	23.6
Germany	11.4	$15.1^{(a)}$	UK	16.4	22.2
Italy	5.3	5.4	US	16.4	18.3

TABLE 2.3. Part-time workers as a percentage of total employment according to
national definitions. Source: OECD, *Employment Outlook*, 1998. (a) 1993

Average yearly hours per incumbent worker may vary under the influence
of changes in the number of hours included in the full-time contract or as a
consequence of a varying proportion of part-time workers in the economy.
Table 2.4 attempts to summarize these simultaneous influences.

As can be seen, in most cases both the decrease in the average annual
hours of the full-time workers and the increase in the number of part-time
jobs have contributed to the downward trend in average working hours
during the century.

It would be interesting to further analyze the two idiosyncratic situations
of the United States and Sweden. In the latter, the positive variation is
largely due to increased hours included in part-time contracts, strongly
weighted by a large number of women participating in the labor market,
and to a significant fall in absenteeism after the last recession (Anxo, 1995).

In the case of the United States, the data have sometimes been displayed
in apparently contradicting terms. Schor (1991, p.1) claims that: "in the
last twenty years the amount of time Americans have spent at their jobs has
risen steadily... Working hours are already longer than they were forty years
ago". This particular account has not found much support in subsequent
or alternative enquiries. In a thorough and detailed study, Coleman and
Pencavel (1993) showed that between 1940 and 1988 the annual average
working time per worker has been "virtually constant". McGrattan and
Rogerson (1998) find that between 1950 and 1990, average weekly hours per
worker in the United States fall from 40.71 to 36.64. Many other relevant
details pertaining to working hours patterns and disaggregated tendencies
may be found in these two last references.

Many proponents of a mandatory reduction in working time have in mind
some idea of work-sharing. In a preliminary empirical approach, it can be
said that a definite negative relationship between employment and working

		Overall change in hours (1+2+3)	Change in hours (full-time workers) (1)	Change in hours (part-time workers) (2)	Change in share of part-time workers (3)
Belgium	1983–93	-7.5	-2.5	0.2	-4.9
Canada	1983–93	-1.1	0.7	0.5	-2.3
Denmark	1985–93	-6.6	-7.1	-0.9	1.4
France	1983–93	-4.1	0.4	0.7	-4.4
Germany	1983–93	-10.9	-6.1	-0.9	-3.9
Greece	1983–93	-1.0	-1.6	-0.4	1.3
Ireland	1983–93	-7.4	-1.0	-0.4	-6.0
Italy	1983–93	-3.7	-3.0	0.4	-0.9
Luxemburg	1983–93	-2.1	-0.9	-0.1	-1.1
Netherlands	1987–93	-6.6	0.0	3.2	-11.3
Portugal	1983–93	-6.9	-6.5	0.6	-0.3
Spain	1987–93	-6.0	-3.8	-0.4	-1.8
Sweden	1987–94	7.7	1.8	3.6	2.3
UK	1983–93	-1.5	3.8	-0.5	-5.0
US	1983–93	7.3	4.7	1.3	1.2
Average (all)	1983–93	-3.1	-1.4	0.5	-1.7

TABLE 2.4. Contributions of various factors to recent changes in average annual hours of employees. Source: OECD, *Employment Outlook*, 1998

hours would provide major support in favor of this policy. The following graphs display working hours and employment for five countries on the basis of the ILO *Yearbook of Labor Statistics*, 1997.

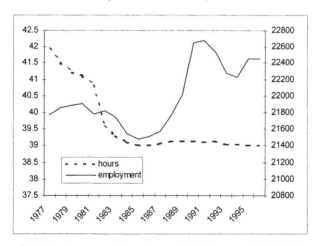

Working hours and employment in France, 1977–1996

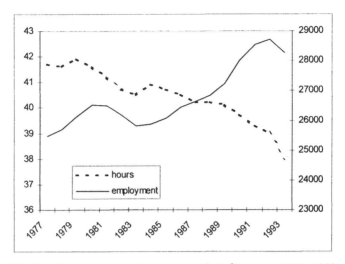

Working hours and employment in West Germany, 1977–1993

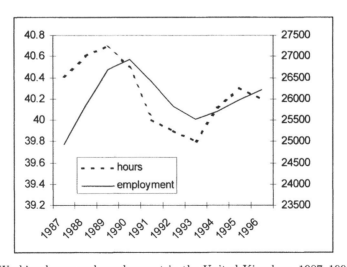

Working hours and employment in the United Kingdom, 1987–1996

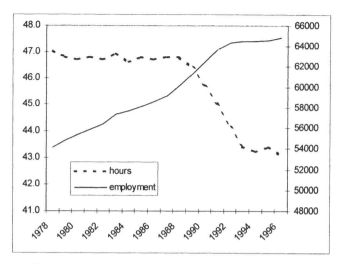

Working hours and employment in Japan, 1977–1996

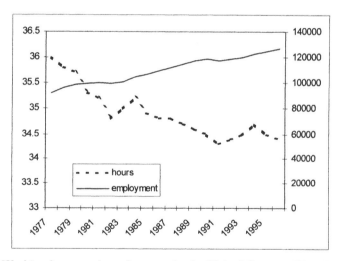

Working hours and employment in the United States, 1977–1996

Inspection of these graphs unfortunately gives little help in determining whether working time and employment are negatively correlated. In the United Kingdom, the two series seem to be positively correlated, in West Germany and Japan negatively correlated, in France and the United States only loosely correlated. In Japan, the abrupt fall in hours may have cushioned the rise in unemployment during the current crisis.

2.2 Hours of work: structure

In most countries, the standard duration of work is close to 40 hours per week, and men work longer days than women (OECD, 1998). There are important differences between countries, as emphasized by Eurostat, the European statistical office (Table 2.5).

Hours per week:	1–35	36–39	40	41–45	46+	Total
Europe 15	8.1	31.4	32.2	8.9	19.4	100%
Germany	8.2	38.9	34.7	4.1	14.1	100%
France	7.6	61.5	8.4	8.8	13.7	100%
Italy	10.3	20.4	40.8	7.9	20.6	100%
Netherlands	1.2	35.4	50.9	1.6	10.9	100%
Spain	6.0	8.9	60.7	7.2	17.2	100%
Sweden	2.8	13.5	67.6	6.5	9.6	100%
UK	9.1	21.9	13.8	20.1	35.1	100%

TABLE 2.5. The pattern of weekly working time in 1997, selected European countries (full-time employees; actual hours per week). Source: *Labor Force Survey* 1997, Eurostat (1998)

Hours of work also vary according to the activity sector and the socio-professional category. According to the Eurostat Labor Force Survey (1998), in the Europe of 15, actual hours of work were in 1997 the highest in agriculture (44.8 hours) and lowest in the service sector (39.7) and in manufacturing (36.8 hours).

Nobody would be surprised to learn that executives work the longest hours. Less easy to explain is the relatively reduced weekly hours of the less qualified people, as shown in Table 2.6. This pattern is valid throughout the European region (Greece excepted); the most striking situation is in the Netherlands, where average weekly working time of less-qualified workers is only 23.0 hours.

The same pattern applies to the United States economy. According to Rones at al. (1997), in 1993, 45% of the managers and sales persons performed over 49 hours per week (as compared with a 40 hours statutory week); on the other hand, only 16% of the less qualified employees work such a long time.

Analyzing the trends of working hours, Coleman and Pencavel (1993) report that since 1940, hours fell for those with relatively little schooling and rose for well-educated people. As they mentioned, "a rising trend in the work hours of the well-educated also squares with reports of longer hours

	France	Ger.	Italy	UK	EU-15
Managers and administrators	44.6	43.4	41.4	45.6	43.9
Academic and scientific professions	35.6	38.2	29.7	40.2	36.6
Associated professional and technical	37.1	36.1	38.1	38.9	36.9
Clerical and secretarial	35.5	34.2	37.2	33.5	35.1
Selling	35.0	33.0	38.3	27.7	33.2
Agricultural and fishing workers	37.2	39.2	38.7	37.1	38.9
Craft and related	38.8	38.4	40.0	43.8	39.7
Plant and machine operatives	39.0	39.2	39.9	44.0	40.2
Unskilled workers	31.5	31.1	36.6	29.9	32.4
Armed forces	45.9	41.1	...	45.3	42.4
Total	36.7	36.3	37.4	37.4	36.8

TABLE 2.6. Wage earners: average weekly hours per socio-professional category in 1997. Source: *Labor Force Survey* 1997, Eurostat (1998)

among professional and managerial workers" (Coleman and Pencavel, 1993, p.282).

Costa (1998) points to the recent tendency of low-paid workers to do fewer hours than highly-paid workers, as compared to the relatively long hours done by the same category of wage earners at the end of the nineteenth century (Table 2.7). The author comments that the largest decline in hours worked took place before 1973, probably in the 1920s. The bulk of the reduction is attributable to low wage-earners.[1]

2.3   Do people *think* they work too much?

Workers' preferences are undoubtedly an important factor accounting for differences between countries with respect to working hours pattern. A first attempt to infer such preferences is based on surveys. As will soon be made clear, different statistics often seem to contradict one another.

In 1989, the International Social Survey Programme (ISSP) organized a survey among the OECD countries. They asked every individual: "Think of the number of hours you work and the money that you make in your main job, including regular overtime. If you had only one of three choices,

---

[1] Costa (1998) argues that the observed shift in hours is due to a large extent to changes in the supply, as opposed to changes in the demand for hours resulting from technological improvements.

hourly wage deciles	1890s	1973	1991
<10 (bottom)	10.99	8.83	8.05
10–20	10.46	8.47	8.47
20–30	10.50	8.54	8.53
30–40	10.63	8.38	8.61
40–50	10.31	8.34	8.59
50–60	9.99	8.33	8.61
60–70	10.29	8.33	8.47
70–80	10.07	8.32	8.66
80–90	9.64	8.26	8.64
>=90 (top)	8.95	8.22	8.72
90th/10th	0.81	0.93	1.08
90th/50th	0.90	0.99	1.01
50th/10th	0.94	0.94	1.07

TABLE 2.7. Distribution of usual-length work day by hourly wage deciles, American men aged 25-64. Source: Costa (1998) who used data from the US Bureau of Statistics surveys in the 19th century

which of the following would you prefer: (1) work longer hours and earn more money, (2) work the same number of hours and earn as much money, (3) work fewer hours and earn less money". A summary of the answers – as a percentage of total answers – is presented in Table 2.8.

	Answer:		
	more hours more pay	same hours same pay	fewer hours less pay
Austria	22.59	71.53	5.88
Germany	13.50	76.41	10.09
Italy	31.03	62.43	6.53
Ireland	30.37	64.64	4.99
Netherlands	17.54	70.16	12.29
Norway	24.36	68.70	6.93
UK	23.77	68.05	8.17
US	32.67	61.83	5.51

TABLE 2.8. Preferred working time and income. Percentage of total answers. Source: Bell and Friedman (1994)

According to this survey, in many countries, about one third of the employees are not satisfied with present hours of work; it is worth noticing that the unsatisfied would, in general, prefer to increase working hours; the

Netherlands appears to be the country with the largest minority of workers desiring to work less.

Kahn and Lang (1996a, 1996b) mention several surveys carried out in the eighties in the United States and Canada which show that approximately half of all workers would like to work a different number of hours per week if they could continue to receive their usual hourly wage. About two thirds of the rationed workers would like to work more hours and only one third would like to work fewer hours. Drolet and Morissette (1997) present the results of the Survey of Work Arrangements held in November 1995 by Statistics Canada: two thirds of paid workers in Canada declared they were satisfied with their work hours; 27% favored more hours for more pay and only 6% preferred fewer hours for less pay. This pattern is robust as it holds for each of the ten provinces, age group, education level, industrial and professional group.

As indicated by a number of opinion polls, the North American pattern, with workers wishing to work more at the going wage rate, seems to have also prevailed in the eighties in Japan (Takagy, 1993).

The European Commission organized various ad hoc labor market surveys, covering inter alia working time issues, in 1984, 1989 and 1994. A questionnaire was addressed to over 10 000 employees in all sectors of the EU. An interesting question was: "Assuming that the present hourly wage rate remained unchanged, would you like to work less, as long or longer?" Table 2.9 pinpoints the tendency of European workers to work shorter hours, a result that seems at odds with the ISSP query. However, the fact that 21% would like to work longer hours cannot be neglected: obviously, worker rationing goes both ways, even though overwork seems to be prevailing in this survey.

	1989	1994
Total	100%	100%
Answer:		
- less	37	29
- as long	51	48
- longer	8	21
- no reply	4	2

TABLE 2.9. Preferred working time (overall). Source: European Commission (1995)

The tendency is stable throughout Europe (Table 2.10), with the notable exception of France, where 67% of the respondents would like to work more.[2]

Country	Answer:				
(actual hours[a])	Total:	Less	As long	Longer	No reply
W. Germany (1552)	100%	30	62	7	1
France (1520)	100%	21	11	67	1
Italy (1682)	100%	29	50	17	4
Netherlands (1395)	100%	21	67	12	0
Spain (1746)	100%	32	52	12	4
UK (1728)	100%	33	53	13	1

TABLE 2.10. Preferred working time, selected countries, 1994. Source: European Commission (1995). (a) Pro memoria: actual yearly working hours per employed person (in UK, hours per wage earner)

Inference from such surveys is difficult since, when asked "If the choice were offered at the next wage round between an increase of pay for the same hours of work and shorter working time for the same pay you get now, which would you prefer?", most people prefer the pay increase, even if in answer to the former question they had declared that they would prefer less hours (Table 2.11). Most European countries stick to this pattern, with the notable exceptions of Denmark and the Netherlands which favored working time reductions.

Of course, the results of such enquiries should be interpreted very cautiously, since the answers are highly sensitive to external factors, such as the general economic and political environment, the economic cycle, the

---

[2]In a special study devoted to the UK labor market and based on data from the British Household Panel Survey (BHSP) of 1991, Stewart and Swaffield (1997) found that most male British workers are subject to overwork. They estimate a mean value of desired working time by manual men of 43 hours per week, less than actually performed by this category of workers.

	1989	1994
Total	100%	100%
Answer:		
- increase in pay	55	56
- shorter working time	34	36
- undecided	9	8
- no reply	2	0

TABLE 2.11. Perceived hours vs. pay increase trade-off in the European Union. Source: European Commission (1995)

personal situation of the respondent, the way the question was worked out, the "political" fashions and norms at work, etc.

2.4 Conclusion

In recent years, increased concern about working time issues has inspired an impressive development of empirical analyses and data collection. The picture obtained is not so simple as is often presumed. The long-standing downward trend in working time generally observable up to the aftermath of World War II, has been replaced in recent years by other less predictable and more diversified patterns of development.

Inquiries about working time preferences have not always been tailored to make Walrasian rationing easily traceable. It can be said however that the price mechanism, in the institutional context of the countries included in the survey, has not proved generally able to eliminate either external rationing (unemployment prevails in Europe and in Japan), or internal rationing, since overwork or underemployment of incumbent employees is constantly reported. Disaggregated data do not confirm any built-in tendency of the productive sector to push workers into systematic overwork, but reveal a variety of situations calling for further theoretical analysis.

Such theoretical investigation is all the more necessary since the paradoxical situations in which external unemployment and internal overwork coexist are to be observed currently, giving a practical importance to assessing the foreseeable impact of a mandatory working time limit on joblessness.

3
Working time policy: an overview

3.1   Why regulate working time?

From material presented in Chapter 2, it appears that during the twentieth century, recorded hours of work have steadily and considerably decreased throughout the industrialized world. This fall might be interpreted as a spontaneous development in an increasingly decentralized economic system, within a general equilibrium framework, since both supply and demand considerations are able to account for a downward trend. State intervention could also have influenced this outcome. The rationale for government interference in working time determination exists and has been inspired over time by varying conceptions and objectives.

The role of law in this matter was first intended to protect the workers from excessive working days judged detrimental to their health and welfare in the long run. Such overwork preoccupations seem to have prevailed in Western Europe from the middle of the nineteenth century to the reconstruction era in the aftermath of World War II. Throughout this period, increasingly protective limits were imposed first by the British Parliament, often followed in particular by the regulations devised in continental Europe.[1]

Assuming perfect competition in a pure Walrasian interpretation of economic life, these rules can be understood as protecting the workers against

---

[1] For instance, the notion of a fixed working week and a standard weekend resting time was established in Britain by 1890 or so (Cross, 1989).

themselves, since actual working time, considered as a market equilibrium magnitude, is supposed to reflect their own preferences (for details, see Chapter 4). The market sector of the economic machinery destroys leisure or home production, in order to produce marketable goods and services. To justify state intervention, we have to think that under the rule of free market forces, this process goes too far. Short-sighted workers may not be able to fully evaluate the global effect of long working hours on health or personal development. In this case, the government, as guarantor of the public interest, is entitled to overrule the system and superimpose its consumption/leisure preferences on those of the workers.

As we have seen in Chapter 1, according to the interpretation of Karl Marx, working time limits would protect the workers against the employers' greed for profits. Some neoclassical writers themselves have referred to the bounded rationality of employers, unable to realize that, due to exertion or other efficiency considerations, shorter working days do not necessarily imply substantially reduced output.[2] In such a case, equilibrium working time does not sustain the economic system in a Pareto-optimal configuration.

Limited rationality of workers, unable to understand their long term welfare requirements, or limited rationality of employers, overestimating the consequences on output of reduced working time, have been, and still are, alleged foundations for the regulation of working hours.

In periods of high unemployment however, such welfare considerations tend to be overshadowed by the more pragmatic goal of job creation obtained from a hypothetical man-hours substitution process. For instance, during the Great Depression, this idea was widely circulated. As early as 1933, the International Labor Office considered a proposal by the Italian government advising a uniform hours standard intended to reduce competition and to reabsorb unemployment. Trade unions fiercely called for a 40 hour week, and, like today, required that no wage cut should accompany the reduction of hours (Cross, 1989).

More recently, in particular after the second oil shock, faced by high and persistent unemployment, a number of governments have resorted again to working time regulations which were perceived as a politically sustainable way to create or defend jobs.[3] Most often, these policies are grouped together under the term of "work-sharing", which can be defined as any policy involving a redistribution of employment through a reorganization of working time. Some measures, like a general reduction in working hours, voluntary part-time working and job sharing, aim at reducing daily or weekly hours of work. These measures might foster the demand for workers only if the technological process and cost structures are such that profit

---

[2] See the comment of John Hicks (1932) on the concept of "optimal working day".

[3] Additional and more detailed information on working time policies can be found in the OECD 1998 Employment Outlook, the Policy Bulletin of the European Employment Observatory and the 1999 issues of the European Industrial Relations Review.

maximizing firms tend to compensate the law induced scarcity of available hours by new hires. However, in some cases, this substitution is not feasible in the short run; some other longer term measures such as paid-leave arrangements, career break or early retirement may be attempted, not being subject to the same shortcomings. In this case, firms would be more likely to replace an incumbent worker who leaves the firm (temporarily or definitively) by a new one.

3.2 Work-sharing methods in international comparison

The general reduction in working hours is probably the most intuitively appealing work-sharing method; during the last two decades it has benefited from significant popular support, especially in countries plagued by high unemployment.

The typical work-sharing regulation involves limitations on working hours for all workers, most often with the declared objective of creating jobs. Such regulations are often based on three elements: statutory working hours (in general a weekly norm beyond which an overtime premium wage is due), an overtime premium to be paid for hours longer than the statutory level and a quota of maximum permitted overtime hours (on a weekly or yearly basis). Such reductions may be negotiated between workers and the trade unions or may be imposed by law. For instance, throughout the nineties, German trade unions have successfully pushed for a reduction of the statutory working week to 35 hours. During the same period, in Japan, the governmental support for a reduced 40 hour working week has finally shifted the balance in favor of the trade unions, which have also succeeded in reducing working time in the last few years. In France, a law passed in 1998 set up a method for introducing a statutory 35 hour week by 2002 at the latest. The Italian government is seriously considering a similar move. In 1999, unions in Finland, Greece, Spain, Sweden, Belgium and Switzerland are advocating a similar policy (they are in general silent on the possibility of a consecutive reduction in the wage bill that should accompany the reduction in hours). More details on the policy of working time reduction will be presented in the next section, containing three country cases.

Some countries have encouraged voluntary part-time working, implementing various incentives intended to prompt workers to reduce their working hours, while encouraging employers to hire replacement workers. This method is very popular in the Netherlands where the government strives to guarantee part-timers equal treatment with full-timers. In Belgium, the government introduced in 1994 an incentive grant for employees accepting a move from a full-time to a part-time job. In 1997, the law was further extended: workers reducing their working time by at least 20% and up to 50% are entitled to a two-year incentive grant proportional to the extent of the working time reduction. In Austria, under the Solidarity Model (1998), employees reducing their working hours and the replacement workers hired are entitled to a solidarity premium for a period of up to two years from the date of recruitment of the latter; this premium is equivalent to a share of the unemployment benefits pro rata to the extent of the working time reduction. In some countries, employers must pay a fixed contribution per employee (for public health, pensions, unemployment benefits), at least under a certain wage-income threshold. Such a practice is obviously detrimental to the extension of part-time jobs. Consequently, many attempts have been recorded lately, aiming at replacing such thresholds with contributions proportional to the wage income, sometimes coupled with an exemption for low wage workers (in Canada, Finland and France).

Job sharing in a strict sense is a special part-time arrangement where two persons share the tasks of a full-time job, dividing the full-time wage on a proportional basis. While this practice has developed in the last few years, only Finland has passed a law to organize such deals.

One recent innovation in the realm of work-sharing policies in Germany was the adoption in 1996 of a part-time early retirement scheme. Under this regulation, older workers are encouraged to work on a part-time basis, in order to push firms to recruit younger people. Employees aged over 55 may cut working time by 50% for a five-year maximum period. They will be paid by the firm on the basis of their actual hours, but the government will reimburse 20% of their pay and pension contributions if employers also award a further 20% of pay and recruit young people.

In some other cases, work-sharing is not considered in relation to short lapses of time (day or week) but in a life-cycle perspective. In this approach, some employees, deemed more able to cope with joblessness are encouraged to leave, and firms are encouraged to replace them with unemployed persons. For instance, under paid-leave arrangements, workers take extended periods of paid leave, most often with a vocational training objective, with unemployed people being recruited to replace them. In Austria, employees may take a six month to one year training leave, without pay; during this period they may benefit from a training indemnity, proportional to the parental indemnity. Other countries like Belgium, the Netherlands or Finland have taken the same steps. Career breaks refer to workers taking periods of unpaid leaves, for various reasons (care for children, undertaking a trip, etc.). Many countries have set up early retirement schemes, where workers near the retirement age are allowed to cease work with a reduced pension during the intermediate years. In such cases, working time policy does not purport to create new jobs but only aims at redistributing the job rationing among different subpopulations.

As will be seen in the following chapters, this text focuses on the choice of working time defined in a short period interpretable as a day or a week; therefore, the later analytical chapters will place special emphasis on working hours regulation, in particular on the general reduction in working time and on the ability of this measure to increase employment.

3.3   Working time reduction: three country cases

General reductions in working hours are often very popular policies; while strongly opposed by firms, they benefit from significant public support in many developed countries. Trade unions also back them, or at least a special variant, where reduction in working hours is to be achieved with a constant wage bill. In this case, the impact on the economy is not simple, since the suggested measure implies simultaneously a new value of the working time constraint and an increase of the hourly wage rate. Policy makers are thus in the difficult situation of arbitrating between the various social partners. Three country cases allow us to highlight the complex character of public decisions intended to support work-sharing policies, in particular by means of a general reduction in working hours. We choose three countries where the work-sharing paradigm seems to be particularly influential.

3.3.1   France: reducing working time by law

Like many other developed countries, France inherited a legal system aiming at protecting the workers from excessive burdens, essentially through weekly hours limits and overtime premium constraints imposed on employers.[4]

In the context of the global economic slump in the early 1980s, the French Parliament, however, decided in 1981 that the statutory working time should be reduced from 40 to 39 hours per week, with an overtime wage fixed at 1.25 of the regular rates. The law also introduced a fifth week of paid vacation and reduced the retirement age from 65 to 60 years. The maximum overtime was limited to 130 hours per year. Unfortunately, the law did not prove able to curb soaring unemployment and the following governments gave up the idea of mandatory reduction of working time.[5] They finally adopted a more flexible policy also aiming at reducing hours, but by means of powerful incentives.

In general, regulations passed after 1981 granted the firms agreeing to reduce the duration of work substantially alleviated social contributions, contingent upon maintaining or increasing employment. In some sense, this

---

[4] The French passed a first working time regulation in 1848, when the maximum daily duration was set at 12 hours.

[5] According to an empirical analysis by Crépon and Kramarz (1999), workers who were working 40 hours a week in March 1981 (when the reduction was decided) are less likely to be employed in 1983, than identical workers who, in 1981, were working 39 hours.

type of regulation aimed at internalizing the social cost of joblessness. The firms able to create jobs by working time reduction are given a share of the savings they induce in favor of the unemployment compensation budget. The most important incentive program was laid down in June 1996 ("Loi Robien"). Firms which simultaneously reduce the duration of work (by 10%) and hire, benefit from a significant social charge credit (amounting to 30–40% of the employer's contribution). This labor cost reduction is granted for a rather long activity interval, up to seven years (Freyssinet, 1997). Although there was no obligation for firms and workers to engage in negotiations under the terms of this law, by the end of June 1998, some 2900 agreements had been signed under this regulation, covering 278 000 workers and creating or safeguarding 15 500 jobs, according to the French Ministry of Employment and Solidarity.

As the early results of this law seemed rather short of its expected benefits – unemployment in France was still very high (11.8% in May 1998) – the socialist government embarked on an active process inspired by the work-sharing paradigm, more *dirigiste* and more in the spirit of the 1981 law. The so-called "Loi Aubry" of June 13, 1998 and the corresponding implementation decrees simultaneously set a new weekly norm (35 hours per week), imposed a method (compulsory collective bargaining) and introduced accompanying measures, mainly public support for the most diligent firms.

The law fixes the statutory working week at 35 hours as of January 1, 2000 for firms with more than 20 workers and as of January 1, 2002 for all firms. It is important to note that the figure of 35 hours represents the statutory, not the obligatory, working time: firms are allowed to hire workers for more than 35 hours, but must pay the higher wage rate for this extra time (1.25 times the normal rate).[6]

Having established this norm, the law requires enterprises to bargain with their respective social partners (in most cases, trade unions) over the conditions under which the reduction is to take place. Negotiations on working time must be carried out at the level of the firm, but in some cases, branch or national level negotiations can also take place. In addition, a company is entitled to a five-year tax credit if it cuts working hours by at least 10% and creates jobs or avoids redundancies of at least 6% of its workforce.

According to a report by the French Ministry for Employment and Solidarity, on July 21, 1999 more than 11 500 firm level agreements had been signed on working time, covering almost two million employees. At branch level, 101 agreements had been concluded by July 1999.[7] In many sectors,

---

[6] By June 1999, the government proposed some inflection to the initial text. Hence, firms will benefit from a one-year transition period, during which the wage premium on weekly hours exceeding the 35 and below 39 will be only 10% (instead of 25%).

[7] For information update, see http://www.35h.travail.gouv.fr.

the government judged them consistent with its objectives of supporting employment and decided on their extension to all firms of the branch.

However, the most important adopted branch agreement was also the most litigious. With 1.8 million employees and a turnover close to $37 billion, the engineering branch is the most important industrial activity in France. An agreement was signed in July 1998 between UIMM, the employers' union and three main worker trade-union confederations (FO, CFTC, CGC). As requested, the statutory working time will become 35 hours per week, but the number of authorized overtime hours was extended from 94 hours to 180 hours per year and worker. Overtime can be compensated either by holidays in the subsequent period or by extra wages. Furthermore, the 35 weekly hours imply a reference annual period of 1645 hours, with firms able to vary weekly hours at their convenience within an upper limit of 10 daily hours. Also, the agreement lays down the possibility of special labor contracts establishing a lump-sum payment for predetermined tasks, independently of the implied working time. Many other sectors have now applied for extensions of this particular agreement. For the time being, the government has refused to acknowledge them, on the grounds that such agreements will not boost the demand for workers. Somewhat ironically, the law triggered a bargaining process ending in an agreement finally granting more flexibility to the firms and not satisfying the government objective of actual working time reduction of the incumbent workers.

The main goal of the Aubry law was to create or save jobs, by limiting the labor service supply by incumbent workers. Whether this goal has been achieved or not, it is of course very difficult to assess. According to the above mentioned official statistics, by July 1999, the measure would have created or saved 100 000 jobs. But firms may have wished to disguise spontaneous job creations as jobs related to the law just in order to take advantage of government benefits. Between July 1998 and July 1999, unemployment in France fell by some 0.5%. However, this favorable outcome cannot be dissociated from the overall improvement of the French economy, recording a yearly growth rate of 2.1%. According to recent OECD (1999) empirical estimations, "...the job dividend [of the Aubry law] is uncertain. The reform could contribute only moderately to reducing unemployment, especially given the eventual weakening of potential and actual output that it will entail if it leads to significantly higher unit labor costs".

It may be noticed that the Aubry law seems to have brought some unexpected benefits to firms: if the law forced employers and trade unions to negotiate on working time, traditional limits on night or weekend hours have simultaneously been lifted. This provided a good opportunity to identify and exploit efficiency gains related to greater flexibility. As a result, most of the agreements on reduced hours included clauses allowing for higher working hour variance in time. The law provoked a wave of reorganizations at firm level that may have improved their competitiveness.

The evolution of the legal framework and political preoccupations pertaining to working time sketched for France have also affected other European countries, a prominent example being Italy. In this country, legislation on working time dates back to a 1923 Royal Decree limiting working time to eight hours and weekly working time to 48 hours. This legislation has not been revised since, social partners preferring to regulate working time through collective bargaining. The working week has therefore gradually been reduced as a result of negotiations between unions and employers at sectorial level. Today, these negotiations materialize in statutory working weeks close to the "traditional" 40 hours spread over five days in most sectors. At the beginning of 1999, the government came up with a proposal very similar to the French law, which would bring down to 35 hours the statutory week by 2001. Unlike France, the law would merely set a target, unions and employers being free to negotiate on how they can introduce the system gradually. For the time being, weekly hours keep on falling as a result of the negotiations between workers and unions.

3.3.2   Germany: negotiated working time reduction

A long-standing legal framework for working time in this country rested upon a law adopted in 1938, establishing a maximum duration of work of 48 hours per week. In 1994, this law was revised, mainly to allow for more flexibility in the organization of work. The German law can be described as very permissive, and this would explain why unions felt obliged to start a campaign for the reduction of working time. During the last two decades work-sharing has been increasingly perceived as an efficient way to fight unemployment and sectorial negotiations of the labor contracts have systematically included working time issues.

In 1977, the DGB (the main trade union confederation in Germany) drew up a "Proposal for Restoring Full Employment", which included the possibility of reducing working hours. Starting with 1984, German unions began to push more effectively toward reducing standard hours on an industry by industry basis, with the declared goal of raising employment. Unions in Germany bargain at the industry level and, as in France, the terms of the collective contract apply not only to members but to almost all workers as well. The first important agreement was signed in 1985 in the engineering sector at the end of an important strike initiated by the powerful trade union of engineering workers, IG Metall. Statutory weekly hours were reduced to 38.5 but more flexibility was conceded in the organization of the manufacturing process. This agreement was followed by others coined in similar terms in the printing, manufacturing and service industries.

By 1990 Germany had entered a period of recession, a fertile ground for work-sharing policies. A flagship experiment was carried out by the car maker Volkswagen, which in 1993 introduced a cut in working hours (and pay) in favor of job guarantees (Blyton and Trinczek, 1997). Given the sales forecast of 1993, the company's estimated overemployment for 1994 was about 20%. By the end of 1993, 30 000 out of 100 000 jobs were under threat. The negotiated solution consisted in adopting a standard 28.8 hours week (initially for two years). This shorter week, which corresponds roughly to a 20% reduction in hours, came with a 16% reduction in the yearly gross income (mainly by eliminating bonuses and special premiums, while maintaining the monthly wage constant). Most of the workers said they were satisfied with this arrangement. By 1995, a new agreement had been signed, with more advantages accruing then to the employers, for instance, the reference week shifted to 30 hours and the company was allowed to increase hours to 38.8 hours per week if necessary, without having to pay a premium for overtime.

In 1990, the trade union IG Metall and employers in this branch negotiated a sectorial agreement which aimed at reducing hours of work to 35 hours per week without loss of pay. By early 1995, such framework agreements on work sharing had been signed in ten industrial sectors in Germany, covering 6.5 million workers. In general, these agreements led to a reduction in the actual hours. Unions announced that they had managed to get "full wage compensation", equivalent to an increase in the wage rate. Using German Socio-Economic Panel data for 1984–1994, Hunt (1999) found that for a one hour reduction in the statutory working time, actual working time of the manufacturing worker fell by 0.88 to one hour. Moreover, a one hour reduction was in general associated to a 2.2% increase in the basic hourly wage, relative to sectors with no hours reduction. This wage response could be responsible for the lack of empirical cogent evidence concerning a subsequent increase in employment (in fact, in some cases, employment could even have been reduced). According to Hunt (1999, p.145): "Germany's work sharing experiment has thus allowed those who remained employed to enjoy lower hours at a higher hourly wage, but likely at the price of lower overall employment".

3.3.3   Japan: another way of negotiating

The Labor Standards Law of 1947 introduced the principle of eight hours a day and 48 hours per week in Japan for the first time; at the same time, the Ministry of Labor was given the responsibility for the regulation of working hours.

Even if the overall working hours of Japanese workers steadily decreased after the 1960 peak of 2318 yearly hours, in the eighties Japan still distinguished itself in the developed world by very long hours of work. By 1987, the actual annual working hours of production workers in Japan were roughly 420 hours longer than in the United States and Germany (Maddison, 1995). Overtime was much longer in Japan than in other major countries and annual paid vacations much shorter.

In 1987, working time legislation was modified to allow for gradual reductions in statutory working time, and it established a long run objective
of 40 hours per week. Initially, statutory working time was lowered from 48
to 46 hours. At the same time, the minimum holidays went from six to ten
days per year, increasing by one day per seniority year, up to 20 days per
year. Hours exceeding the statutory level were to be paid at a premium rate
at least 25% above the normal wage. Constraints on working hours were
further tightened in 1989, when a new law limited the number of overtime
hours to 450 hours per year.

It is important to remark, however, that at this period, unemployment in
Japan was quite low. In this context, work-sharing could not be a desired
outcome; on the contrary, the government would have preferred to avoid
the inflationary pressures that any increase in the demand for workers could
entail. Why, then, was the law modified? One important motivation of the
Japanese government to support a general reduction in working time was
to avert increasing criticism from abroad: Japan was running huge trade
surpluses with its main partners, and some of them claimed that the reason
for this imbalance could be found in the unduly long hours supplied by
Japanese workers (Takagi, 1993). In addition, some other voices claimed
that working time reduction would improve the structure of global demand
by reducing exports and increasing leisure related domestic consumption,
would support workers' welfare by qualitative improvements in working life,
and would maintain social vitality (Sugeno, 1992).

In the nineties, the motivation for shorter hours has tended to change
as Japan entered a very severe and persistent recession. Statutory hours
were reduced to 44 weekly hours in 1991. Under the pressure of increasing
unemployment, a "Five Year Plan for Improvement of Living Standards"
was implemented in 1992 advocating a more rapid shift towards the target
of 40 hours week established in 1987. In 1993, the quota on overtime hours
was brought down to 360 hours. While the Labor Standards Law prescribes
that employers pay a premium of at least 25% above the normal wage, by
the mid-nineties many firms were paying a 30% premium on overtime hours
and a 40% premium on Saturday, Sunday and holiday work.

The policy of the macro-management of hours seems to have succeeded
in reducing working time in the context of a deep economic crisis. By 1996,
the total working hours in Japan and the United States were brought in
line: according to the 1999 Asahi Shimbun Japan Almanac, in 1996 annual
working hours in manufacturing in America amounted to 1986 compared
to 1993 in Japan, the latter still penalized by a smaller number of holidays.
Overtime hours in the US manufacturing sector now exceed overtime hours
in Japan.

As in Germany, the revision of the Labor Standards Law was in general
opposed by employers while obtaining the support of most union leaders.
An important role in the process of negotiating and amending the law was
held by the Ministry of Labor who strongly supported the policy. Inter alia,

the public body promised that if the unions and the management agreed on reducing working time to 40 hours per week, it might agree to deregulate other elements of the working hours policy to allow more flexible allocations of hours (Kume, 1998).

3.4   Working time: regulation vs. flexibility

As mentioned before, working time regulations have been introduced firstly with the aim of protecting people against the side effects of hours which are too long, and later in order to stimulate employment within the work-sharing paradigm. However, when state interventions interfere with market equilibrium in the allocation of hours, additional costs are inflicted on firms, on workers, or on both. This would explain why, in the most regulated economies, we can often hear an opposing argument in favor of more flexibility, as a means of making the functioning of labor markets more efficient.

In the last decade, many countries have moved toward greater hours flexibility in order to allow firms to make a better fit between their labor requirements and the demand for output. As mentioned by Bosch (1997), working time has always been adjusted to match fluctuations in production. To cope with demand peaks, firms systematically have recourse to overtime; they may also hire full-time or part-time temporary workers or extend the working hours of the part-time workers. Of course, such fluctuations in the demand for labor services would be more important in the service sector than in manufacturing, since production in the former is more labor intensive and stocks cannot be accumulated.

Traditional forms of expanding the duration of work – weekend, evening, night and holiday working – were usually regulated in most developed countries. As reported by the OECD (1995, 1998), in the last few years, a number of countries have eased bans on such schedules, either by regulatory interventions or by collective bargaining at the branch level. When such working time was permitted in a number of situations, the discomfort was compensated by premium pay. In addition, several original work organization schemes are currently being tried out by firms throughout the world, for instance: work during standard breaks, staggered operation of costly equipment and staggered vacations.

A popular measure concerns so-called "annualization", wherein employers are allowed to vary weekly working hours (within certain limits) while holding the annual amount of time at a predetermined level. This work organization is particularly useful for highly seasonal activities and may rule out the need for adjusting employment by laying off people in periods of low demand and hiring relatively untrained people in periods of high demand. For instance, in Austria the revision of the Working Time and Rest Periods

Act (April 1997) authorized the one year reference period in working time calculations. The model requires a limit of 48 normal hours per week and nine or ten working hours per day, the actual distribution of hours resulting from collective negotiations. In France, annualization was introduced in 1982 and was successively extended in 1987 and 1993. The law establishes a maximum yearly duration of work, based on the week of 44 hours; the statutory weekly duration is 39 hours; actual hours may fluctuate around this average, extra hours giving the right to premium hours compensation. According to the government's proposal (July 1999), by 2001–2002 working hours may fluctuate within the week around the statutory 35 hours; in this case, hours exceeding 1600 hours per year should be considered as overtime and be paid at the premium wage. In Germany, annualization was introduced through negotiations; in 1985 the reference period for working time was set in the engineering industry at two months, then extended to six months in 1987 and to one year in 1994 (Bosch, 1997). In Japan, employers are allowed to increase hours above the statutory duration (the reference periods being the week, the month or the quarter) without paying overtime provided that on average working time does not exceed the statutory time (Sasajima, 1995). Negotiations between employees and employers with respect to changes in the work schedule are compulsory. Other countries, like Belgium, Italy and the Scandinavian ones, have also introduced one year reference periods as concerns the distribution of hours.

Workers also require more flexibility in the choice of work schedules. In recent years, more firms have also agreed on flexible work schedules, where workers may vary the time they begin or end work. For instance, according to the May 1997 Current Population Survey (CPS), in the United States about 25 million full-time wage workers had benefited from such arrangements, that is 27% of the workforce. This figure contrasts sharply with the 15.1% recorded in 1991. It should be noted that while most managers, executives and administrators had flexible working schedules, operators, craft, repair workers, and low qualified workers were the least likely to have flexible work schedules. In France, according to a survey by the National Institute of Statistics (Insee), in 1995, 8.1% of the wage earners had the choice of freely determining working hours (Boisard and Fermanian, 1999).

3.5   Conclusion

Under the pressure of high unemployment in the eighties and nineties, governments in continental Europe and Japan have supported trade union calls for a reduction in working hours. The Scandinavian countries and Austria implemented rather "soft" work-sharing policies, where fiscal incentives or subsidies were provided to employers or employees who voluntarily agreed on hours reductions. In a more authoritarian way, constraints on statutory weekly hours were legally imposed in France (in 1981 and 1998) or conceded by employers under the pressure of strike-threatening unions in Germany. In Japan, working hours regulation was initiated by the government with an objective of convergence with the main economic partners; during the economic crisis in the 1990s, it appears to have cushioned the unemployment impact of the drastic reduction in demand for labor services.

In contrast, hours of work in the United Kingdom are highly deregulated. There is no statutory working week and unions and firms freely negotiate complex wage and work schemes to cope with demand fluctuations. Indeed, working time policy in this country seems to be guided by the need for improved flexibility, rather than by an objective of job creation.

The United States and Canada have rather simple regulations on working time, and have not reinforced the constraints in the last twenty years. For instance, in the United States the only piece of legislation with important effects on working time is a provision of the Fair Labor Standards Act of 1938, according to which working time exceeding 40 hours per week must be paid at time and a half. In these countries, the policy of working time reduction does not generally receive much public support and unions themselves are rather silent on the question (Hunt, 1998). As a consequence, the few contemporary proponents of this policy prefer to point to the risk of overwork on morale or intellectual development rather than to the potential gains in terms of employment.

The situations portrayed in this chapter correspond to a wide spectrum of state intervention on working time. In the contemporary context of high unemployment, the main objective of the regulation of working time is to "share" jobs. The efficiency of such a policy depends on many factors. Developed countries differ with respect to their economic structure: they are more or less integrated into the world economy, they have a more or less important public sector, they have a more or less generous social welfare system, and so on. In particular, they have different labor market structures: some of them are highly unionized, others are not. Working time and wage negotiations may take place at different levels: national, sectorial or firm. This important diversity should be taken into account in any serious attempt to assess the potential outcome of a working time policy.

In the following chapters, after analyzing the factors determining working time in the absence of hours constraints, we will highlight the impact of mandatory working time reductions on employment and other important macroeconomic variables in different economic contexts.

4

The standard neoclassical view of the labor market

Standard neoclassical analysis of the labor market rests on the atomistic frictionless Walrasian representation of the economy. With both goods and labor markets competitively organized, no individual agent or group of agents may unilaterally influence prices, including the hourly wage rate. It will be shown that as a consequence of the currently accepted axioms, firms appear to be indifferent with respect to the composition of the flow of labor services in hours or employment. Working time in this context is essentially determined on the supply side of the market.

This chapter has two main objectives: the received theory of labor market equilibrium is summarized in a perspective placing particular emphasis on working time determination, and therefore needing a careful description of worker preferences; simultaneously, a whole set of notations and axioms used throughout this text receive a formal definition.

4.1   Introductory considerations

4.1.1   The demand for labor services: the perfect homogeneity assumption

On the demand side of the labor market, firms apply a technology requiring a homogeneous flow of labor services L. This flow is sufficiently defined by the product between a number of employed workers n and a number of working hours h; workers are homogeneous and individual effectiveness in time is also assumed constant. This perfect homogeneity assumption of labor input means that one hour supplied by any individual, for instance, in the beginning of the working day is a perfect substitute for another hour supplied by any other individual at the same time, or in the afternoon. In this case, $L = nh$.

The return to additional labor services is positive but decreasing. In the simplest case, when labor is the only explicit productive factor, measuring the flow of output by y, the productive technique is represented by a function $y = F(L)$. This function is supposed to be concave, implying $F'(L) > 0$ and $F''(L) < 0$.

The cost of labor services is assumed limited to a wage bill of the form $C(n, h) = wnh = wL$, where w stands for the real wage rate. The cost is linear in labor services. Consequently, in the (Oh, On) space, for a constant value of L, any hyperbola defined by $nh = L$ may be considered simultaneously as an isoquant defined by $F(nh) = F(L)$ or as an isocost $C(n, h) = wnh$.

Profit maximizing firms buy labor services provided the productivity of an additional unit is greater than its price. This maximizing behavior may be represented by the profit function $\pi = F(L) - wL$. Implicitly, the goods market being in equilibrium, firms are able to sell all their output at the market price and no constraint applies to the level of activity. Profit maximization therefore requires as first order condition:[1]

$$\frac{d\pi}{dL} = F'(L) - w = 0 \tag{4.1}$$

In equation (4.1), the well-known equality of the real wage rate and marginal productivity does not apply to workers, but to the more abstract notion of labor services.

A more explicit form of the profit function is obtained by considering the profit under the form $\pi = F(nh) - wnh$, i.e. as a function of the two directly controlled variables n and h.

First order conditions are:

$$\frac{\partial \pi}{\partial n} = hF'(nh) - wh = 0 \tag{4.2}$$

$$\frac{\partial \pi}{\partial h} = nF'(nh) - wn = 0 \tag{4.3}$$

In this context, $\partial \pi / \partial n$ and $\partial \pi / \partial h$ are respectively called the "extensive margin" and the "intensive margin" of the firm, respectively representing the sensitivity of profit to employment and to working time.

Profit maximization occurs when both margins have been eliminated. It is easy to check that when condition (4.1) holds, both extensive and

---

[1] Concavity of the production function entails concavity of the profit function and first order conditions are sufficient to determine its unique global maximum.

intensive margins are eliminated. The sufficient condition for profit maximization in this context is the use of a determined amount of labor services L^*, such that condition (4.1) holds, implying $F'(L^*) = w$ or $L^* = F'^{-1}(w)$. This quantity of labor services is uniquely determined, since $F''(L) < 0$ everywhere implies that the function $F'(L)$ is monotonously decreasing.

The demand for labor services is subject to the "law of demand": differentiating (4.1) yields $dL^*/dw = 1/F''(L^*) < 0$, a *local property* of the demand function.

More generally, if we consider two different possible wages, w_1 and w_2, since $L^*(w)$ is the unique solution to profit maximization, we can write:

$$F(L_1^*) - w_1 L_1^* > F(L_2^*) - w_1 L_2^* \qquad (4.4)$$

$$F(L_2^*) - w_2 L_2^* > F(L_1^*) - w_2 L_1^* \qquad (4.5)$$

Adding equation (4.4) and equation (4.5), we get:

$$(w_2 - w_1)(L_2^* - L_1^*) < 0 \qquad (4.6)$$

This is a *global property* holding $(\forall w_1, \forall w_2)$. Higher wages always imply a reduced demand for labor services.

The composition of the flow of labor services, i.e. the precise demand for workers n^* and the firm's demand for hours h^*, is left undetermined; the firm is indifferent and could accept any combination (n, h) such that $nh = L^*$, since such combinations entail the same labor cost and the same output.

The above mentioned law of demand appears to be supported by empirical analyses (see the survey by Hamermesh, 1986).

4.1.2   Equilibrium and rationing

We call "internal equilibrium" a situation in which the optimum working time from the worker's point of view denoted h^s coincides with the optimum working time from the firm's point of view h^*. Insider rationing takes place outside of internal equilibrium, for instance when firms impose more hours than desired by the workers; this situation will be called "overwork". The opposite case in which the firm would impose a suboptimal working time from the worker's point of view is called "insider underemployment".

We call "external equilibrium" the situation in which all the persons wanting to work are really employed. Outside rationing on the labor market may take the well-known form of "open unemployment" measured by the difference between the number of people wanting to work and the number of workers hired by firms. Open unemployment is politically much more conspicuous than the insider underemployment and may be more detrimental to social welfare, but it must be kept in mind that it does not necessarily exhaust the rationing of labor services in the market.

In its most idealized version, the neoclassical analysis explains the elimination of any rationing in the following way: on the supply side, workers wish to provide working time as long as the utility increase related to the supplementary consumption derived from an additional hour of work exceeds the working effort disutility. As will be shown in detail in the next section, any value of a constant wage rate w implies an optimum working time from the worker's point of view denoted $h^s(w)$. It simultaneously determines a demand for labor services $L^*(w)$. Each firm can adjust working time to the value $h^s(w)$ at no cost and is induced to do so since worker mobility implies that any employer trying to impose another working time would either lose its employees or be obliged to compensate them for non-optimal working time, reducing its own competitiveness.[2]

The actual working time is therefore determined by worker preferences; internal equilibrium obtains and the demand for workers by the firm is therefore:

$$n^*(w) = \frac{L^*(w)}{h^s(w)} \qquad (4.7)$$

If we consider that the productive sector is composed of f identical firms and if N individuals want to participate in the job market whatever the wage rate, external equilibrium obtains for values w^* such that:

$$n^*(w) = N/f \qquad (4.8)$$

The basic neoclassical assumptions do not guarantee that the solution of equation (4.8) is unique. Uniqueness is granted if the demand for workers $n^*(w)$ is monotonously decreasing in w. Since

$$\frac{dn^*(w)}{dw} = \frac{1}{[h^s(w)]^2}\left[\frac{\partial L^*(w)}{\partial w}h^s(w) - L^*(w)\frac{\partial h^s(w)}{\partial w}\right]$$

a sufficient condition is $\dfrac{\partial L^*(w)}{\partial w}h^s(w) < L^*(w)\dfrac{\partial h^s(w)}{\partial w}$ $\forall w$, or in equivalent elasticity terms, $\eta_w^{L^*} < \eta_w^{h^s}$: the wage elasticity of the demand for labor services should be lower than the wage elasticity of the individual hours supply. Of course, since the law of demand implies a negative elasticity of the demand for labor services with respect to the wage rate, $\eta_w^{h^s} \geq 0$ is a fortiori sufficient for uniqueness.

We represent in Figure 4.1 the equilibrium wage rate for a decreasing demand for workers: total workforce N depends upon demographic trends, technological changes affect $L^*(w)$; changes in tastes modify $h^s(w)$ and consequently the function $n^*(w)$. Equation (4.8) and Figure 4.1 lend themselves to comparative statics analysis. In any case, the actual working time

---

[2] A clear account of this view may be found for instance in Stigler (1966), chapter 16.

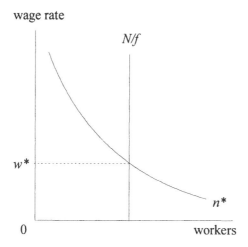

FIGURE 4.1. Equilibrium wage

is finally explained by $h^s(w^*)$. The traditional neoclassical analysis relative to working time appears to be related to the supply side of the market. It is therefore necessary to give more development to the analysis of individual labor supply functions.

4.2   The neoclassical hours supply

4.2.1   Main assumptions about workers' constraints and preferences

In a one period representation (a symbolic day), worker satisfaction is explained solely by the availability of two homogeneous commodities, respectively called consumption and leisure, denoted by c and l.

The consumption unit may be interpreted either as a truly unique good, or as a composite commodity standing for all the goods available in this economy. Each day, the individual may receive an autonomous flow of resources obtained from family support, subsidies, income from real or financial assets whose total value in consumption units is denoted y, and a labor earned income denoted wh, where w is a constant real wage (in consumption units per hour) and h the duration of work. Consumption is therefore limited by $c \leq y + wh$. The fact that the worker cannot influence the market wage rate may be viewed as a particular case of the common "price-taking" assumption.

Leisure l is the number of unworked hours within the day, or the private time the individual spends outside the working place. Denoting total available time by T and working time by h, we get the basic identity: $T = l + h$ or, normalizing T to unity, $1 = l + h$.

Worker preferences are represented by a utility function in consumption and working time $U(c, h)$, subject to the following axioms:

Axiom 1 *Continuity: $U(c, h)$ is defined $\forall c > 0$ and $\forall h \in]0, 1[$ and is twice continuously differentiable.*

Axiom 2 *Strong non-satiation: $\forall c > 0$ and $\forall h \in]0, 1[$, marginal utilities $U_c > 0, U_h < 0$; ceteris paribus, more consumption is preferred to less consumption and less labor is preferred to more.*[3]

As a consequence of axioms 1 and 2, it is possible to define, for any constant value S of the utility level, a "working time compensating consumption function", $c(h)$ uniquely defined by:

$$U[c(h), h] = S \tag{4.9}$$

In the (Oh, Oc) space, the compensating function $c(h)$ is an indifference curve corresponding to the constant utility level S. Its derivative $c'(h) = \left(\dfrac{dc}{dh}\right)_{U=S}$ is called the marginal rate of compensation of working time. Differentiating (4.9) with respect to h yields the value of this derivative in marginal utility terms:

$$c'(h) = -\frac{U_h[c(h), h]}{U_c[c(h), h]} \tag{4.10}$$

From axiom 1, the slope of an indifference curve is well defined, and from axiom 2, this slope is always positive.

The concept of the indifference curve makes it possible to introduce in a convenient way a third important assumption.

Axiom 3 *Convexity of the indifference curves.*

Preferences of the worker are such that the marginal rate of compensation is an increasing function of h, therefore $c''(h) > 0 \; \forall h$. Differentiating (4.10) with respect to h shows that a necessary and sufficient condition for this inequality to hold is in terms of the utility function:

$$\det \begin{pmatrix} 0 & U_c & U_h \\ U_c & U_{cc} & U_{ch} \\ U_h & U_{hc} & U_{hh} \end{pmatrix} > 0 \tag{4.11}$$

It is also currently assumed that for constant hours, successive increases in consumption bring decreasing utility gains, that is $U_{cc} < 0$ and that for

---

[3] Individual preference may be alternatively represented by a utility function having consumption and leisure as arguments $U(c, l)$. In this case $U_c > 0$, $U_l > 0$.

constant consumption, successive increases in working time bring decreasing variations in utility, $U_{hh} < 0$. This supplementary assumption however is not necessary for the results obtained in this chapter. It does not imply axiom 3 and is not implied by it.[4]

Figure 4.2 represents indifference curves compatible with the three axioms.

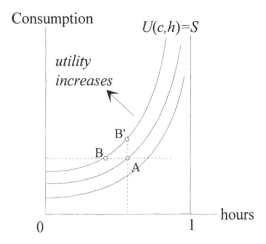

FIGURE 4.2. Network of indifference curves

Utility in B is higher than in A, because the same consumption level is obtained in a shorter working time. Point B' is also preferred to A, because the same amount of work comes with more consumption. Any point on a curve that lies to the northwest of another one is preferred to any point on a curve to the southeast.

Convexity of the indifferences curves illustrates the increasing marginal rate of compensation: the consumption required for an additional hour of work is larger when working time is already large (for instance, at point B' in Figure 4.2) than if working time is low (point B). At the extreme, when working time is close to unit, leisure is scarce and the typical worker claims a high compensation for an increased working time.

Finally, different workers may have different preferences and thus different indifference maps in the (Oc, Oh) space. For instance, two individuals with the same initial working time and consumption, if asked to work one more hour may be more or less demanding in consumption terms. Often, to simplify matters, we will consider homogeneous workers, but in some

---

[4] A simple example is given by the utility function $U = c(1 - h)$, satisfying axiom 3, but with non-decreasing marginal utilities.

instances in this text, heterogeneity of preferences will be explicitly introduced.

4.2.2 Optimal working time: the individual supply of hours

We examine first the direct problem of the worker considered as a "wage taker" in its analytical form:

$$\begin{cases} \max_{h,c} U(c,h) \\ \text{with:} \quad c \leq y + wh \\ \text{and with: } c \geq 0, \ h \in [0,1] \end{cases} \tag{4.12}$$

where y stands for an autonomous income.

Non-satiation (axiom 2) being incompatible with a solution such that $c < y + wh$, we infer that the constraint is binding, and we represent the market constraint by the equality $c = y + wh$.

Under axioms 1, 2 and 3, the solution of problem (4.12) exists and is unique, defining the optimal working time (individual supply) and the optimal consumption of the worker, denoted (c^*, h^s).

We consider first interior solutions, such that $h^s \in]0,1[$ and $c^* > 0$.

Introducing the Lagrangian multiplier λ, we may write the necessary first order condition applying to the following expression:

$$\mathcal{L} = U(c,h) - \lambda[c - y - wh]$$

i.e. the partial derivatives of $\mathcal{L}$ with respect to c, h, λ must vanish:

$$\begin{align} \mathcal{L}_c &= U_c(c^*, h^s) - \lambda^* = 0 \tag{4.13} \\ \mathcal{L}_h &= U_h(c^*, h^s) + \lambda^* w = 0 \tag{4.14} \\ \mathcal{L}_\lambda &= c^* - y^* - wh^s = 0 \tag{4.15} \end{align}$$

More insight regarding the solution can be gained by eliminating λ^* from equations (4.13) and (4.14), obtaining:

$$w = -\frac{U_h(c^*, h^s)}{U_c(c^*, h^s)} \tag{4.16}$$

The right hand term is the marginal compensation rate between consumption and hours at constant utility, therefore, at the worker optimum:

$$w = \left(\frac{dc}{dh}\right)_{U=S} = c'(h^s) \tag{4.17}$$

It may be checked (using axiom 3) that second order conditions are fulfilled.[5]

---

[5] First and second order conditions may also be determined by substitution, in considering the free maximization of $U(wh + y, h)$ as a function of h.

The solution has been represented in Figure 4.3. The budget constraint is a straight line of slope w and intercept y. The optimal working time can be observed at the point where an indifference curve is tangential to this line; on this indifference curve satisfaction is the highest possible given the market constraint.

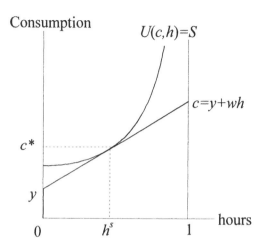

FIGURE 4.3. Hours supply

First order conditions may not apply in the case of a corner solution. It is easily seen that if $c'(0) > w$, since $c''(h) > 0$, condition (4.17) cannot hold for any positive working time. In this case, the optimum working time is nil and the satisfaction of the individual is $U(y, 0)$. In order to induce the individual to supply a positive working time, we must have $w > c'(0) = -\dfrac{U_h(y, 0)}{U_c(y, 0)}$. This condition implicitly defines a minimum wage $\underline{w} = c'(0)$, called the reservation wage, below which the individual prefers full-time leisure. This corner solution is represented in Figure 4.4.

Under axioms 1, 2 and 3 the supply of hours h^s is a continuous function of two arguments, the autonomous real income y and the wage rate w :[6]

$$h^s = h^s(w, y) \qquad (4.18)$$

The same property applies to the implicit optimum consumption: $c^* = c^*(w, y)$.

---

[6] See Mas-Colell et al. (1995), chapter 3, Appendix A for a proof of continuity in analogous cases.

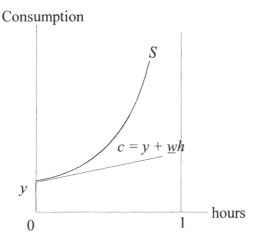

FIGURE 4.4. The reservation wage

The supply curve is usually understood as the partial relationship $h^s(w)$ between the working hours offered by the individual and the wage rate. A great deal of attention has been given, in particular, to the sensitivity of the labor supply with respect to the wage rate, $\partial h^s(w, y)/\partial w$.

4.2.3   The compensated working time supply

In order to analyze in depth the shape of the labor supply curve, we suggest introducing first the auxiliary concept of "compensated working time supply".

Let us consider a new problem: determine in the (Oc, Oh) space the point $(\hat{c}, \hat{h})$ minimizing the autonomous income y necessary to enable the worker to attain utility level S, when the wage rate is w.

In analytical form, this problem can be written:

$$\left\{\begin{array}{l} \min\{y\} \\ \text{with:} \qquad y = c - wh \\ \text{and with: } U(c, h) \geq S \end{array}\right. \qquad (4.19)$$

The utility constraint is clearly binding and first order conditions must be fulfilled in the following Lagrangian form:

$$\mathcal{L} = c - wh - \sigma\left[U(c, h) - S\right]$$

$$\begin{array}{lll} \mathcal{L}_c & = & 1 - \sigma U_c(\hat{c}, \hat{h}) = 0 \qquad (4.20) \\ \mathcal{L}_h & = & -w - \sigma U_h(\hat{c}, \hat{h}) = 0 \qquad (4.21) \\ \mathcal{L}_\sigma & = & U(\hat{c}, \hat{h}) - S = 0 \qquad (4.22) \end{array}$$

Elimination of σ from the first two equations shows that $w = -\dfrac{U_h(\hat{c}, \hat{h})}{U_c(\hat{c}, \hat{h})}$, and using equation (4.10):

$$w = c'(\hat{h}) \tag{4.23}$$

As a consequence of our assumptions, the compensated labor supply function is a continuous function of its arguments:

$$\hat{h} = \hat{h}(w, S)$$

Differentiating equation (4.23) gives the sign rule:

$$\frac{\partial \hat{h}}{\partial w} = \frac{1}{c''(\hat{h})} > 0 \tag{4.24}$$

The objective function takes its minimum value $\hat{y} = \hat{c} - w\hat{h}$; from the continuity of the compensated equilibrium and from its definition, the objective function is itself continuous in S and w and is denoted $\hat{y} = \hat{y}(w, S)$.

Proposition 4 *It can be shown that $\partial \hat{y}/\partial w = -\hat{h}$.*
   Proof. *Since $\hat{y} = \hat{c} - w\hat{h}$:*

$$\frac{\partial \hat{y}}{\partial w} = \frac{\partial \hat{c}}{\partial w} - \hat{h} - w\frac{\partial \hat{h}}{\partial w} \tag{4.25}$$

Differentiating (4.22) with respect to w yields: $U_c\dfrac{\partial \hat{c}}{\partial w} + U_h\dfrac{\partial \hat{h}}{\partial w} = 0$; hence from (4.20) and (4.21), $\dfrac{1}{\sigma}\left[\dfrac{\partial \hat{c}}{\partial w} - w\dfrac{\partial \hat{h}}{\partial w}\right] = 0$ and finally, from (4.25):

$$\frac{\partial \hat{y}}{\partial w} = -\hat{h} \tag{4.26}$$

■

4.2.4   The response of the individual labor supply to the wage rate

We are now able to analyze the effect of a change of the wage rate on the optimum working time, using the following identity:[7]

$$\hat{h}(w, S) = h^s\left[w, \hat{y}(w, S)\right] \tag{4.27}$$

---

[7] For an illustration of dual methods in the context of standard consumption theory, see Mas-Colell et al. (1995), chapter 3.

This basic identity means that the point $(\hat{c}, \hat{h})$ may be given two possible interpretations: it is the solution of (4.19) and also the solution of (4.12) if $y = \hat{y}(w, S)$.

Differentiating both members with respect to w, we obtain:

$$\frac{\partial \hat{h}}{\partial w} = \frac{\partial h^s}{\partial w} + \frac{\partial h^s}{\partial y} \frac{\partial \hat{y}}{\partial w}$$

and using equation (4.26):

$$\frac{\partial h^s}{\partial w} = \frac{\partial \hat{h}}{\partial w} + \hat{h} \frac{\partial h^s}{\partial y} \qquad (4.28)$$

If the wage rate increases, the worker's response may be considered as the sum of two components.

The first component is a pure substitution effect: given that one hour of work is better paid, the compensated individual tends to substitute leisure with consumption and would like to work more: $\partial \hat{h}/\partial w > 0$.

The second is an autonomous income effect. The sign of this income effect is left undetermined by the accepted axioms on preferences. If leisure is an "inferior" commodity, increased income prompts workers to supply more working hours, $\partial h^s/\partial y > 0$; in this case, there is no ambiguity about the sign of the individual labor supply response, as both effects go in the same direction, $\partial h^s/\partial w > 0$.

However, in the opposite case in which leisure is a "normal" commodity, in other words, if people tend to increase their demand for leisure when their autonomous income increases, $\partial h^s/\partial y < 0$. In this case, the net effect of the wage increase depends on the magnitude of the two components, $\partial h^s/\partial w \lessgtr 0$.

Figure 4.5 depicts a situation in which leisure is a normal commodity, and in which the substitution effect prevails.

When the wage rate increases from w_1 to w_2, the substitution effect would increase working time to h_3, but the income effect tends to offset this first term, final working time being h_2; in this case h_2 is still larger than h_1.

In the presence of a positive autonomous income ($y > 0$), equation (4.28) lends itself to an analysis in elasticity terms: multiplying both members of equation (4.28) by w/h, this takes the form:

$$\eta_w^{h^s} = \eta_w^{\hat{h}} + \theta \eta_y^{h^s} \qquad (4.29)$$

where $\theta = wh/y$ represents the ratio of labor earned income over autonomous income, $\eta_w^{h^s}$ stands for the uncompensated wage elasticity of hours of work, $\eta_w^{\hat{h}}$ is the income compensated wage elasticity (income is

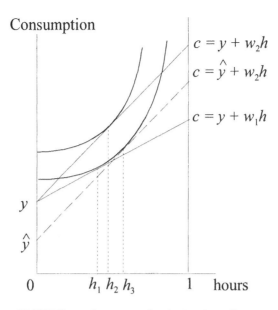

Consumption

$c = y + w_2 h$

$c = \hat{y} + w_2 h$

$c = y + w_1 h$

y

$\hat{y}$

$0 \qquad h_1\, h_2\, h_3 \qquad 1 \qquad$ hours

FIGURE 4.5. Income and substitution effects

adjusted to hold utility constant), while $\theta \eta_y^h$ is the so-called "total income elasticity" (Pencavel 1986).

If there is no autonomous income, $y = 0$, $\theta = +\infty, \eta_y^{h^s} = 0$ but by definition, $\theta \eta_y^{h^s} = w \dfrac{\partial h^s}{\partial y}$.

4.2.5 Empirical estimates of labor supply functions

As mentioned in Chapter 1, the first forms of this analysis were suggested by Lionel Robbins (1930) who argued quite convincingly that only empirical analysis could reveal the actual form of the relationship between wages and the working hours supply; since an early attempt to estimate hours supply functions by Douglas (1934), an impressive number of studies have been devoted to this issue. According to Pencavel (1986, p.3) "labor supply has become the most active area of all labor economics research".

Most empirical estimates use cross-sectional data to reveal the supply behavior in the short run. These studies analyze workers' participation or annual hours of work as they are affected by wage rates (w in our notation) or unearned income (y). As emphasized by Ehrenberg and Smith (1994), the most reliable studies are those which focus on hours supply of men, since the supply decision of women is highly sensitive to child-rearing and household work arrangements for which data are sketchy at best.

Pencavel (1986) quotes fourteen studies on the hours response of American men carried out in the seventies and eighties. The central tendency of estimates of the uncompensated wage elasticity of hours of work lies between $[-0.17, 0.08]$, and a simple average of all estimates (except a positive outlier) is $\eta_w^{h^s} = -0.12$. According to the same author, from these studies it may be reasonably inferred that $\eta_w^{\hat{h}} = 0.11$ and the total income elasticity is $\theta\eta_y^h = -0.23$. Apart from two papers, all the other studies found that the income effect is negative, thus leisure appears to be a normal good. He also surveys several studies on British men, and finds support for a similar conclusion, in favor of a seemingly backward bending supply curve.

As far as women are concerned, supplied working time seems to exhibit positive response to wage increases. Killingsworth and Heckman (1986) and Blundell (1993) survey several studies carried out in the eighties and early nineties, most of them reporting positive uncompensated elasticities and negative income elasticities. For instance, the uncompensated wage elasticity of hours of work reported in the eight studies surveyed by Blundell lies in the interval $[0.10, 0.71]$, with an outlier of 1.44. Of course, the behavior of women appears to be highly sensitive to marital status, the number of children and the age of children. As a rather general feature, all these cross-sectional analyses for men and women conclude that both income and substitution effects are small.

Long run supply behavior is difficult to grasp, insofar as many factors are unstable. As mentioned in Chapter 2, in the last 200 years, hours of work have declined throughout the Western world while wages and GDP per inhabitant have risen steadily. If one reasonably assumes that technical progress is responsible for an upward shift of the demand for labor services, in the light of this chapter, the observed tendency would suggest that the hour supply curve must be backward bending. However, in the eighties the downward trend in working hours tended to stabilize and even to reverse in some countries. The elementary neoclassical model could be made consistent with this observation if the supply becomes at least locally more rigid. Costa (1998) brings out some evidence in favor of this view.

	All workers	Hourly workers
1890s	−0.304	−0.536
1973	−0.087	−0.023
1991	−0.017	+0.104

TABLE 4.1. Elasticity of daily hours worked with respect to the hourly wage. American men aged 25-64. Source: Costa (1998)

4.2.6 Surplus from work

As mentioned before, when the wage rate is higher than the lower reservation limit, workers supply a positive amount of time, $h^s(w) > 0$; this

optimum working time enables the individual to increase his utility from
the value $S_0 = U(y, 0)$ to $S^* = U(y + wh^s, h^s)$.

The surplus from work is defined by the autonomous income increase v
which would compensate the individual for being prevented from working
at all. It is implicitly defined by:

$$U(y + v, 0) = S^*$$

This compensation is represented in Figure 4.6.

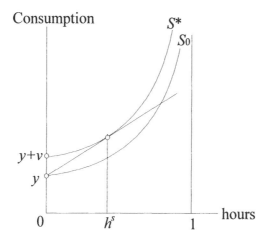

FIGURE 4.6. Surplus from work

A general expression for the compensation of wage variations may be obtained from properties of the objective function in the compensated problem (4.19). For instance, if the wage rate decreases from the initial value
w_1 to the final value w_2, by definition of the function $\hat{y}(w, S)$, the necessary
compensation is $\gamma(w_1, w_2) = \hat{y}(w_2, S_1^*) - \hat{y}(w_1, S_1^*)$ where S_1^* is the satisfaction level reached in the initial equilibrium: $S_1^* = U[y + w_1 h^s(w_1), h^s(w_1)]$.

Since $\partial\hat{y}/\partial w = -\hat{h}$, this may be written $\gamma(w_1, w_2) = -\int_{w_1}^{w_2} \hat{h}(w, S_1^*)dw$. It

can be represented by the grey shaded area at the left of the compensated
supply curve and between the two horizontal lines of ordinates w_2 and w_1
(Figure 4.7), where it may be seen that $\hat{h}(w, S^*) = 0$ for small values of w.

In this perspective, surplus from work may be viewed as the compensation for a wage variation going from an initial value w_1 to zero:

$$v = \gamma(w_1, 0) = \int_{w=0}^{w_1} \hat{h}(w, S_1^*)dw$$

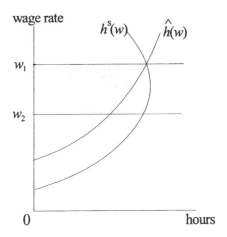

FIGURE 4.7. Compensation of a wage rate decrease

4.3   Comments on the elementary neoclassical model of hours supply

4.3.1   The composite good: a caveat about relative prices

We have used in the above analysis the familiar notion of the real wage rate. In using the compact notation $S = U(c, h)$ we consider either that only one good exists in the economy or that c stands for the consumption of a composite commodity. In the latter case, a utility function $U(c, h)$ may be defined in the following way. Recording the consumption of the m goods by $(x_1...x_i...x_m)$, we consider first a neoclassical utility function $V(x_1...x_i...x_m, h)$ (with $V_h < 0$) representing constant preferences and denote $(x_1^*...x_i^*...x_m^*)$ the vector of consumption, solution of the problem:

$$\begin{cases} \max_{x_1...x_i...x_m} \quad V(x_1...x_i...x_m, h) \\ \quad \text{with:} \sum_{i=1}^{m} p_i x_i \leq c \end{cases} \quad (4.30)$$

where c and h are considered predetermined and where p_i represents the money price of the ith good. From standard demand theory, $(x_1^*...x_i^*...x_m^*)$ is uniquely determined and is a continuous function of c, h and all prices p_i. It is possible to define $U(c, h)$ by $U(c, h) = V(x_1^*...x_i^*...x_m^*, h)$; this new function is an "indirect utility function", c standing for a money flow of income available for consumption. This function is well defined for a given price structure and satisfies axioms 1, 2 and 3.[8]

---

[8] Proof of this statement is a technical exercise omitted here.

In what sense can we say that a constant wage rate implies a constant labor supply when c stands for a composite commodity ?

To illustrate the problem in intuitive terms, consider the following case. A worker is so fond of golf that in an initial situation, he spends as much money playing his favorite sport as purchasing food. In a first assumption, we imagine that the price of food is increased by 20%, other prices being constant. His nominal wage rate is adjusted in order to make the consumption and leisure-time bundle of the initial reference state exactly possible. In a second assumption, the hourly cost of golf is increased by 20%, other prices being constant. Once again, his nominal wage rate is adjusted in order to make the consumption and leisure-time bundle of the initial reference state exactly possible. We can say that the worker is compensated in both cases, and that the real wage rate has been in some sense kept constant. Can we predict that this worker's labor supply is affected in the same way?

When the price of food increases, the compensated worker tends to reduce somewhat his consumption because of the substitution effect, but eating less or eating lower quality food does not impinge so directly on the duration of meals and on the demand for leisure. When the price of golf increases, the compensated worker with neoclassical preferences is going to reduce time spent on golf courses and this could very well induce him to supply more working hours.

In order to examine the effects of changes in prices, the worker's problem may be rewritten in terms of the direct utility function:

$$
\left\{
\begin{aligned}
&\max_{x_1...x_i...x_m,h} V(x_1...x_i...x_m,h) \\
&\text{with: } \sum_{i=1}^{m} p_i x_i = Wh + Y
\end{aligned}
\right.
\qquad (4.31)
$$

In problem (4.31), the wage rate W and the income Y are in money terms. The first order conditions applying to the Lagrangian form associated to this problem are:

$$
\begin{aligned}
&V_i - \lambda p_i = 0, \ \forall i = (1,...,m) \\
&V_h + \lambda W = 0 \\
&\sum_{i=1}^{m} p_i x_i^* = Wh^s + Y
\end{aligned}
\qquad (4.32)
$$

The resulting labor supply function is of the form:

$$
h^s = h^s(p_1...p_i...p_m, W, Y)
\qquad (4.33)
$$

This function clearly verifies the following homogeneity property:

$$
\forall \mu > 0, \ h^s(\mu p_1...\mu p_i...\mu p_m, \mu W, \mu Y) = h^s(p_1...p_i...p_m, W, Y)
\qquad (4.34)
$$

Therefore, when the prices of all goods change proportionally, the following relationship holds:

$$h^s(\mu p_1...\mu p_i...\mu p_m, W, Y) = h^s\left(p_1...p_i...p_m, \frac{W}{\mu}, \frac{Y}{\mu}\right) \qquad (4.35)$$

In this case, controlling the labor supply function for variations of the price level may simply be carried out by dividing the nominal wage and the monetary autonomous income by $\mu = 1 + \pi$, where π is a well-defined inflation rate.

When the price structure is modified, it is possible to show that for constant preferences (constant direct utility function), the relationship between the labor supply and the "real wage rate" is not stable, when the real wage rate is understood as the nominal wage rate deflated by a conventional price index.[9] To develop this point, we differentiate equation (4.32) in the case where $m = 2$:

$$\begin{pmatrix} V_{11} & V_{12} & V_{1h} & -p_1 \\ V_{21} & V_{22} & V_{2h} & -p_2 \\ V_{h1} & V_{h2} & V_{hh} & W \\ -p_1 & -p_2 & W & 0 \end{pmatrix} \begin{pmatrix} dx_1^* \\ dx_2^* \\ dh^s \\ d\lambda^* \end{pmatrix} = \begin{pmatrix} \lambda^* dp_1 \\ \lambda^* dp_2 \\ \lambda^* dW \\ x_1 dp_1 + x_2 dp_2 - h^s dW - dY \end{pmatrix}$$

or, after inversion of the left hand side matrix:

$$\begin{pmatrix} dx_1^* \\ dx_2^* \\ dh^s \\ d\lambda^* \end{pmatrix} = \begin{pmatrix} m_{11} & . & . & m_{14} \\ . & . & . & . \\ . & . & . & . \\ m_{41} & . & . & m_{44} \end{pmatrix} \begin{pmatrix} \lambda^* dp_1 \\ \lambda^* dp_2 \\ \lambda^* dW \\ x_1^* dp_1 + x_2^* dp_2 - h^s dW - dY \end{pmatrix}$$

In general,

$$dh^s = \lambda^* (m_{31} dp_1 + m_{32} dp_2 + m_{33} dW) + m_{34}(x_1^* dp_1 + x_2^* dp_2 - h^s dW - dY) \qquad (4.36)$$

If we consider that the only variation is $dp_1 > 0$, Slutsky compensation would consist in increasing the nominal wage in such a way that $dW = (x_1^*/h^s)dp_1$, but in this case, $dh^s = \lambda^*\left(m_{31} + m_{33}\dfrac{x_1^*}{h^s}\right)dp_1 \neq 0$. This reaction may be understood as a substitution effect between leisure and good 1.

This means that when relative prices of goods are changed, a constant "real wage" does not imply constant labor supply. Dividing the nominal

---

[9]The widespread Laspeyres price index weights prices on the basis of the initial consumption basket of the representative consumer.

wage by a price index tends to control the labor supply for income effects associated with price variations but not for substitution effects. In cross-section samples, all the workers face the same set of prices and differences in nominal wage are equivalent to differences in the real wage rate; in time series, the price structure cannot generally be assumed constant and some shifts in the apparent labor supply diagram could be spuriously attributed to changes in workers' tastes.

4.3.2 Labor supply, wages and competing home production

In the explanation of working time presented in subsection 4.2.2, the consumption/leisure trade-off takes place with a market constraint in which the income not related to labor (y) is exogenous. In a pioneering text, Becker (1965) outlined that the conditions in which "leisure" is allocated to various activities may have a significant impact on welfare and on labor supply. In the light of his paper, the elementary neoclassical model may be modified to account for domestic production of the consumption good, and to emphasize other relevant effects of changes in wages and domestic productivity on the time spent on outside jobs. This sort of situation is often considered as particularly relevant in Less Developed Countries where the production terms in firms hardly surpass those attainable in domestic production.

A simple model was worked out by Gronau (1986) and builds on the following set of assumptions:

– Consumption objectives can be achieved either directly by domestic production or indirectly, by selling hours of work in the labor market, and then converting the wage income into the consumption commodity.

– The individual applies a technology transforming domestic work into goods, described by: $c_d = F(h_d)$, where h_d are domestic working hours. We assume $F(0) = 0, F' > 0, F'' < 0$.

– He can alternatively sell labor services in the labor market at the wage rate w. Denoting on-the-job working time by h_m, resulting consumption is $c_m = wh_m$.

– Total consumption is thus $c_\bullet = c_d + c_m$ and total time devoted to productive activities is $h_\bullet = h_d + h_m$. Of course, leisure is: $l = 1 - (h_d + h_m) = 1 - h_\bullet$.

– Assumed homogeneity of consumption goods and equal disutility of working time in the two places makes it possible to represent the satisfaction of the worker by the neoclassical utility function $u(c_\bullet, h_\bullet)$.

The worker's decision is represented by:

$$\left\{ \begin{array}{l} \max\limits_{h_d, h_m} u(c_\bullet, h_d + h_m) \\ \text{with: } c_\bullet = F(h_d) + wh_m \end{array} \right. \tag{4.37}$$

The corresponding Lagrangian form is:

$$\mathcal{L} = u(c_\bullet, h_d + h_m) - \lambda[c_\bullet - F(h_d) - wh_m] \qquad (4.38)$$

entailing first order conditions:

$$u_c = \lambda \qquad (4.39)$$
$$u_h = \lambda F'(h_d) \qquad (4.40)$$
$$u_h = \lambda w \qquad (4.41)$$

Thus from equation (4.40) and equation (4.41) we have $F'(h_d) = w$ which defines h_d^s, and from (4.39) and (4.41), $MRS = \left(\dfrac{dc}{dh}\right)_{U=S} = -\dfrac{U_h}{U_c} = w$ which defines total hours supply $h_\bullet^s$. Then $h_m^s = h_\bullet^s - h_d^s$.

The solution is depicted in Figure 4.8:

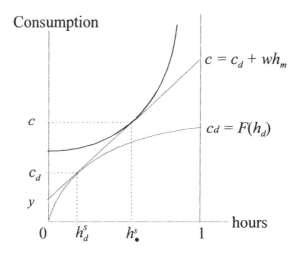

FIGURE 4.8. Optimal working time: at home and on-the-job

In order to analyze the response of the market supply of labor h_m^s to wage rate fluctuations, it is possible to consider the two logically consecutive stages of the worker's decision. The first decision consists in working at home for a time h_d^s, solely determined by $F'(h_d) = w$. This first decision determines the market line and its intercept on the vertical axis noted y. In a second stage, the worker's choice may be interpreted as a standard working time decision in which the "autonomous" income y becomes a function of the wage rate w denoted $y(w)$. With the help of Figure 4.8 it can be checked that $y(w) = F(h_d^s) - wh_d^s$ and therefore $\dfrac{dy}{dw} = [F'(h_d^s) - w]\dfrac{dh_d^s}{dw} - h_d^s = -h_d^s$.

Considering the total working time as a function of w, we can write the following identity:

$$h_\bullet^s(w) = h^s[w, y(w)] \tag{4.42}$$

Therefore $\dfrac{dh_\bullet^s(w)}{dw} = \dfrac{\partial h^s}{\partial w} + \dfrac{\partial h^s}{\partial y}\dfrac{dy}{dw} = \dfrac{\partial h^s}{\partial w} - h_d^s\dfrac{\partial h^s}{\partial y}$. The term $\dfrac{\partial h^s}{\partial w}$ itself can be decomposed to substitution and income effects according to equation (4.28): $\dfrac{\partial h^s}{\partial w} = \dfrac{\partial \hat{h}}{\partial w} + h_\bullet^s\dfrac{\partial h^s}{\partial y}$. We then have:

$$\frac{dh_\bullet^s}{dw} = \frac{\partial \hat{h}}{\partial w} + (h_\bullet^s - h_d^s)\frac{\partial h^s}{\partial y} = \frac{\partial \hat{h}}{\partial w} + h_m^s\frac{\partial h^s}{\partial y}$$

Also, $F'(h_d^s) = w$ implies $\dfrac{dh_d^s}{dw} = \dfrac{1}{F''(h_d)}$.

Since $h_m^s = h_\bullet^s - h_d^s$, we finally obtain:

$$\frac{dh_m^s}{dw} = \frac{dh_\bullet^s}{dw} - \frac{dh_d^s}{dw} = \frac{\partial \hat{h}}{\partial w} + h_m^s\frac{\partial h^s}{\partial y} - \frac{1}{F''(h_d^s)} \tag{4.43}$$

The effect of an increased wage rate on the supply of market hours by workers having their own productive abilities is decomposed into three terms. Only the income effect, restricted to hours sold on the market may be negative. The order of magnitude of the third term can be overwhelming if the technology is close to linearity, $F''(h_d)$ taking small values. The response of labor supply for this type of worker may therefore be very different from the standard prediction.

4.3.3   Reservation wage and lump-sum cost of working: a quantum

The standard labor supply theory implies strong continuity properties; in particular, when the wage rate decreases toward its reservation value as defined in subsection 4.2.2, the supplied working time continuously diminishes and approaches zero. Very short working durations are however rarely observed, a fact which can be interpreted in labor supply terms if we introduce more details into the worker's feasible set description. We consider that the worker incurs a fixed cost z if working. This lump sum may be interpreted as the cost of having to commute to the workplace and arrive with a suitable appearance, but it may more significantly include the loss of support or subsidy granted to the unemployed. In this case the labor supply is $h^s(w, y - z)$ if the resulting satisfaction equals or exceeds the satisfaction level recorded when not working at all, but saving the fixed cost. This more encompassing notion of reservation wage $\widetilde{w}$ is therefore defined as the solution of the following equation:

$$U\left[y - z + wh^s(w, y - z), h^s(w, y - z)\right] = U(y, 0)$$

Worker's behavior in the presence of lump costs can be represented by the supply function:

$$h^s = \begin{cases} h^s(w, y - z), & \text{for } w \geq \tilde{w} \\ 0, & \text{for } w < \tilde{w} \end{cases}$$

When the wage rate decreases towards the reservation limit, labor supply tends to an indivisible quantum of working time, denoted $\tilde{h}$. Figure 4.9 illustrates the determination of $\tilde{w}$ and $\tilde{h}$.

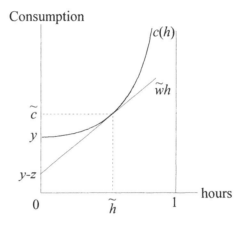

FIGURE 4.9. Reservation wage with "commuting" costs

We show how the reservation wage rate in the case where unemployment benefits are lost by the incumbent workers modifies the representation of outside equilibrium in the labor market. According to equation (4.7), the firm demand for workers takes the form:

$$n^*(w) = \frac{L^*(w)}{h^s(w)}$$

The demand for workers does not exist where $w < \tilde{w}$ since in this case $h^s(w) = 0$. The number $n^*(\tilde{w})$ represents the maximum amount of workers willingly hired by the representative firm.

The supply of workers per firm (each providing $h^s(w)$) is:

$$n^s = \begin{cases} N/f, & \text{if } w \geq \tilde{w} \\ 0, & \text{if } w < \tilde{w} \end{cases}$$

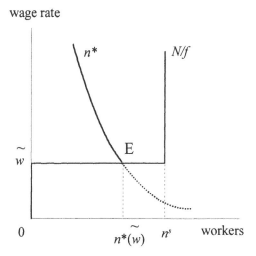

FIGURE 4.10. Involuntary unemployment

that is, the participation rate becomes nil for wages inferior to the reservation wage rate.

If the demand for workers is weak, the special situation depicted in Figure 4.10 may arise: $n^*(\tilde{w}) < N/f$. Workers are indifferent between holding a job or not; those who do not have one $(n^s - n^*(\tilde{w}))$ can either be called involuntary unemployed, insofar as they would take an available job at the going wage, or voluntary unemployed, since their situation is a consequence of their preferences and since they incur no welfare loss from unemployment.[10]

It may be checked that $\tilde{w} = c'(\tilde{h})$ and convex indifference curves imply that $\tilde{w}$ and $\tilde{h}$ are both increasing in z. In the Appendix to this chapter, the reservation wage and the corresponding quantum of working time are explicitly calculated as functions of the fixed cost z for a simple theoretical utility function.

4.4   Conclusion

In this chapter, emphasis was placed on the analysis of the labor supply, which dominated the early period of neoclassical economics. We show how considerations on consumption/leisure preferences themselves may explain the variety of durations of work, for a non-differentiated flow of labor services provided to firms. One of the main shortcomings of this elementary neoclassical view is its incapacity to account for obvious worker rationing

---

[10]See De Vroey (1998) for an analysis of the two terms in historical perspective.

and systematic conflicts over working hours. These difficulties come from the obvious oversimplification of the demand side. In the late sixties, some authors begin to pay more attention to the composition of the flow of labor services. The next chapter proposes a brief description of these advances and develops an original description of the productive process, introducing the concept of "output density function".

4.5   Appendix: Examples of theoretical utility functions

We suggest examining basic utility functions able to convey the three axioms concerning preferences adopted in this chapter and to illustrate simply some of the proposed concepts. The time unit is the day so $h \in]0,1[$.

- **U = c(1 − h)**

Axioms 1, 2 and 3 hold; a fixed level of satisfaction S defines a compensating function (or an indifference curve) $c(h) = S/(1 - h)$.

The first derivative $c'(h) = \left(\dfrac{dc}{dh}\right)_{U=S} = S(1 - h)^{-2}$ and the second derivative $c''(h) = 2S(1 - h)^{-3}$ are both defined and positive for $h \in]0,1[$.

The corresponding hours supply function is $h^s(w,y) = (w-y)/2w$, where y is an autonomous income.

For $w \geq S$, the compensated labor supply function is $\hat{h}(w,S) = 1 - \sqrt{S/w}$.

In the absence of fixed costs entailed by working, the reservation wage is $\underline{w} = y$. If the fact of working implies the loss of z consumption units (foregone unemployment benefits), a new value of the reservation wage can be computed. This value is the solution of: $U\left[y - z + wh^s(w), h^s(w)\right] = U(y,0)$; applying the assumed utility function, it may be shown that the relevant solution of this equation is $\widetilde{w} = z+y+2\sqrt{zy}$, an increasing function of z; the quantum of labor supplied for this value of the wage rate is $\widetilde{h} = \dfrac{z + \sqrt{zy}}{z + y + 2\sqrt{zy}}$. It may be checked that $z = 0 \Rightarrow \widetilde{w} = y$ and $\widetilde{h} = 0$.

- **U = (c − c$_0$)$^\alpha$(1 − h)$^{1-\alpha}$, $\alpha \in]0,1[$**

This utility function introduces a term c_0 which may be interpreted as a subsistence consumption; preferences are not defined for $c < c_0$.

A given satisfaction level S defines an indifference curve $c(h) = c_0 + S^{\frac{1}{\alpha}}(1 - h)^{\frac{\alpha-1}{\alpha}}$.

The slope of the indifference curve is therefore: $c'(h) = \left(\dfrac{dc}{dh}\right)_{U=S} = S^{\frac{1}{\alpha}}\left(\dfrac{1-\alpha}{\alpha}\right)(1 - h)^{-\frac{1}{\alpha}} = \left(\dfrac{1-\alpha}{\alpha}\right)\left(\dfrac{c - c_0}{1 - h}\right) > 0 \ \forall h \in]0,1[$, the parameter α tuning the slope of the indifference curve.

The compensating function is convex $c''(h) = S^{\frac{1}{\alpha}} \left(\dfrac{1-\alpha}{\alpha^2} \right)(1-h)^{-\frac{1+\alpha}{\alpha}} >$ $0\ \forall h \in]0,1[$.

The hours supply function is $h^s(w,y) = \alpha + [(c_0 - y)(1-\alpha)]/w$; therefore, $\partial h^s/\partial w$ is nil if $y = c_0$, negative if $y < c_0$ and positive if $y > c_0$.

The reservation wage is $\underline{w} = (y - c_0)(1 - \alpha)/\alpha$, increasing with y.

This utility function is able to illustrate the mercantilist view of labor supply mentioned in Chapter 1. Consider the case where $y = 0$ (workers have no autonomous income). In this case, $h^s(w,0) = \alpha + c_0(1-\alpha)/w$ implying $\lim_{\alpha \to 0} \{h^s(w,0)\} = c_0/w$. This limit depicts a situation in which no finite increase in consumption would be able to compensate an increased working time when the subsistence requirement is satisfied. It involves $\eta_w^{h^s} = -1$.

- **Quasi-linear utility functions**

It is often convenient to use quasi-linear utility functions, i.e. functions of the form $U(c,h) = c - v(h)$, where $v(h)$ is a convex function such that $v(0) = 0$, $v'(h) > 0$, $v''(h) > 0$. Such functions generate convex compensating functions (or indifference curves) defined for any given value of S by $c(h) = S + v(h)$ and therefore $c'(h) = v'(h)$ and $c''(h) = v''(h) > 0$. The hours supply function is $h^s(w) = v'^{-1}(w)$, with $dh^s/dw = 1/v''(h) > 0$.

In a space (Oh, Oc), the satisfaction level related to an indifference curve has a consumption equivalent visualized by the ordinate $c(0) = S$. The surplus derived from Walrasian supply in the labor market is also visualized on the vertical axis. (An application of these functions to working time theory will be provided in Chapter 7.)

5
Working time, production and cost functions

5.1   Contemporary demand side contributions to working time analysis

5.1.1   The critique of the elementary neoclassical approach

The standard textbook analysis of the demand side of the labor market draws exclusively on standard production functions, in which the flow of labor input is entirely defined as the product of the number of employed people and the number of hours worked per day, or other implicit time unit. As seen in Chapter 4, with such production functions, and assuming standard labor cost functions, the wage-taking firm is totally indifferent to the composition of the labor input. Competition can therefore bring about the optimal working day from the worker's point of view, corresponding to the notional labor supply.

Production and cost functions are in fact symbolic and highly simplified representations of the economically relevant aspects of complex production processes. They are generally conceived as parsimonious tools, able to integrate the most basic properties of firm behavior into broader descriptions of the economic system. As building blocks of involved models, their own complexity must be kept at sufficiently low levels.

More formally, production functions – in the standard form – explain which flow of output y can be obtained by applying a stock of capital K, and a flow of labor services L. This relationship is represented by a concave, twice differentiable function $F(K, L)$. The neoclassical standard form implies, in particular, the following assumptions:

1. The stock of capital is generally considered to be composed of K homogeneous equipment units.

2. The flow of labor services is (most often implicitly) supposed to be of the form $L = nh$, where n is the number of homogeneous workers and h is the number of homogeneous hours.

3. The total cost incurred by the producer is explained by the same variables, and the currently used functions are of the form $C(K, L) = wL + (\delta + r)K$. Its first term is the wage bill, where w stands for the hourly real wage rate. The second term is the rental cost of capital including an exponential depreciation component represented by δK and a financial cost rK, where r is the prevailing real interest rate. By a suitable choice of units, the price of the capital unit is equal to one.

Under these assumptions, the profit function is also concave: $\pi(K, L) = F(K, L) - wL - (\delta + r)K$.

From standard microeconomic analysis, we know that first order conditions are therefore sufficient to characterize a profit global maximization input mix. The corresponding point $(K^*, L^*) = \arg\max\{\pi(K, L)\}$ is the unique solution, and is such that $K^* = K^*(w, \delta + r)$ and $L^* = L^*(w, \delta + r)$ are continuous functions of their arguments. Since hours supplied by outsiders or by insiders are perfect substitutes in the productive process, and since labor costs are wL, isoquants and isocosts in space (Oh, On) coalesce in the hyperbola representing the equation $L^* = nh$. In this case, as explained in detail in Chapter 4, firms are strictly neutral in terms of working time, and indetermination on (n, h) can be lifted by the workers' preferences.

Historical evidence has revealed, however, the existence of persistent conflicts between employees and firms over working time (Chapter 2). Two types of disequilibrium especially should be considered: *overwork*, i.e. the situation where the duration of work determined by the firm exceeds the Walrasian labor supply and *insider underemployment*, the opposite rationing in which the worker is constrained to more leisure than demanded for the current wage rate. Explaining the actual working time and imperfect equilibrium in a decentralized economy has thus required improved descriptions of labor costs or production processes.

As far as costs structures are concerned, most authors apply the two-part form pioneered by Rosen (1968):

$$C(w, n, h) = n(wh + \theta) \tag{5.1}$$

where the product of the real wage rate w and individual hours h represents the total wage bill (or wage compensation), and θ stands for the "fixed costs of labor".

The wage rate may itself be considered as predetermined, or depending on other variables, including in particular the duration of work.

Fixed costs of labor are expenses depending only on the number of workers and independent of the working time; in some sectors such costs may be quite substantial.[1] An exhaustive list of these costs is impossible to draw up, but we can mention: costs incurred in providing the workers with individual equipment and job environment (personal computer, office room, lunch facilities, etc.), management of the personnel files, etc. Firms often have to provide workers with some form of specific training; they consequently incur in the steady state various costs proportionate to the staff and to the staff turnover, as well as a financial cost induced by investment sunk in human capital.

It is worth noticing that the distribution of labor costs in fixed and variable forms is also affected by government interference and regulation. In most OECD countries, social charges collected from employers for financing the social welfare and unemployment compensation schemes are individually limited by a ceiling. For those workers with wages below this ceiling, social charges are still proportional to the wage income, therefore behaving like variable costs; for workers with wages above the ceiling, the contribution appears as a lump-sum tax, thus behaving like a fixed cost.

In a thorough analysis of non-wage costs, Hart (1984) published quantitative estimations of these fixed labor costs in the UK and the US. In 1981, the ratio of variable to total (variable plus fixed) costs was around 0.89 if payments for days not worked are excluded, or 0.80 if payments for non-worked days are included.

In relation to the productive process, it must be kept in mind that some early authors, before and throughout the neoclassical period, have proved quite aware of its complex underlying structure and their points of view were coined in explicit terms:

> Two hundred grenadiers pulling ropes for a few hours have been able to lift the Luxor obelisk on the Place de la Concorde; a few grenadiers pulling for two hundred hours could not. (Pierre Joseph Proudhon, 1840)
>
> ...if a man continually works beyond a certain point, the intensity of his work will be reduced to such an extent that the gain in longer hours will be more than offset by the loss in hourly output, so that if he had worked less his average output would have been greater. (Lionel Robbins, 1929, p.26)

---

[1] See Oi (1962) for an early analysis of the labor input as a quasi-fixed factor.

Increased leisure means increased facilities for rest and recreation; rest and recreation improve physical strength and increase alertness; these in their turn react upon efficiency... Some men might turn out more if the hours were longer, some men more if they were shorter; but if the total output is maximized at a given length of day, that length is the optimum. (John Hicks, 1932, p.105)

5.1.2 Basic Generalized Production Functions

Such considerations are at the core of various generalizations of the production functions which contemporary labor market analysis has worked out. By definition, Generalized Production Functions (G.P.F.) do away with the implicit assumption of perfect substitution between workers and hours (in logarithms). In general terms, G.P.F. are functions of the form:

$$y = \varphi(n, h, K)$$

where y is the daily flow of output, n is a continuous variable approximating the number of hired workers, h is the daily working time per individual and K is the worker's capital endowment. Different authors have suggested a particular G.P.F., able in their view to capture the particular features of the productive process they want to emphasize.

For instance, Hoel (1986) argues that production in the manufacturing sector should be represented as:

$$y = hF(n) \tag{5.2}$$

$F(\ )$ being a concave function. In his interpretation, equipment is not homogeneous, the firm employing a stock of machines of varying quality and staff is subject to diminishing returns, because successive workers are equipped with tools of decreasing efficiency. On the other hand, the output is linear in working time, and this function does not express the effect of exertion on production. It must be noticed that Hoel's function is also compatible with another (non-exclusive) interpretation according to which the concavity of $F(\ )$ should be attributed to the productivity structure of a heterogeneous labor force or to labor coordination effects and not to heterogeneous equipment.

According to Calmfors and Hoel (1989) output depends on hours and employment according to the function $y = F(nh, shK)$, where the integer s stands for the number of shifts and K is the stock of capital. The product sh indicates in fact the number of hours per day for which the equipment is used. In the case of a production function homogeneous of degree one, we have for instance: $F(nh, shK) = (nh)^a(shK)^{1-a}$, $(a < 1)$, and the obtained form is also linear in working time:

$$y = hF(n, sK) \tag{5.3}$$

Shift work is often present in those activities where the costs of stopping and starting production are high (for instance, production of nuclear electric power requires permanent monitoring; steel production also requires continuous production flow). Protective services (police, firefighters and emergency health care) also require shift work. However, the bulk of contemporary production does not rely on such an organization. According to data published by the US Bureau of Labor Statistics, in 1997, 82.9% of the full-time paid workers in the United States were on regular daytime schedules. Only 2.9% of them were on rotating shifts and 8.1% did evening or night shifts. The same pattern was observed in France, where the National Institute of Statistics (Insee) recorded that, in 1995, only 10.4% of the wage earners worked on regular shifts (Boisard and Fermanian, 1999).

Hoel and Vale (1986) observed that firms incur an output loss when recruiting new employees, as a result of time diversion in training the newly hired in the workplace. Such losses are thus proportional to the firm's turnover q, and would justify a production function in which only effective working time contributes to explain output:

$$y = F[(h - tq)n] = F(nh - tqn) \qquad (5.4)$$

In equation (5.4), q is the turnover rate and t represents the necessary training time per employee. In such a case, the output elasticity with respect to hours η_h^y should be larger than the output elasticity with respect to workers η_n^y, since from equation (5.4) $\eta_n^y = (1 - tq/h)\eta_h^y$ and therefore $\eta_h^y > \eta_n^y$.

As already mentioned, in the conventional neoclassical analysis, the standard definition of labor services is the total number of hours, i.e. $L = nh$, and, whatever the production function applied to this flow of labor services, $\eta_n^y = \eta_h^y$. Rather than using the general form of G.P.F., the improved functions encountered in modern working time analysis are usually based on a specific concept of labor services to be included as an argument of the production function. This concept acknowledges the fact that the contribution of hours and workers to the flow of labor services may justify a more flexible representation than the simple multiplicative form, i.e. $L = L(n, h)$ with $L_n > 0$ and $L_h > 0$.

In this new setting, the marginal contribution to labor services of additional hours obtained from the employment of a new worker or by extending the average working time of incumbent workers may significantly differ. In this perspective, labor services are often described by the form introduced by Ehrenberg (1971):

$$L = ng(h) \qquad (5.5)$$

In this multiplicative form, the "effectiveness function" $g(h)$ indicates the individual contribution of a worker to the flow of labor services. It is generally assumed that $g(0) = 0$ and $g'(h) > 0$, additional time generating additional output. As emphasized by Hart (1987), it is also most often supposed that $g''(h) > 0$ for some $h \leq h_0$, "warming-up" or other favorable effects prevailing and increasing the marginal efficiency for durations inferior to a threshold h_0: in this case, successive equal time increments generate increasing increments of labor services. For "long" durations $h > h_0$, the effects of exertion and perhaps boredom prevail and $g''(h) < 0$, that is the contribution of successive time units to the flow of labor services diminishes (Figure 5.1).[2]

The time structure of the two effects (warming-up and exertion) explains the variations in average efficiency $g(h)/h$. In this context, it is possible to define the number of hours h_1 which maximizes average efficiency. Since $h_1 = \arg\max\{g(h)/h\}$, from the first order condition for an interior solution, i.e. if $h_1 \in]0, 1[$, this maximization implies $g(h_1) = h_1 g'(h_1)$. If the effectiveness function is such that $g''(h) > 0$ for $h < h_0$ and $g''(h) < 0$ for $h > h_0$ it is possible to show that $h_1 > h_0$. For $h < h_1$, increasing hours entail increasing average efficiency, and beyond this threshold, increasing hours decrease average efficiency. In the light of this comment, it must be noticed that exertion may sometimes occur even if average productivity increases.

Figure 5.1 summarizes the relationship between such an efficiency function $g(h)$, the marginal efficiency $g'(h)$ and average efficiency $g(h)/h$. It must be noticed that, from the l'Hôpital rule, $\lim_{h \to 0} \dfrac{g(h)}{h} = \lim_{h \to 0} g'(h) \geq 0$.

Researchers have suggested different specifications for the effectiveness function. For instance, FitzRoy and Hart (1985) and Hart (1987) have introduced two positive parameters τ and ϵ, considering that $g(h) = 0$, for $h < \tau$ and $g(h) = (h - \tau)^\epsilon$, for $h > \tau$ with $0 < \epsilon < 1$. Time τ is interpreted as closing a "set-up" interval. Although this form reflects exertion as soon as $h > \tau$, since in this case $g''(h) < 0$, average productivity increases during a first time interval, then diminishes for $h > \dfrac{\tau}{1 - \epsilon} > \tau$.

Other authors introduced constant elasticity functions, like $g(h) = h^\beta$, where $\beta < 1$ is interpreted as a dominant fatigue effect, and $\beta > 1$ as a dominant warming-up effect (see Booth and Schiantarelli, 1987; Andersen, 1987; FitzRoy, 1993; D'Autume and Cahuc, 1997).

It should be noted in general terms that the introduction of the currently proposed efficiency functions is nothing but a special way of building a G.P.F., defined for instance by $\varphi(n, h, K) = F[ng(h), K]$. The empirical meaning of the labor services as an argument of a production function is however questionable, since a degree of freedom is introduced in defining jointly the production function and the labor services input. For instance the constant output elasticity function $y = K^\gamma n^\alpha h^\beta$ is a simple

---

[2] This form has already been advocated by Chapman (1909).

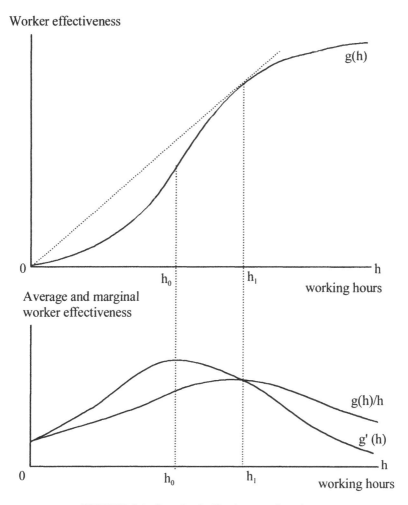

FIGURE 5.1. Standard effectiveness function

G.P.F., which can be interpreted in different ways. We can define labor services by $L = nh^{\beta/\alpha}$; in this case the corresponding production function is $y = K^{\gamma}L^{\alpha}$. Alternatively, labor services may be defined by $L = n^{\alpha/\beta}h$, the corresponding production function being $y = K^{\gamma}L^{\beta}$. The only empirically determinable relationship is therefore the G.P.F. version relating observable output y to observable inputs K, n, h. The two suggested interpretations in terms of labor services are apparently opposed, since in one case, these labor services are linear in n, in the other case linear in h. They describe however the same productive process. Labor services as a malleable and measurable input are therefore defined in accordance with some convention. For instance, if there exists in the economy a productive process in which the labor services are directly considered as productive without any collateral factors or intermediation, $L = ng(h)$ may be defining efficiency $g(h)$ from the output obtained in this particular process by n individuals working h hours. The flow L, used as an argument of a production function related to other activities, may be interpreted in such a case as a form of opportunity cost of production.

It is important to remark that the notion of labor services has been extensively used by economists who developed "efficiency wage" models of the labor market (see for pioneering papers Solow, 1979; Akerlof, 1982; Shapiro and Stiglitz 1984). In their view, worker effort in the workplace would be an increasing function of the wage rate relative to some reference income obtained from alternative activities. This positive relationship between wages and effort has been justified either by better morale under the gift-exchange paradigm, or by the increasing opportunity costs of shirking when effort on the job is private information to the worker. There were a few attempts to combine working time and efficiency wage approaches based on more sophisticated G.P.F. For instance, in their production function (equation 5.4), Hoel and Vale (1986) considered that the quit rate q is a decreasing function of the wage rate. Also, Schmidt-Sørensen (1991) proposed an effectiveness function where individual labor services depend not only on hours of work as in standard working time models, but also on relative wages as in efficiency wage models.

5.1.3 Empirical estimates of constant output elasticity Generalized Production Functions

On the empirical side, many researchers, following Feldstein (1967), have estimated constant output elasticity functions in which hours and employment are separately dealt with. The suggested basic functional form is:

$$y = F(K, n, h) = AK^{\eta_K} n^{\eta_n} h^{\eta_h} \tag{5.6}$$

Table 5.1 recapitulates the main results (we only report the most significant values of the quoted studies).

	$\hat{\eta}_K$	$\hat{\eta}_n$	$\hat{\eta}_h$	Data
Feldstein (1967)	0.25	0.76	1.90	UK cross-section, 1960
Craine (1973)	0.12	0.68	1.89	US manufacturing panel 1949-1967
Leslie and Wise (1980)	0.32	0.64	0.64	UK panel, 1948-1968
Åberg (1987)	0.25	0.75	0.71	Swedish panel 1963-1982
Hart and McGregor (1988)	0.60	0.45	0.99	W. German panel 1968-1978

TABLE 5.1. Estimated output elasticities

These empirical findings may be interpreted in the terms of former theoretical considerations. If we suppose that the labor services are linear in workers we may define $L = nh^\beta$, and the former production function may be written as $y = K^{\eta_K} L^\alpha$ with $\alpha = \eta_n$. In this case, the elasticity of labor services with respect to hours $\beta = \eta_h/\eta_n$, i.e. the ratio of output elasticities with respect to hours and employment. Except for the findings of Leslie and Wise (1980), in which $\eta_h = \eta_n$ supported the traditional neoclassical view ($\beta = 1$), all these studies revealed that the estimated output elasticity ratio $\hat\beta = \hat\eta_h/\hat\eta_n > 1$, suggesting a strong warming-up effect in the vicinity of the equilibrium.

The results of Hart and McGregor (1988) support the form proposed by Hoel (1986), given that $\hat\eta_h$ is close to one, while $\hat\eta_n$ is smaller than one.

Of course, such empirical estimations are based on observations limited to small variations around central values; they provide us with limited information about the global shape of effectiveness or production functions, and can have only a local reliability in the design of working time policies.

The purpose of this chapter is to examine the foundations underlying generalized production and cost functions extensively used by all contemporary working time analyses. From a first simple but formal representation of production choices, we move towards more practical tools, emphasizing the implicit assumptions adopted at each stage. We show in particular that G.P.F. might themselves be grounded on a deeper description of production, formalized through the concept of "density". It is in some instances easier and more intuitive to enunciate assumptions about technology at this first stage, and this concept yields a more flexible and interpretable rendition of various productive processes.

5.2   A formal representation of the production decision

5.2.1   Describing production and cost structures

The production decision is a choice among a considerable number of possible combinations of elements belonging to different sets. A formal approach is useful to fully evaluate the standard neoclassical assumptions, to do away with some ambiguous expressions and to introduce more detailed assumptions in more general settings.

Consider first the simplest case, consisting of putting people to work without equipment. A production decision may be represented after defining:

 – a time set $T = \{1, ...t..., H\}$ whose elements are individualized equal time intervals (hours) where it is legally and physically possible to work in a day, and

– an individual set $I = \{1, ...i..., N\}$ whose elements are distinguishable workers available to be hired.

The employer's decision consists in determining which person will be working in each time interval. Formally, this decision is represented by a subset P of the Cartesian product $D = I \otimes T$. An empty subset $P = \emptyset$ means that there is no work at all; $P = D$ would mean that every individual works all the time. The employer may also decide to distribute workers into different teams and establish hierarchies within teams and between them, but this aspect will be neglected for simplicity.

Such a Cartesian product is represented in Table 5.2.

$i \backslash t$	1	...	t	...	H
1	$(1,1)$				$(1,H)$
i			(i,t)		
N	$(N,1)$				(N,H)

TABLE 5.2. Production decision: matching hours and workers

In this framework, $(i,t) \in P$ means that an individual i does work at time t.

Restricting ourselves to describing single output technologies, a formal production function may be defined as a set function, i.e. a mapping $\phi(P)$ of the Cartesian product $I \otimes T$ into $\mathbb{R}_1^+$. Similarly, a cost function is a set function i.e. a mapping $C(P)$ of the Cartesian product $I \otimes T$ into $\mathbb{R}_1^+$. Profit maximization consists in determining $P^* = \arg \max_P \{\phi(P) - C(P)\}$; it implies cost minimization, i.e. $P^* = \arg \min_P \{C(P)\}$ with $\phi(P) = \phi(P^*)$.

5.2.2   Conventional production and cost functions

Conventional production and cost functions used in received theory attempt to explain output or cost, not from the set P itself, but from functions of one or several real variables themselves obtained from P, and supposed to convey the relevant information about the production decision. What is assumed is the existence of variables $x_1 = h_1(P), ..., x_i = h_i(P), ..., x_n = h_n(P)$, and of functions $f(\,,....,\,)$ and $g(\,,.....,\,)$ such that:

$$
\begin{aligned}
\phi(P) &= f(x_1, ..., x_i, ..., x_n) \\
C(P) &= g(x_1, ..., x_i, ..., x_n)
\end{aligned}
$$

The arguments of usual production functions are in fact proxies expected to represent production sets with sufficient information to account for the main relevant features of the production process.

The simplest case is the situation assumed by the standard neoclassical function where $\phi(P) = f(L)$ with $L = card(P)$, the number of elements in P, and $C(P) = wL$, w being a constant wage rate.

Generalized Production Functions assume in a more flexible way $\phi(P) = \varphi(n, h)$, when n and h represent workforce and working time unambiguously defined from P.

5.2.3   Characterizing technologies and cost structures

We denote the set of incumbent workers at time t by:

$$z(t) = \{i \mid (i, t) \in P\}$$

The set of retained workers or workforce z is then defined by $z = \{i \mid (i, t) \in P\}$ for some t or $z = \cup_{t \in T} \{z(t)\}$.

Symmetrically, the working schedule of the ith individual is:

$$s(i) = \{t \mid (i, t) \in P\}$$

The operating schedule of the firm is defined as the set of hours s where there is some work ($z(t)$ is non-empty). Therefore $s = \{t \mid (i, t) \in P\}$ for some i or $s = \cup_{i \in z} \{s(i)\}$.

A "constant" workforce n exists if $z(t)$ contains n elements or zero according to the value of t. A "permanent" workforce is a particular case of a constant workforce in which all included workers have the same working schedule coinciding with the operating schedule of the firm: $s(i) = s \; \forall i$.

Tables 5.3, 5.4 and 5.5 where individuals are represented by capital letters illustrate the defined notions and the distinction between a constant workforce and a permanent workforce, the elements of P being represented by blackened cases.

$i \backslash t$	1	2	3	4	5
A	■				
B	■	■			
C	■	■	■		
D		■	■		
E			■		

TABLE 5.3. Constant workforce

In Table 5.3 the workforce n is constant at $n = 3$, but the individual working schedules are different: $s(A) = \{1\}$; $s(B) = \{1,2\}$; $s(C) = \{1,2,3\}$; $s(D) = \{2,3\}$; $s(E) = \{3\}$. The operating schedule of the firm is $s = \{1,2,3\}$; it coincides with $s(C)$ only, and $z = \{A,B,C,D,E\}$.

In Table 5.4, the workforce is constant and permanent, insofar as $s = \{2,3,4\} = s(A) = s(B) = s(C)$; $z = \{A,B,C\}$.

$i \backslash t$	1	2	3	4	5
A		■	■	■	
B		■	■	■	
C		■	■	■	
D					
E					

TABLE 5.4. Constant and permanent workforce

In Table 5.5, $s = \{1,2,3,4,5\}$ whereas $s(A) = \{1,3,4\}$; $s(B) = \{2,3,5\}$; $s(C) = \{4\}$; $s(D) = \{1\}$; $s(E) = \{5\}$; $z = \{A,B,C,D,E\}$

$i \backslash t$	1	2	3	4	5
A	■		■	■	
B		■	■		■
C				■	
D	■				
E					■

TABLE 5.5. Irregular working time

The "operating time" of the firm is the number of hours in the operating schedule and is denoted h. In Tables 5.3 and 5.4, $h = 3$; in Table 5.5, $h = 5$.

5.2.4   More definitions

• Homogeneous workers

Workers are homogeneous at time t for the technology $\phi(\ )$ if $\forall P$, $\forall i$, $\forall i'$ such that $(i,t) \notin P$, $(i',t) \notin P$:

$$\phi\{P \cup (i,t)\} = \phi\{P \cup (i',t)\} \tag{5.7}$$

Workers are generally homogeneous if (5.7) holds for all t.

Here i and i' represent insiders if $(i,t') \in P$ for some $t' \neq t$ or $(i',t'') \in P$ for some $t'' \neq t$, outsiders in the opposite case.

- **Homogeneous time**

Hours are homogeneous for individual i and for the technology $\phi(\ )$ if $\forall P$, $\forall t$, $\forall t'$ such that $(i,t) \notin P$, $(i,t') \notin P$:

$$\phi\{P \cup (i,t)\} = \phi\{P \cup (i,t')\} \tag{5.8}$$

Hours are generally homogeneous if (5.8) holds for all i.

- **General homogeneity**

Labor services are homogeneous if $\forall P$, $\forall(i,t) \notin P$, $\forall(i',t') \notin P$:

$$\phi\{P \cup (i,t)\} = \phi\{P \cup (i',t')\} \tag{5.9}$$

Condition (5.7) implies that all the individuals are perfect substitutes at time t; this could not be true for $t' \neq t$ (for instance, if t' is the hottest hour of the day and if i and i' are unequally susceptible to heat).

Condition (5.8) always holding implies that the incremental output obtained from the addition of an hour worked by any individual does not depend on t.

Conditions (5.7) and (5.8) always holding are equivalent to condition (5.9).

- **Relative workers' homogeneity**

Condition (5.7) is rather strong; it involves the assumption that an extra hour obtained from somebody having already worked many hours brings the same incremental output as that obtained in the same interval from a fresh outsider. It does not allow for any form of warming up or exertion of human abilities in the production process. The influence of t on individual productivity may have two different meanings: consider for instance that t indicates late hours in the evening and that the output obtained at t by harvesters is comparatively small. This could be interpreted as the consequence of two facts.

The first influence could be related to dim light at sunset creating an adverse circumstance for work; this is an intrinsic property of time t.

The other (non exclusive) interpretation is related to the fact that harvesters may have worked for the full day and be tired. A relative concept of workers' homogeneity may therefore be suggested.

Workers are relatively homogeneous if $\forall P$ such that $s(i) = s(i') \Rightarrow \phi\{P \cup (i,t)\} = \phi\{P \cup (i',t)\}$. In this case, workers are perfect substitutes if they have the same working schedules. The definition may be generalized to all t.

- **Additive technologies**

A technology is worker additive if $\phi\{\cup_{i\in z}[s(i)]\} = \sum_{i\in z}\phi[s(i)]$.

It is worker subadditive if $\phi\{\cup_{i\in z}[s(i)]\} < \sum_{i\in z}\phi[s(i)]$ and it is worker superadditive if $\phi\{\cup_{i\in z}[s(i)]\} > \sum_{i\in z}\phi[s(i)]$.

Proudhon's parable (page 71) is clearly related to a worker superadditive technology, as well as the celebrated texts by Adam Smith in which the efficiency of large scale production is brought out.

Similarly, a technology is time additive if $\phi\{\cup_{t\in s}[z(t)]\} = \sum_{t\in s}\phi[z(t)]$.

It is time subadditive if $\phi\{\cup_{t\in s}[z(t)]\} < \sum_{t\in s}\phi[z(t)]$ and it is time super-additive if $\phi\{\cup_{t\in s}[z(t)]\} > \sum_{t\in s}\phi[z(t)]$.

Hicks' observation (page 72) clearly refers to a time subadditive technology.

When, and only when, a technology is generally additive (worker and time additive), we can write

$$\phi\{P_1 \cup P_2\} = \phi\{P_1\} + \phi\{P_2\} - \phi\{P_1 \cap P_2\}$$

These properties may be assumed globally ($\forall P$) or locally (within some subset of $I \otimes T$).

- **Worker linear technology**

Technology $\phi(\ )$ is linear in workers if there exists a constant $\alpha(t)$ such that $\forall P$, for any constant value of t and $\forall i$ such that $(i,t) \notin P$, $\phi\{P \cup (i,t)\} = \phi(P) + \alpha(t)$.

- **Time linear technology**

Similarly, technology $\phi(\ )$ is linear in hours if there exists a constant $\beta(i)$ such that $\forall P$, for any constant value of i and $\forall t$ such that $(i,t) \notin P$, $\phi\{P \cup (i,t)\} = \phi(P) + \beta(i)$.

- **General linearity**

Technology is linear if it is linear in workers and in hours. In this case, $\forall i$ and $\forall t$, $\beta(i) = \alpha(t)$ and $\phi(P) = \alpha L$.

Additivity and (general) homogeneity imply linearity.

5.2.5 Working with equipment

The role of equipment in production and cost functions is conventionally introduced through a unique continuous variable K, standing for the material environment of the labor force, measured in homogeneous units.

In order to extend our formal representation, we have to introduce a set E of distinguishable equipment units: $E = \{1, ...k, ...K\}$.

A production decision is represented by a subset P of the Cartesian product $D = I \otimes T \otimes E$. Therefore, $(i, t, k) \in P$ means that individual i is working at time t with equipment k. If $(i, t, k) \in P$ and $(i, t, k') \in P$, individual i at time t is using simultaneously equipment k and k'. With this notation, we can define:

- **Collective equipment**

If $(i, t, k) \in P \ \forall i \in z$ and $\forall t \in s$, k is collective equipment (used by all elements of the workforce when working).

- **Individual equipment**

If $(i, t, k) \in P \Rightarrow (i', t, k) \notin P$, k is individual equipment (cannot be used simultaneously by two different workers).

- **Personal equipment**

If $(i, t, k) \in P \Rightarrow (i', t', k) \notin P$, k is personal equipment (cannot be used at all by different workers).

For instance, a building may be collective equipment, a hammer individual equipment; a personal computer may exemplify personal equipment.

Equipment, as well as workers, has working schedules $s(k)$; in some instances, $s(k) = T$, the equipment is constantly in use. In some instances, shift work permits full utilization of permanent equipment; individuals of the same shift are assigned one of three non-overlapping working schedules s_1, s_2 and s_3 such that $s_1 \cup s_2 \cup s_3 = s(k) = T$.

Taking into consideration the effect of equipment in production and cost is usually done by introducing a unique variable K as an argument of production and cost functions. It has been seen that the distinction between collective and individual equipment may play a significant role in the cost functions, since individual equipment is included in the concept of the "fixed cost of labor". Most often capital is omitted; it is implicitly assumed constant and its effect is conveyed by the form of the proposed function.

5.3   Production and cost functions

5.3.1   Individual contribution functions

Individual contribution functions may be used to explain output in the following way:

$$\phi(P) = \sum_{i \in z} \sum_{t \in s(i)} f[i, t, s(i), z(t)] \qquad (5.10)$$

Output is related to the individual contributions of all elements of the work-force, the contribution to output of individual i at time t being influenced by its working schedule $s(i)$, and by the entire set of other workers also working at time t, $z(t)$. In spite of its summation signs, expression (5.10) is not confined to additive technologies.

Worker additivity is the special case in which the individual contribution does not depend on other workers who are simultaneously active: $\phi(P) = \sum_{i \in z} \sum_{t \in s(i)} f[i, t, s(i), \bullet]$.

Time additivity obtains if individual contributions are not affected by the worker's time schedule: $\phi(P) = \sum_{i \in z} \sum_{t \in s(i)} f[i, t, \bullet, z(t)]$.

General additivity is reflected by $\phi(P) = \sum_{i \in z} \sum_{t \in s(i)} f[i, t, \bullet, \bullet]$.

5.3.2   Generalizing the representation of labor cost structure

The notions of additivity, linearity and homogeneity also apply to cost functions. If a legal premium applies to hours worked during the night, hours are not homogeneous. In studies pertaining to labor market discrimination, particular cost structures have been introduced in which, due to ethnic prejudices, wages to be paid to elements of one ethnic group have to be increased if they have to work in a team with elements of another group (see the survey by Cain, 1986). In such a case, the additivity property of labor cost functions is clearly ruled out.

A rather general cost function may be suggested:

$$C(P) = \sum_{i \in z} \sum_{t \in s(i)} w[i, t, s(i), z(t)] \qquad (5.11)$$

This function can explain the cost in a complete market system where each individual may be paid a different price for each hour according to his working schedule $s(i)$ and the worker's environment $z(t)$. If the cost of individual i at time t does not depend on the other employees simultaneously at work, $z(t)$ is omitted.

The standard cost function assumed in textbook examples is implicitly .$C(P) = wL$ with $L = card(P)$; it assumes a flat structure, $w = w\,[i, t, s(i), \bullet\,]$, whereas (5.11) encompasses cost differences related to individuals, hours and individual working schedules.

The Marxian notion of a market for "labor power" (introduced in Chapter 1) implies $C(P) = wn$, w being the cost of subsistence, $n = card(z)$; the cost of labor is not altered by variations of working schedules.

5.4 Output density functions and cost density functions

For continuous arguments, the individual contribution functions may be turned into density functions; integrating density functions yields G.P.F. Whereas output density functions may be mathematically equivalent to generalized production functions, conveying the same information about the productive process, it will be shown that they lend themselves in some instances to more intuitive interpretations.

5.4.1 The general form

Introducing continuous time and a (more symbolic) continuous individual index, restricting ourselves to subsets P implying permanent workforce n during a time interval $[t_0, t_0 + h]$, we can write (5.10) in the form:

$$y = \phi(P) = \int_{i=0}^{n} \int_{t=t_0}^{t_0+h} f(i, t, n, h)\, di\, dt \qquad (5.12)$$

In this form, a common working schedule is determined by t_0 and h, the set of workers $z(t)$ is constant and is determined by n, the integration domain is rectangular in the (Ot, Oi) space and $f(i, t, n, h)$ is called an Output Density Function (O.D.F.).

Along the same lines, the expression (5.11) has a cost density version:

$$C = \int_{i=0}^{n} \int_{t=t_0}^{t_0+h} w(i, t, n, h)\, di\, dt \qquad (5.13)$$

The standard form in which $w(i, t, n, h) = w$ yields by integration: $C = wnh$.

5.4.2 Time profile of output density

In the context of a permanent workforce, the partial derivative $\partial f(i, t, n, h)/\partial t$ indicates how the flow contribution to output of individual i changes over time for a given working schedule h, owing to warming-up, exertion or other facts. We denote by $\left\{ t : \dfrac{\partial f(i,t,n,h)}{\partial t} > 0 \right\}$ the "warming-up set" of individual i and by $\left\{ t : \dfrac{\partial f(i,t,n,h)}{\partial t} < 0 \right\}$ the "exertion set" of individual i. These sets coincide for relatively homogeneous workers.

Partial derivative $\partial f(i,t,n,h)/\partial h$ indicates how the individual contribution in density terms is affected at each point in time by variations of the total working time. As suggested by the quotation from Lionel Robbins (page 71), this partial derivative may be expected to be negative.

5.4.3 The Hicksian "optimal" day

O.D.F. forms make it possible to construe an analytical interpretation of the Hicksian "optimal" working day conceived as the output maximizing value of h, denoted h^*. A necessary condition for this maximization is, according to Leibniz's rule applied to (5.12):

$$\frac{dy}{dh} = \int_{i=0}^{n} f(i, t_0 + h^*, n, h^*)di + \int_{i=0}^{n} \int_{t=t_0}^{t_0+h^*} \frac{\partial f(i,t,n,h^*)}{\partial h} didt = 0 \quad (5.14)$$

The first term is expected to be positive and measures the sensitivity of the output to change in work duration, if this change had no impact on the workers' contribution (density) at each point in time.

Hicks' line of reasoning clearly supposes $\partial f(i,t,n,h^*)/\partial h < 0$; the second term is therefore negative and records the impact of an increased working schedule on density in the whole integration domain.

5.4.4 Individual profile of output density

For a given value of t, the density $f(i,t,n,h)$ also has the individual index as an argument. The influence of i on the density has two possible interpretations: on the one hand, labor forces may be heterogeneous; in this case the definition of $f(i,t,n,h)$ rests on an implicit ordering of workers, called to participate in production according to a stable rule; on the other hand, the index i may indicate a properly ordered series of different jobs or places, each one being occupied by a worker. In this case, the index i stands for a job matched by a worker. Variation in density may be related to this job structure and not necessarily to individual intrinsic efficiency.

If $f(i,t,n,h)$ does not depend on i, we can write $\displaystyle\int_{i=0}^{n} f(\bullet,t,n,h)di =$ $nf(\bullet,t,n,h)$ and (5.12) takes the form $y = n \displaystyle\int_{t=t_0}^{t_0+h} f(\bullet,t,n,h)dt$; furthermore, if the technology is worker additive, the described technology is linear in workers and this expression is further simplified, $y = n \int_{t=t_0}^{t_0+h} f(\bullet, t, \bullet, h) dt$. In this case, the condition (5.14) applies under the simplified form:

$$\frac{\partial y}{\partial h} = f(\bullet, t + h^*, \bullet, h^*) + \int_{t=t_0}^{t_0+h} \frac{\partial f(\bullet, t, \bullet, h^*)}{\partial h} dt$$

5.4.5 A simple optimal working schedule

If the technology is linear in workers, an optimal (i.e. profit maximizing) collective working schedule may be characterized in the following way, considering also a linear labor cost function. In intensive variables (profit, output and cost per worker), we can write:

$$\pi = \int_{t=t_0}^{t_1} f(t, t_1 - t_0) dt - w(t_1 - t_0)$$

If we consider profit maximizing by the choice of a unique profit maximizing working interval, with $h = t_1 - t_0$, first order conditions imply:

$$\frac{\partial \pi}{\partial t_0} = w - f(t_0^*, t_1^* - t_0^*) - \int_{t=t_0^*}^{t_1^*} \frac{\partial f(t, t_1^* - t_0^*)}{\partial h} dt = 0 \qquad (5.15)$$

and:

$$\frac{\partial \pi}{\partial t_1} = f(t_0^*, t_1^* - t_0^*) - w + \int_{t=t_0^*}^{t_1^*} \frac{\partial f(t, t_1^* - t_0^*)}{\partial h} dt = 0 \qquad (5.16)$$

Increasing t_0 saves on labor cost (w); the output is reduced by a shortened working time $f(t_0^*, t_1^* - t_0^*)$, but increased by the effect of shorter hours on the density integrated on the whole interval. If the technology rigidly determines the output density, the terms under the integral sign are nil.

5.5 The two dimensional demand for labor in the general case

Ignoring equipment and conventionally setting $t_0 = 0$, we interpret the G.P.F. as:

$$\varphi(n, h) = \int_{i=0}^{n} \int_{t=0}^{h} f(i, t, n, h) di dt$$

implying in particular: $\varphi_h(n, h) = \int_{i=0}^{n} f(i, h, n, h) di + \int_{i=0}^{n} \int_{t=0}^{h} \frac{\partial f(i, t, n, h)}{\partial h} di dt.$

The right hand interpretation having the advantage of explicitly distinguishing the effect of h on total output as an integration limit and its effect as a parameter of output density.

In the same way, it is possible to define the generalized cost function by

$$C(n, h) = \int_{i=0}^{n} \int_{t=0}^{h} w(i, t, n, h) di dt.$$

5.5.1 The cost minimization problem

The cost minimization problem of a predetermined output y is:

$$\begin{cases} \min_{(n,h)} C(n, h) \\ \text{with } n \geq 0, h \geq 0 \\ \text{and } \varphi(n, h) \geq y \end{cases} \tag{5.17}$$

Let us denote by $(\hat{n}, \hat{h})$ the solution.

Considering first the cost minimization problem, any interior solution must satisfy first order and second order conditions.

- **First order conditions**

First order conditions applying to the Lagrangian form $\mathcal{L} = C(n, h) - \sigma [\varphi(n, h) - y]$ must hold for interior solutions $\hat{n} > 0, \hat{h} > 0$, the output constraint being saturated:

$$C_n(\hat{n}, \hat{h}) - \hat{\sigma} \varphi_n(\hat{n}, \hat{h}) = 0 \tag{5.18}$$

$$C_h(\hat{n}, \hat{h}) - \hat{\sigma} \varphi_h(\hat{n}, \hat{h}) = 0 \tag{5.19}$$

$$\varphi(\hat{n}, \hat{h}) = y \tag{5.20}$$

Taking the total derivative of equation (5.20) with respect to y and using (5.18) and (5.19), it is possible to show that $\partial C(\hat{n}, \hat{h})/\partial y = \hat{\sigma}$ (the value of the Lagrangian multiplier being identified as marginal cost).

Existence and uniqueness of solutions are related to concavity properties of the production and cost functions.[3]

First order conditions for an interior solution may also be brought out by considering the isoquant and isocost curves implied by the two functions. Let $\psi(h)$ be defined by $\varphi\{\psi(h), h\} = \varphi(\hat{n}, \hat{h}) = y$, and $\xi(h)$ by $C\{\xi(h), h\} = C(\hat{n}, \hat{h})$; we can then write:

$$\psi'(h) = -\frac{\varphi_h\{\psi(h), h\}}{\varphi_n\{\psi(h), h\}} \tag{5.21}$$

$$\xi'(h) = -\frac{C_h\{\xi(h), h\}}{Cn\{\xi(h), h\}} \tag{5.22}$$

The convexity properties of the isoquant and of the isocosts are related to the first and second order partial derivatives of the production and cost function. It may be shown in differentiating (5.21) and (5.22) that:

$$\psi''(h) = \varphi_n^{-3} \det \begin{pmatrix} 0 & \varphi_n & \varphi_h \\ \varphi_n & \varphi_{nn} & \varphi_{nh} \\ \varphi_h & \varphi_{hn} & \varphi_{hh} \end{pmatrix} \tag{5.23}$$

$$\xi''(h) = C_n^{-3} \det \begin{pmatrix} 0 & C_n & C_h \\ C_n & C_{nn} & C_{nh} \\ C_h & C_{hn} & C_{hh} \end{pmatrix} \tag{5.24}$$

If we introduce the cost function:

$$m(h) = C\{\psi(h), h\} \tag{5.25}$$

the first order condition is:

$$m'(h) = \psi'(h)C_n\{\psi(h), h\} + C_h\{\psi(h), h\} = 0 \tag{5.26}$$

In other terms $\psi'(h) = -\dfrac{C_h}{Cn} = \xi'(h)$; the isoquant and the isocost are mutually tangent.

In a point where first order conditions (5.18) and (5.19) hold, $\psi'(h) = \xi'(h)$.

---

[3] For instance, it is easily checked that with the standard wage-taking cost function $C = wnh$ and production functions of the form $\varphi(n, h) = n^{\alpha}h^{\beta}$, such interior solutions do not exist for $\alpha \neq \beta$.

- **Second order conditions**

A necessary second order condition for a local cost minimum is $m''(h) > 0$. Differentiating (5.26), we can write for a point where first order conditions hold:

$$m''(h) = C_n \left[\psi''(h) - \xi''(h) \right] > 0 \qquad (5.27)$$

Since $C_n < 0$, this condition is fulfilled if the isoquant is more convex than the isocost at the point where they are mutually tangential. First order and second order conditions are jointly sufficient for a local minimum of the cost function under output constraint. In the opposite case where $\xi''(h) > \psi''(h)$ first order conditions characterize a local maximum of the cost under the output constraint, as can be checked graphically.

5.5.2 Profit maximization

The profit function $\pi = \varphi(n,h) - C(n,h)$ makes it possible to define a two dimensional demand for labor services, i.e. (n^*, h^*) solution of:

$$\begin{cases} \max_{(n,h)} \{ \pi(n,h) = \varphi(n,h) - C(n,h) \} \\ \text{with } n \geq 0, h \geq 0 \end{cases} \qquad (5.28)$$

- **First order conditions**

$$\pi_n(n,h) = \varphi_n(n,h) - C_n(n,h) = 0 \qquad (5.29)$$

$$\pi_h(n,h) = \varphi_h(n,h) - C_h(n,h) = 0 \qquad (5.30)$$

These equations can be interpreted as the absence of both "extensive" and "intensive" profit margins.

- **Second order conditions**

The determinant of the Hessian matrix:

$$\begin{pmatrix} \varphi_{nn} - C_{nn} & \varphi_{nh} - C_{nh} \\ \varphi_{hn} - C_{nh} & \varphi_{hh} - C_{hh} \end{pmatrix} \qquad (5.31)$$

should be negative definite, the special form of (5.31) for a standard cost function $C = wnh$ being:

$$\begin{pmatrix} \varphi_{nn} & \varphi_{nh} - w \\ \varphi_{nh} - w & \varphi_{hh} \end{pmatrix} \qquad (5.32)$$

5.5.3 Profit maximization and the total demand for hours

Proposition 5 *Within the concavity domain of the profit function, with* $C = wnh$, *an increase in the wage rate* w *necessarily diminishes the optimum labor flow* $L^* = n^* h^*$, *generalizing the standard Law of Demand.*

Proof. Consider two distinct values of the wage rate, w_1 and w_2 inducing respectively profit maximizing values (n_1^*, h_1^*) and (n_2^*, h_2^*). The profit function being concave, we can write:

$$\varphi(n_1^*, h_1^*) - w_1 n_1^* h_1^* > \varphi(n_2^*, h_2^*) - w_1 n_2^* h_2^* \tag{5.33}$$

$$\varphi(n_2^*, h_2^*) - w_2 n_2^* h_2^* > \varphi(n_1^*, h_1^*) - w_2 n_1^* h_1^* \tag{5.34}$$

Adding (5.33) and (5.34) gives:

$$(w_2 - w_1)(n_2^* h_2^* - n_1^* h_1^*) < 0 \tag{5.35}$$

This global result implies the local sign rule:

$$\frac{dL^*}{dw} = \frac{d(n^* h^*)}{dw} < 0 \tag{5.36}$$

■

This result doesn't specify the separate response of h^* and n^* to variations of w. It will be shown later on that this indeterminacy may be removed for special generalized cost and production functions. L is here a flow of hours and not a labor services input.

5.6 The two dimensional demand for labor with a specific G.P.F.

5.6.1 From a simple O.D.F. to the specific G.P.F.

In order to bring more intuition to this abstract analysis, we will introduce a particular G.P.F., grounded in a stylized description of a standard production process, then we will study the demand for hours and workers when the cost of labor is of the standard linear form $C = wnh$.

We consider a generally additive technology represented by the simplified output density function:

$$f(i, t) = e^{-\gamma i}(1 - vt^2) \tag{5.37}$$

where i is the individual continuous index, $i \in [0, n]$ and t is the moment of the day when output density is recorded, $t \in [0, 1]$.

Since capital is omitted, the parameter γ can be interpreted as measuring the impact of the quality structure of the equipment – workers being matched with tools of decreasing efficiency – or a diminishing quality of co-ordination. We suppose therefore $\gamma > 0$. In this case, the decreasing return set encompasses the interval $[0, n]$.

The parameter v tunes the effect of exertion on the density function. Whatever i, density goes to zero when t tends to $\sqrt{1/v}$. It is therefore assumed that $v \geq 1$. The exertion set encompasses the interval $[0, h]$. Figure 5.2 illustrates this particular density function for $\gamma = 0.5, v = 1$.

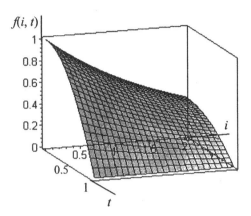

FIGURE 5.2. A special O.D.F.

Integrating density (5.37) across individual and time indexes, we obtain the special Generalized Production Function:

$$\varphi(n, h) = \int\limits_{i=0}^{n} \int\limits_{t=0}^{h} e^{-\gamma i}(1 - vt^2)didt = \frac{1}{\gamma}(1 - e^{-\gamma n})(h - v\frac{h^3}{3}) \qquad (5.38)$$

The output density approach is clearly vindicated by the fact that it is extremely difficult to infer the assumptions on technology implicit in (5.38). It is possible to check that the function $\varphi(n, h)$ is strictly concave in (n, h) within a well-defined domain, although the original density function is not concave in (i, t).

5.6.2 Profit maximization and the demand for workers and hours

As already mentioned, cost functions could also be based on a cost den-sity concept, such that: $C = \int\limits_{t=0}^{h} \int\limits_{i=0}^{n} w(i, t)dzdt$. To simplify the example we assume a constant wage rate, implying a flat job structure and a flat time structure of the cost density. This simplified cost function has been traditionally adopted, especially in studying the stylized context where a monopoly union determines the wage rate and concedes to the employer "the right to manage" (to determine n and h):

$$C = \int_{t=0}^{h} \int_{i=0}^{n} w \, di \, dt = wnh \tag{5.39}$$

We show hereafter that the special technology we have introduced through an O.D.F. representation yields an interior solution in the profit maximization problem *with* this standard labor cost function.

The profit function is $\pi(w, n, h) = \varphi(n, h) - wnh$ or, in G.P.F. terms:

$$\pi(w, n, h) = \frac{1}{\gamma}(1 - e^{-\gamma n})(h - v\frac{h^3}{3}) - wnh \tag{5.40}$$

Figure 5.3 represents profits for various values of n and h (we set $\gamma = 0.5$ and $w = 0.25$).

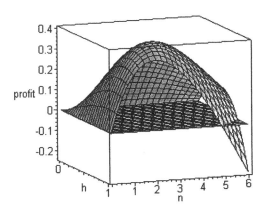

FIGURE 5.3. Profit function

For an interior solution, we denote the profit maximizing values of the endogenous variables $n^*(w)$ and $h^*(w)$.

The solution should verify the first order conditions:

$$\pi_n = 0 = e^{-\gamma n}(h - v\frac{h^3}{3}) - wh \tag{5.41}$$

$$\pi_h = 0 = \frac{1}{\gamma}(1 - e^{-\gamma n})(1 - vh^2) - wn \tag{5.42}$$

In Figure 5.4, we represent at point M the optimum values for our special case, and the network of isoprofit curves in the (n, h) space. The isoprofit curve is defined by the equation: $\varphi(n, h) - wnh = \bar{\pi}$. (The plot is made for $\bar{\pi} = 0.35, 0.37, 0.38, 0.40$).

Concavity of the profit function implies convexity of sets defined by: $\varphi(n, h) - wnh \geq \bar{\pi}$.

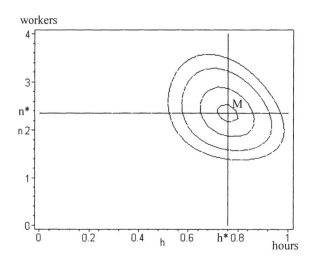

FIGURE 5.4. Isoprofit network for predetermined wage

The slope of the tangent to an isoprofit curve indicates the value of the marginal rate of substitution:

$$\left(\frac{dn}{dh}\right)_{\pi=const} = -\frac{\varphi_h - wn}{\varphi_n - wh} = -\frac{\text{Intensive margin}}{\text{Extensive margin}} \qquad (5.43)$$

5.6.3 Comparative statics of profit maximization: the impact of varying wages

We consider now the comparative statics resulting from our special O.D.F. (5.37). For different values of the real wage w, the point $M = (n^*, h^*)$ moves. This relation is plotted (mm curve) in Figure 5.5 (where we also represent a set of isoprofit curves for $w = 0.25$ and $w = 0.4$).

Eliminating w we obtain the $n - h$ relationship in the implicit form (for $v = 1$):

$$\frac{1}{\gamma}(1 - e^{-\gamma n})(1 - h^2) - ne^{-\gamma n}(1 - \frac{h^2}{3}) = 0 \qquad (5.44)$$

The special density we have introduced entails $dh^*/dw < 0$ and $dn^*/dw < 0$ thus lifting indeterminacy from equation (5.36).

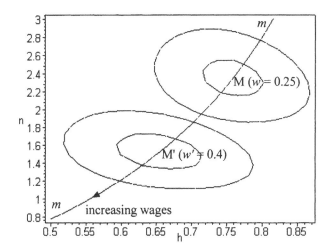

FIGURE 5.5. Optimal staff and working time under wage variation

5.6.4 On the impossibility of a decentralized equilibrium in the labor market with a constant wage rate

The former analysis puts forward a possible source of conflict in the labor market, if the wage rate is a linear price of labor. As shown, firms manifest an explicit demand for hours and workers; only, by fortunate coincidence, this two dimensional demand simultaneously matches the individual supply of hours *and* the global supply of workers.

More precisely, if profits are of the form $\pi(n, h) = \varphi(n, h) - wnh$, full equilibrium requires the following conditions:

$$\varphi_n(n, h) - wh = 0 \qquad (5.45)$$
$$\varphi_h(n, h) - wn = 0 \qquad (5.46)$$
$$n = n^s(w) \qquad (5.47)$$
$$h = h^s(w) \qquad (5.48)$$

This system of four equations cannot generally be solved by three endogenous variables $\{n, h, w\}$.

Figure 5.6 depicts possible configurations in the labor market when $n^s(w) = \bar{n}$. The northeast quadrant represents the internal supply and demand for individual hours, the northwest quadrant represents the external supply (assumed constant for simplicity) and the demand for workers. At the external (full-employment) equilibrium (point B), insiders work longer than desired hours; at the internal equilibrium (point A), unemployment $\bar{n} - n_A$ is observed. Obviously, in the case depicted in Figure 5.6, a perfectly flexible wage would not be able to simultaneously eliminate rationing in the internal and external markets.

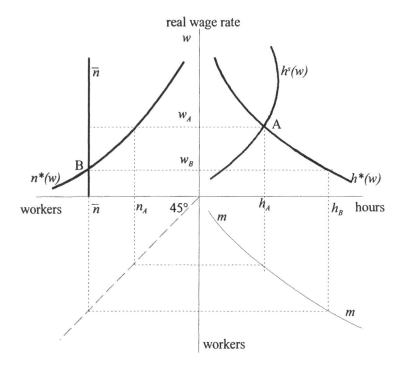

FIGURE 5.6. Internal vs. external equilibrium

The elementary neoclassical case is the special situation in which there exists a function $F(,)$ such that $\varphi(n,h) = F(nh) \; \forall(n,h)$. In this case $\varphi_n(n,h) = hF'(nh)$ and $\varphi_h(n,h) = nF'(nh)$. The equality $w = F'(nh)$ eliminates simultaneously the extensive and the intensive margins, solving the first two equations of the former system.

5.7   Conclusion

In this chapter, focus was set on the complexity of the productive process. From a formal description, we evolved towards more tractable but reductive concepts emphasizing, however, the respective roles of hours and employment. In the next chapters, generalized production functions and generalized cost structures will be extensively in use, a better knowledge of these concepts being a basic precondition of a precise understanding of actual labor contracts and of any prediction pertaining to the effects of mandatory working time reductions.

Mandatory working time reductions aim at increasing employment, in a man-hours substitution process. In a decentralized economy, the firms being able to subject employment to their profit maximization policy, we can write the following identity:

$$n^*(\bar{h}) = \hat{n}\left[\bar{h}, y^*(\bar{h})\right]$$ (5.49)

The left hand element of this equation represents the demand for workers by the profit maximizing firm as a function of the working time constraint $\bar{h}$; the right hand element interprets employment as the demand for workers minimizing the cost of producing the profit maximizing output $y^*(\bar{h})$.

Differentiating (5.49) with respect to $\bar{h}$ yields the following decomposition:

$$\frac{dn^*(\bar{h})}{d\bar{h}} = \frac{\partial \hat{n}\left[\bar{h}, y^*(\bar{h})\right]}{\partial \bar{h}} + \frac{\partial \hat{n}\left[\bar{h}, y^*(\bar{h})\right]}{\partial y}\frac{\partial y^*(\bar{h})}{\partial \bar{h}}$$ (5.50)

The impact of an imposed working time variation on employment is the sum of a pure substitution effect (the first term on the right hand side) and of a "production effect" represented by the second term. The most sanguine proponents of working time reduction as a job saving measure usually buttress their optimism on the substitution effect, little being said with respect to the production effect, which is difficult to evaluate on an intuitive basis.

Chapters 6, 7 and 8 will focus on the first term of the right hand side of equation (5.50), the output level being considered as constant. Chapters 9 and 10 detail the whole effect of working time restrictions, when the output level is itself adapted to its profit maximizing value.

6
Working time in a cost minimization problem

In Chapter 5, a formal approach helped to represent production processes and cost structures in a less simplified context than is usually assumed in conventional microeconomics. In this chapter, generalized production and labor cost functions are applied to the general problem of labor expense minimization by the firm. Cost minimization is always a necessary condition for profit maximization, but it may also apply directly to the "Keynesian" case, in which firms are constrained in the goods market, being able to sell only limited quantities, at least in the short run. In this case, their optimal decision is limited to choosing the minimum cost input mix.

In section 6.1 we highlight the role played by fixed costs of labor only in explaining the optimal labor contract from the firm's point of view and the employer's tendency to extract longer hours than are willingly supplied by the workers. Section 6.2 examines the particular case where the employer is constrained to provide workers with a working time duration equal to their individual supply and emphasizes the inefficient character of this situation. Section 6.3 introduces a slightly more elaborate model, where the production function is also generalized to allow for imperfect man-hours substitution.

6.1   Neoclassical production function with fixed costs of labor

We begin the analysis with a very simple model of working time determination, where the principal extension of the traditional neoclassical analysis consists in introducing a more general labor cost structure. As mentioned in Chapter 5, in a static framework, labor costs are made up of wage costs and various fixed costs proportional only to the number of people at work, but independent of working time.

In this simple framework, the labor market is supposed to be competitive. Firms must therefore submit labor contracts that workers are willing to accept, that is, must provide them with a utility level higher or equal to some reservation utility. This reservation utility level is open to various interpretations: in a perfectly homogeneous and flexible labor market economy, this level should be understood as endogenous; it is an expression of the satisfaction level obtained by workers at full employment and is a common constraint imposed on all firms. In other cases, with external unemployment, it should be associated with unemployment compensation and with maximum leisure time. In more structured economies, the constraining utility level would be the outcome of negotiations between unions, firms and the state, a kind of social contract.

More formally, let us denote by s this minimum utility requirement. Worker preferences may be represented by a neoclassical utility function $u = u(c, h)$, having as arguments consumption possibilities c and working time h. Following standard neoclassical assumptions, $u_c > 0$, $u_h < 0$. The length of the reference period will be normalized, which implies a maximum working time $h = 1$.

Then, condition $u(c, h) \geq s$, often called "participation constraint", implies an acceptancy region in the plane (Oc, Oh) bordered by a frontier $c(h)$ implicitly defined by $u[c(h), h] = s$ and defined in Chapter 4 as the "working time compensating consumption function". Following the neoclassical paradigm, we assume that this compensating consumption is increasing and convex: $c'(h) > 0, c''(h) > 0$, with $c(0) = c_0 \geq 0$ and $\lim_{h \to 1} c(h) = \infty$ (Figure 6.1).

With the participation constraint may be associated a reservation value of the wage rate noted w_r, defined as the minimum hourly wage rate convincing the employee to work; at this wage rate, workers' hours supply h_r is the solution to the problem: $\min_h \{c(h, s)/h\}$ and corresponds to point R in Figure 6.1.

Labor expenses are therefore $E = n(c + \theta)$, where c is workers' daily compensation and θ stands for the fixed costs per worker; these costs have been discussed at length in Chapter 5.

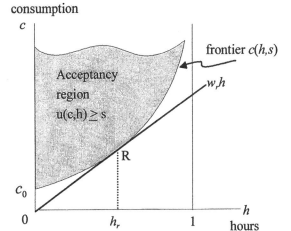

FIGURE 6.1. Optimal working time

The firm production function is $F(L)$, where L measures the flow of labor services and, in this elementary framework, takes the standard neoclassical form of perfect man-hours substitution $L = nh$.

As already mentioned, output is predetermined: $y = \bar{y}$, thus the necessary quantity of labor services is also fixed, $\bar{L} = F^{-1}(\bar{y})$. The firm's decision is thus:

$$\left\{ \begin{array}{l} \min_{h}\{n(c + \theta)\} \\ \text{with} : c \geq c(h) \\ \text{and} : nh = \bar{L} \end{array} \right. \tag{6.1}$$

The compensation constraint being obviously saturated, one may introduce both constraints into the objective to obtain cost as a function of h only:

$$E(h) = \frac{\bar{L}}{h}[c(h) + \theta]$$

This form indicates that the firm has to minimize the per hour cost of labor services. Then the cost minimizing working time must verify the first order condition $E'(h) = 0$:

$$h^* c'(h^*) = c(h^*) + \theta \tag{6.2}$$

implying

$$\frac{c(h^*)}{c(h^*) + \theta} \frac{h^* c'(h^*)}{c(h^*)} = 1$$

and therefore:

$$\sigma(h^*)\eta_h^c(h^*) = 1$$

where $\eta_h^c(h)$ is the elasticity of the compensation function with respect to h and $\sigma(h)$ is the ratio of wage cost to total labor cost per worker.

Graphically, the solution may be easily illustrated using isocost lines, i.e. the sets of values of c and h assigning a constant value $\bar{E}$ to the expenditure function $E = \dfrac{\bar{L}}{h}[c + \theta]$. An isocost line is defined by the explicit function:

$$c = -\theta + \frac{\bar{E}}{\bar{L}} h$$

It can be represented in the (Oc, Oh) plane by a straight line of slope $(\bar{E}/\bar{L})$ and crossing the vertical axis at $c = -\theta$.

The compensating consumption function and two isocost lines are represented in Figure 6.2. The decision of the firm is represented by point F where the solid line is tangent to the compensatory consumption. It corresponds to the lowest cost E^*, compatible with workers' acceptance of the labor contract.

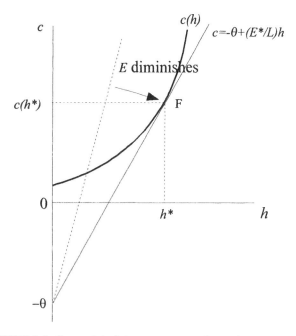

FIGURE 6.2. Cost minimizing contract under utility constraint

It is easily seen from Figure 6.2 that the contract proposed by the firm in this setting has an efficiency property since at F, cost is minimized under the workers' satisfaction constraint and equivalently, workers' utility is maximized under the cost constraint.

However, if we consider that workers' compensation is delivered by means of a linear wage, it can easily be shown that under this contractual arrangement, $\forall \theta > 0$, they would prefer to work shorter hours (and earn a lower compensation) than imposed by the firm.

Let us denote by $h^s(w)$ the individual labor supply function, that is the working time which maximizes the workers' satisfaction for any wage rate, w.

$$h^s(w) = \arg \max_h \{u(wh, h)\}$$

The hourly wage rate w^* required to provide the optimal compensation $c(h^*)$ is defined by $c(h^*) = w^* h^*$ and is equal to the slope of the straight line joining the origin to the point F describing the firm's decision $(c(h^*), h^*)$.

But as clearly shown in Figure 6.3, this configuration implies systematic overwork, that is $h^s(w^*) < h^*$. Obviously, the existence of fixed costs of labor is sufficient to prompt firms to demand more than Walrasian working hours. The point W representing the Walrasian supply by the worker and the point F do not coincide.

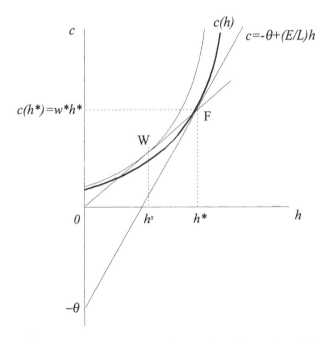

FIGURE 6.3. Optimal contract: firm and worker point of view

Walrasian rationing of the insiders could be reduced by introducing a mandatory constraint on working hours, $\bar{h} < h^*$. In this framework, workers' rationing would disappear at R where the hours constraint and the wage rate would coincide with the reservation values, i.e. h_r and $w_r = c(h_r)/h_r$. This situation is depicted in Figure 6.4, where the point representing the firm's decision has shifted from F to R.

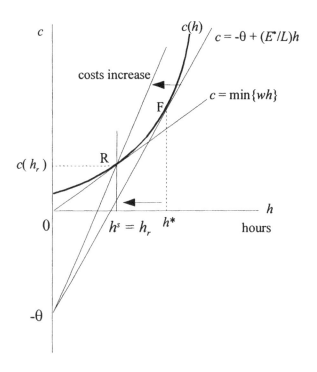

FIGURE 6.4. Constrained working time

In this case, the labor cost E increases while worker rationing as measured by the distance between $\bar{h} = h_r$ and h^s is nil. In this case of perfect man-hours substitution, reduced working time implies, of course, increasing demand for workers.

The only situation in which workers and firms are in full Walrasian equilibrium is the neoclassical special case $\theta = 0$, and in which points W, F and R coalesce.[1]

---

[1] With an overtime premium scheme, point F might be considered as a worker's equilibrium (see Chapter 8).

6.2 Consequences of supply determined working time

The situation in which the firms would be allowed to determine the hourly wage rate, but should comply with the number of hours optimally supplied by the workers is worth further analysis. In this case, the output constrained firm $(F(\bar{L}) = \bar{y})$ solves the following cost minimization problem:

$$\left\{ \begin{array}{l} \min_{w} \{n[wh^s(w) + \theta]\} \\ \text{with: } w \geq w_r \\ \text{and: } nh^s(w) = \bar{L} \end{array} \right. \tag{6.3}$$

Substituting n with $\bar{L}/h^s(w)$, the firm's decision is represented by maximization of $E(w) = \bar{L}\left[w + \dfrac{\theta}{h^s(w)}\right]$.

For an interior solution, the first order condition $E'(w) = 0$ implies

$$\frac{\theta h^{s\prime}(w)}{[h^s(w)]^2} = 1 \tag{6.4}$$

or, in elasticity terms:

$$wh^s(w) = \theta \eta_w^{h^s}$$

or else:

$$\sigma = \frac{\eta_w^{h^s}}{1 + \eta_w^{h^s}}$$

where σ is the share of wage costs in total labor costs and $\eta_w^{h^s}$ the wage elasticity of the hours supply.

The consequences of such a situation are depicted in Figure 6.5. The feasible contracts are limited to the points of the RS curve where the utility of the worker is maximized for the current wage rate. Minimum total labor cost may be obtained (interior solution) for the particular worker's equilibrium W where the RS curve is tangent to an isocost straight line. The incurred labor cost is higher than at point F where the firm minimizes cost by controlling wages and working time.

Comparative statics related to the fixed cost θ can explain how some surplus from work may be obtained by the worker. In the absence of such costs, W clearly coincides with R and the worker is exactly compensated. For higher values of θ, point W moves upwards on the RS curve indicating positive surplus from work. From (6.4), this surplus appears if $\theta > \theta_0 = \dfrac{[h^s(w_r)]^2}{h^{s\prime}(w_r)}$. If θ increases indefinitely, (6.4)$\Rightarrow h^{s\prime}(w) = 0$, isocost lines tend

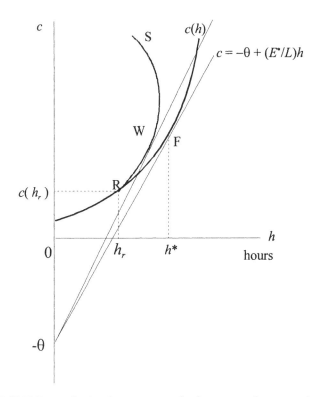

FIGURE 6.5. Optimal contract under hours supply constraint

to be vertical and the wage policy amounts to maximizing the individually supplied working time, in order to reduce the number of workers.

Last but not least, the contract W is not efficient. At this point, it might be shown that the indifference curve and the isocost line are not mutually tangent and border a set of points yielding simultaneously more satisfaction to the worker and reduced labor costs. As inefficient contracts are highly unstable, in the following developments of this book we concentrate on the case of utility constraints on the decision of the firm.

6.3   A more general approach: labor effectiveness

This section extends the cost minimization problem under utility competition to a more general form of the production function.

6.3.1   The cost minimization problem

As in the former case, the production function is $F(L)$, with $F'(L) > 0$, $F''(L) < 0$ where L are labor services. Here we consider that hours and workers are no longer perfect substitutes in the production of labor services. We hold however the multiplicatively separable form introduced in the former chapter: $L = ng(h)$, where $g'(\ ) > 0$. Note that the elasticity of labor services with respect to workers $\eta_n^L = 1$; the elasticity of labor services with respect to hours $\eta_h^L = \dfrac{hg'(h)}{g(h)} = \eta_h^g$. Output is predetermined, implying $L = \bar{L}$. The labor cost function is: $E(n,h) = n[c(h) + \theta]$ where $c(h)$ represents worker compensation and θ are the fixed costs per worker.

The cost minimization problem is therefore:

$$\begin{cases} \min_{h,n} \{n[c(h) + \theta]\} \\ \text{with: } ng(h) = \bar{L} \end{cases} \tag{6.5}$$

The Lagrangian $\mathcal{L} = \{n[c(h) + \theta] - \lambda[ng(h) - \bar{L}]\}$ entails first order conditions:

$$\mathcal{L}_n = c(h) + \theta - \lambda g(h) = 0 \tag{6.6}$$

$$\mathcal{L}_h = nc'(h) - \lambda ng'(h) = 0 \tag{6.7}$$

$$\mathcal{L}_\lambda = ng(h) - \bar{L} = 0 \tag{6.8}$$

Dividing equation (6.7) by equation (6.6) we obtain the following form of first order conditions applying to the cost minimizing working time h^*:

$$\frac{c'(h^*)}{c(h^*) + \theta} = \frac{g'(h^*)}{g(h^*)} \tag{6.9}$$

In terms of elasticities, equation (6.9) may be written equivalently:

$$\sigma(h^*)\eta_h^c(h^*) = \eta_h^g(h^*)$$

with $\eta_h^g(h^*) = \dfrac{h^* g'(h^*)}{g(h^*)}$, $\eta_h^c(h^*) = \dfrac{h^* c'(h^*)}{c(h^*)}$, and $\sigma(h^*) = \dfrac{c(h^*)}{c(h^*) + \theta}$ is the share of wage costs in total labor costs.

6.3.2   Second order conditions

The conditions for cost minimization under output constraint with generalized production and cost functions have been detailed in Chapter 5, and apply here in the special setting at hand. They may be readily specified by considering the labor costs as a function of h only. Since $ng(h) = \bar{L}$, we can consider that the firm minimizes $E(h) = \bar{L}\dfrac{c(h) + \theta}{g(h)}$.

At a point where the first order condition (6.9) holds, i.e. $E'(h^*) = 0$, the second order condition $E''(h^*) > 0$ is equivalent to:

$$c''(h)g(h) > g''(h)\left[c(h) + \theta\right]$$

It is always fulfilled if $g''(h) < 0$. It may be fulfilled for positive values of $g''(h)$, if $g''(h) < c''(h)\dfrac{g(h)}{c(h) + \theta}$.

6.3.3   Graphic solution

As in the case of prefect man-hours substitution, the solution h^* can be obtained graphically by introducing the auxiliary concept of an isocost curve. An isocost curve represents all the pairs (c, h) generating a given labor cost. Let us consider the expenditure function: $E(n, h) = n[c(h) + \theta]$ and substitute n by $\bar{L}/g(h)$. Then, a constant cost curve of E_0 level is defined by:

$$c = \frac{E_0}{\bar{L}}g(h) - \theta \tag{6.10}$$

Notice that the isocost curve has the same shape as the worker effectiveness function $g(h)$. As explained in Chapter 5, this function may be convex for the first hours, then become concave, given that exertion may justify positive but decreasing contribution of additional hours to output. It intercepts the vertical axis at $-\theta$. The smaller the cost, the lower is the curve. Therefore, cost minimization necessitates establishing the lower isocost curve, consistent with the workers' minimum satisfaction constraint. Figure 6.6 shows the solution as the point F. The lowest isocost curve corresponds to the minimum cost E^*. In this picture, workers still perform longer than desired hours, $h^* > h^s(w^*)$, as in the case of perfect man-hours substitution. However, in the case of generalized production functions, this outcome is no longer certain: Figure 6.7 shows the alternative situation of insider underemployment, in which workers would like to work longer than actual hours.

The workers' supply and the firms' demand for hours might coincide only in the exceptional case where the isocost curve is tangent to the compensation function for a duration equal to the reservation hours, h_r. In this case, the slope of the isoscost curve is equal to the slope of the compensation function and is equal to the reservation wage; points W and F coalesce.

6.3.4   An exercise of comparative statics

The impact of varying effectiveness and of fixed labor costs on the optimal duration is easily determined in the particular case where $g(h) = h^\beta$, $\beta < 1$.

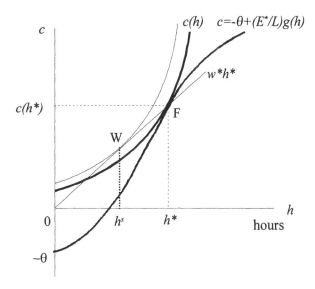

FIGURE 6.6. Optimal working time: overwork

Then condition (6.9) becomes:

$$\frac{c'(h^*)}{c(h^*) + \theta} = \frac{\beta}{h^*} \tag{6.11}$$

Comparative statics of the equilibrium working time may be sketched with respect to changes in the relevant parameters, i.e.: θ, related to the fixed costs of labor and β, related to worker effectiveness in time.

By differentiating equation (6.11), we show that for $\beta < 1$ an increase in hour effectiveness contributes to increasing working time:

$$\frac{dh^*}{d\beta} = \frac{c(h^*) + \theta}{(1 - \beta)c'(h^*) + h^*c''(h^*)} > 0$$

$$\eta_\beta^{h^*} = \frac{\beta\sigma}{\eta_{h^*}^c[(1 - \beta) + \eta_{h^*}^{c'}]} > 0$$

σ being the share of wages in total labor cost. The elasticity $\eta_{h^*}^{c'} = \dfrac{h^*c''(h^*)}{c'(h^*)}$ is positive by the convexity assumption.

As expected, an increase in the fixed cost of labor would push firms to increase working time:

$$\frac{dh^*}{d\theta} = \frac{\beta}{(1 - \beta)c'(h^*) + h^*c''(h^*)} > 0$$

$$\eta_\theta^{h^*} = \left(\frac{1 - \sigma}{\sigma}\right)\frac{\beta}{\eta_{h^*}^c[(1 - \beta) + \eta_{h^*}^{c'}]} > 0$$

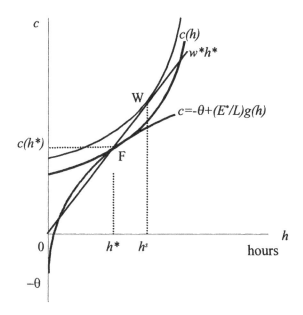

FIGURE 6.7. Optimal working time: insider underemployment

The response of employment to changes in parameters is important for a policy purpose. For a predetermined output, employment is implicitly given by: $g(h^*)n^* = \bar{L}$, thus

$$\frac{dn^*}{dh^*} = -\frac{n^*g'(h^*)}{g(h^*)}$$

or in elasticity terms:

$$\eta_{h^*}^{n^*} = -\eta_h^g$$

Thus, any change in the parameter value which implies a reduction in equilibrium working time would also bring an increase in employment:

$$\eta_\beta^{n^*} = -\eta_h^g\eta_\beta^h \text{ and } \eta_\theta^{n^*} = -\eta_h^g\eta_\theta^h$$

that is, increasing fixed costs and worker effectiveness would decrease the demand for workers.

6.4   Cost minimization with factor substitution

6.4.1   The case with unconstrained working hours

In this subsection we consider more general situations, in which both capital and labor services may be adjusted, output still being considered as predetermined.

Denoting by k the number of equipments units, the flow of capital services is $K = kz(h)$, where $z(h)$ is a "capital effectiveness function". The function $z(h)$ captures the relationship between working time h and the flow of services from the capital endowment. It may be constant, increasing or decreasing. In the simplest case, $z(h) = h$, implying that capital services are linear in hours, unmanned capital being unproductive.

The technology is represented by the generalized production function:

$$y = F(K, L) = F[kz(h), ng(h)] \tag{6.12}$$

where L represents labor services and has the already mentioned form, $L = ng(h)$.

We assume that the rental cost of capital is of the form $(\delta + r)k$; the depreciation of equipment does not depend upon the daily working time.

Under these assumptions, the cost minimization problem is:

$$\begin{cases} \min\limits_{k,n,h} \{k(r + \delta) + n[c(h) + \theta]\} \\ \text{with: } F[kz(h), ng(h)] = \bar{y} \end{cases} \tag{6.13}$$

where $c(h)$ is the compensating consumption function and θ are the fixed costs of labor. The solution (n^*, k^*, h^*) should verify first order conditions relative to the Lagrangian form:

$$\mathcal{L} = k(r + \delta) + n[c(h) + \theta] - \lambda\{F[kz(h), ng(h)] - \bar{y}\} \tag{6.14}$$

First order conditions applying to (6.14) are:

$$\mathcal{L}_n = c(h) + \theta - \lambda g(h)F_L = 0 \tag{6.15}$$
$$\mathcal{L}_k = r + \delta - \lambda z(h)F_K = 0 \tag{6.16}$$
$$\mathcal{L}_h = nc'(h) - \lambda[kz'(h)F_K + ng'(h)F_L] = 0 \tag{6.17}$$

From (6.15) and (6.17), we obtain a special condition for the solution h^*:

$$\frac{c'(h^*)}{c(h^*) + \theta} = \frac{g'(h^*)}{g(h^*)} + \frac{K}{L}\frac{F_K}{F_L}\frac{z'(h^*)}{z(h^*)} \tag{6.18}$$

We denote the share of wage costs in total labor costs by $\sigma(h)$. Defining $L(K)$ by $F(K, L(K)) = \bar{y}$, we denote $\eta_K^L = \frac{K}{L}L'(K) = -\frac{K}{L}\frac{F_K}{F_L} < 0$. Then, the former expression may be written in equivalent elasticity terms,

$$\sigma(h^*)\eta_h^c(h^*) - \eta_h^g(h^*) = -\eta_K^L\eta_h^z(h^*) \tag{6.19}$$

6.4.2   The impact of a mandatory reduction in working hours

In the following, we consider the effects of a binding constraint on working hours, the law imposing a maximal duration, $\bar{h} \leq h^*$. As seen in Chapter 3, in the work-sharing paradigm, such a policy is expected to induce firms to substitute hours with workers. It must be noticed that in our assumptions the reduction of hours for given n and k implies a simultaneous reduction of labor and capital services.

In this case, working time is no longer a control variable and first order conditions (6.15) and (6.16) only apply; from them we can write an expression for the ratio of marginal productivities of the two forms of services:

$$\frac{F_K}{F_L} = \left(\frac{g(\bar{h})}{z(\bar{h})}\right)\left(\frac{r+\delta}{c(\bar{h})+\theta}\right) \tag{6.20}$$

To explore the consequences of mandatory working time reduction, we introduce a simple homogeneous Cobb-Douglas production function: $F(K,L) = K^\alpha L^{1-\alpha}$, implying $\eta_K^L = -\dfrac{KF_K}{LF_L} = -\dfrac{\alpha}{1-\alpha}$ and therefore:

$$\frac{F_K}{F_L} = \left(\frac{\alpha}{1-\alpha}\right)\left(\frac{ng(\bar{h})}{kz(\bar{h})}\right) \tag{6.21}$$

From (6.20) and (6.21), $k = \left(\dfrac{\alpha}{1-\alpha}\right)\left(\dfrac{c(\bar{h})+\theta}{r+\delta}\right)n.$

Substituting k in the constraint $\bar{y} = \left[kz(\bar{h})\right]^\alpha \left[ng(\bar{h})\right]^{1-\alpha}$, we obtain:

$$\ln n = Const + \ln(\bar{y}) - \alpha \ln[c(\bar{h})+\theta] - \alpha \ln[z(\bar{h})] - (1-\alpha)\ln[g(\bar{h})] \tag{6.22}$$

Differentiating (6.22) with respect to $\bar{h}$ finally yields:

$$\eta_{\bar{h}}^n(\bar{h}) = -\eta_{\bar{h}}^g(\bar{h}) - \alpha\eta_{\bar{h}}^z(\bar{h}) - \alpha\left[\sigma(\bar{h})\eta_{\bar{h}}^c(\bar{h}) - \eta_{\bar{h}}^g(\bar{h})\right] \tag{6.23}$$

This last relation in elasticity terms shows the complexity of the response of the cost minimizing firm to a mandatory working time reduction, when the quantity of productive capital is flexible. In some cases, equation (6.23) however takes a simpler form.

For instance, if the constraint applies to an initially free system, (6.19) holds and we can write $\sigma(h^*)\eta_h^c(h^*) - \eta_h^g(h^*) = -\eta_K^L\eta_h^z(h^*)$. Given that in the case of the Cobb-Douglas form $\eta_K^L = -\alpha/(1-\alpha)$, equation (6.23) becomes:

$$\eta_{\bar{h}}^n(h^*) = -\eta_h^g(h^*) - \left(\frac{\alpha}{1-\alpha}\right)\eta_h^z(h^*) \tag{6.24}$$

It may be noted that the man-hours substitution which would take place if capital services were kept constant is indicated by the first term of the right hand side of equation (6.24). The impact of human working time on capital services is indicated by the elasticity η_h^z. If the function $z(h)$ is increasing in h, $(\eta_h^z > 0)$, men are needed to offset fewer hours and capital services.

If $z(h)$ is decreasing in h, $(\eta_h^z < 0)$, man-hours substitution is limited in consequence of increased capital services per time-unit. If we consider the simple case in which $z(h) = h$, and therefore $\eta_h^z(h) = 1 \; \forall h$, the elasticity of employment with respect to working time is:

$$\eta_h^n(h^*) = -\eta_h^g(h^*) - \left(\frac{\alpha}{1-\alpha}\right) \tag{6.25}$$

The additional effect of labor capital substitution on the elasticity $\eta_h^n(\bar{h})$ represented by $\alpha/(1-\alpha)$ is a consequence of fewer capital services supplied by a given stock of equipments when working hours are reduced.

6.5 Conclusion

The cost minimizing approach helps emphasize the role of fixed costs of labor and of varying effectiveness in the determination of working time by the firms, when they are constrained to offer contracts compatible with a minimum satisfaction of workers. It clearly reveals the possibility of various types of insider rationing.

When the production function is neoclassical (builds on the assumption of perfect man-hours substitution), the mere existence of fixed costs explains the employer's tendency to require longer hours than are willingly supplied.

Introducing a more general description of production and allowing for varying effectiveness, the model shows a more complex situation, in which insider rationing may go either way; in particular, if worker effectiveness in time decreases sharply, employers may prefer short working hours despite fixed costs per worker; in this case, the possibility of insider underemployment, with workers working fewer than desired hours per period, cannot be ruled out. This leads to a reversed conflict about working time.

In the cost minimization framework, imposing a binding constraint on working hours may contribute to increase the demand for workers, given the induced scarcity in labor and capital services. The measure is however accompanied by a reduction in profits.

The model at hand is a useful benchmark for more detailed analysis of working time in the context of predetermined output. In the next chapter, we investigate the case of workers who are identically productive but have different consumption/leisure preferences, and we put forward the optimal contract offered by the firm.

7
Cost minimization, heterogeneous workers and asymmetric information

In Chapter 6, we considered homogeneous workers, not only in terms of productive skills but also in relation to their consumption/leisure preferences. Firms were perfectly informed about workers' characteristics and determined the optimal input mix given a unique participation constraint applying to all of them. This chapter considers an extension of cost minimization problems, focusing on the design of optimal compensation schemes when workers differ only in terms of consumption/leisure preferences or reservation utility levels. In this generalized setting, a new issue arises: is the employer entitled to offer a definite contract to a worker or a subset of workers exclusively? Such a policy, when it is feasible, is often termed "discriminatory", identical labor services being finally paid differently. It must be noticed that the mainstream of economic analysis applied to discrimination tends to define this concept in a restrictive way: there is discrimination if the same economically homogeneous good or service is sold (or bought) at different prices. Most models of this tradition tend to account for different wages applying to workers who are identical under all attributes including tastes, apart from some economically irrelevant parameters such as sex or ethnicity (see the survey by Cain 1986). Here, we consider discrimination as the ability of the firm to reserve different contracts for workers of the same skill, but having varied working hours compensation demands.

The feasibility of this cost minimizing policy depends firstly upon the legal and institutional environment of the firm. In some countries, employers are given considerable freedom in their contracting practices and the principle of equal reward for equal work does not really apply. For instance, the French law tolerates unequal treatment of workers as a form of the right to manage in the private sector, except if the differences are based on sex, religion or race. Even in the case where discrimination is not forbidden on a legal basis, its application may be difficult, to the extent that worker types are in general private information, unknown to the employer. In this situation, the firm can only offer a set of contracts defining working time and its compensation, and leave workers free to make their choice. This particular setting is related to a standard category of problems usually included under the heading of "mechanism design", and has been extensively studied by recent microeconomic theory, in particular as applied to second price discrimination by the monopolist. The reader may find detailed analyses of this topic in Fudemberg and Tirole (1991, chapter 7) and Mas-Collel et al. (1995, chapter 14).

The text is organized as follows. In the first section, we introduce the main assumptions and the general Kuhn and Tucker conditions encompassing different particular types of solutions. Section 7.2 deals with the special case where some of the more demanding workers are left unemployed, first in the discriminating case, then when discrimination is ruled out. The last section 7.3 investigates the implications of a policy of mandatory working time reduction.

7.1   The decision problem of the firm

7.1.1   Main assumptions and constraints

We consider the general problem of minimizing the cost of a given output under a set of constraints.

a) Workers are clustered into a finite number of types, according to their consumption/leisure preferences and their minimum utility requirement levels. Preferences of the type i worker are represented by quasi-linear utility functions $u^i(c_i, h_i) = c_i - v_i(h_i)$ where c_i and h_i respectively measure the total wage compensation and the number of working hours per period. In each case $v_i(0) = 0$, $v_i'(h_i) > 0$, and $v_i''(h_i) > 0$. Each type of worker has a reservation utility level s_i defined as the utility levels attainable outside, through unemployment benefits or other job opportunities. A contract is accepted only if $c_i - v_i(h) \geq s_i$.[1]

In the following, to keep the analysis as simple as possible, we consider two types only: $i = (1, 2)$. Then, the firm has to determine labor contracts (c_1, h_1) and (c_2, h_2) subject to *participation constraints* P_1 and P_2:

$$c_1 - v_1(h_1) \geq s_1 \qquad\qquad (P_1)$$

---

[1] Corneo (1995) analyzed the participation decision of heterogeneous workers according to their autonomous income.

$$c_2 - v_2(h_2) \geq s_2 \qquad (P_2)$$

b) If discrimination is impossible, *incentive compatibility constraints* may also appear, as a consequence of free contract choice by workers of all types. These constraints called IC_1 and IC_2 are obtained by writing that the contract earmarked for one type of worker is at least as well appreciated by this type as the contract designed for the other type; this implies in our setting:

$$c_1 - v_1(h_1) \geq c_2 - v_1(h_2) \qquad (IC_1)$$

$$c_2 - v_2(h_2) \geq c_1 - v_2(h_1) \qquad (IC_2)$$

c) The amount of output to be produced is *predetermined* and requires a quantity $\bar{L}$ of labor services. The technology is neoclassical in the sense that hours and workers are perfect substitutes in the production of one unit of labor services. While workers differ regarding their consumption/leisure preferences, they are homogeneous with respect to their effectiveness in time. Denoting by n_1 (n_2) the number of type 1 (type 2) workers, the *quantity constraint,* pertaining to the necessary amount of labor services is obviously binding in any case and holds as an equality:

$$n_1 h_1 + n_2 h_2 = \bar{L} \qquad (QC)$$

d) We assume that workers of the first type are available in number $\bar{n}_1$, workers of the second type in number $\bar{n}_2$. Then, *availability constraints* are

$$n_1 \leq \bar{n}_1 \qquad (AC_1)$$

$$n_2 \leq \bar{n}_2 \qquad (AC_2)$$

The *objective of the firm* consists in minimizing total labor costs:

$$E = n_1 c_1 + n_2 c_2 + \theta(n_1 + n_2)$$

all the above mentioned constraints being fulfilled. As in previous chapters, we denote by θ the fixed cost per incumbent worker, whatever its type.

Non-negative slack variables must be introduced where there are inequality constraints. If e_1 and e_2 stand for unemployed workers in each type, availability constraints AC are:

$$n_1 + e_1 = \bar{n}_1 \qquad (7.1)$$

$$n_2 + e_2 = \bar{n}_2 \qquad (7.2)$$

Surplus from work x_i may arise if workers of some type derive an increased utility from work. Participation constraints as equalities are therefore:

$$c_1 - v_1(h_1) = s_1 + x_1 \tag{7.3}$$

$$c_2 - v_2(h_2) = s_2 + x_2 \tag{7.4}$$

A relative form of surplus exists if one type strictly prefers its contract to the other contracts, i.e. if incentive compatibility constraints are not binding. Introducing slack variables y_1 and y_2, IC_1 and IC_2 may be written as equalities:

$$c_1 - v_1(h_1) = c_2 - v_1(h_2) + y_1 \tag{7.5}$$

$$c_2 - v_2(h_2) = c_1 - v_2(h_1) + y_2 \tag{7.6}$$

First order necessary conditions therefore apply to the following cumbersome expression into which suitable Lagrangian multipliers $\lambda, \mu_i, \varphi_i, \psi_i$ have been introduced:

$$
\begin{aligned}
\mathcal{L} \;=\; & n_1 c_1 + n_2 c_2 + \theta(n_1 + n_2) - \lambda\left(n_1 h_1 + n_2 h_2 - \bar{L}\right) \\
& -\varphi_1\left(n_1 + e_1 - \bar{n}_1\right) - \varphi_2\left(n_2 + e_2 - \bar{n}_2\right) \\
& -\mu_1\left[c_1 - v_1(h_1) - s_1 - x_1\right] - \mu_2\left[c_2 - v_2(h_2) - s_2 - x_2\right] \\
& -\psi_1\left[c_1 - v_1(h_1) + y_1 - c_2 + v_1(h_2)\right] \\
& -\psi_2\left[c_2 - v_2(h_2) + y_2 - c_1 + v_2(h_1)\right]
\end{aligned} \tag{7.7}
$$

7.1.2 Kuhn and Tucker conditions

Kuhn and Tucker conditions on first derivatives of $\mathcal{L}$ with respect to n_1, n_2, h_1, h_2, c_1, c_2 are:

$$c_1 + \theta - \lambda h_1 - \varphi_1 = 0 \tag{7.8}$$

$$c_2 + \theta - \lambda h_2 - \varphi_2 = 0 \tag{7.9}$$

$$-\lambda n_1 + \mu_1 v_1'(h_1) + \psi_1 v_1'(h_1) - \psi_2 v_2'(h_1) = 0 \tag{7.10}$$

$$-\lambda n_2 + \mu_2 v_2'(h_2) + \psi_2 v_2'(h_2) - \psi_1 v_1'(h_2) = 0 \tag{7.11}$$

$$n_1 - \mu_1 - (\psi_1 - \psi_2) = 0 \tag{7.12}$$

$$n_2 - \mu_2 - (\psi_2 - \psi_1) = 0 \tag{7.13}$$

Conditions related to non-negative slack variables $e_1, e_2, x_1, x_2, y_1, y_2$ are:

$$-\varphi_1 \geq 0 \text{ and } e_1\varphi_1 = 0 \tag{7.14}$$

$$-\varphi_2 \geq 0 \text{ and } e_2\varphi_2 = 0 \tag{7.15}$$

$$\mu_1 \geq 0 \text{ and } x_1\mu_1 = 0 \tag{7.16}$$

$$\mu_2 \geq 0 \text{ and } x_2\mu_2 = 0 \tag{7.17}$$

$$-\psi_1 \geq 0 \text{ and } y_1\psi_1 = 0 \tag{7.18}$$

$$-\psi_2 \geq 0 \text{ and } y_2\psi_2 = 0 \tag{7.19}$$

Conditions related to the Lagrangian multipliers are equivalent to the constraints.

7.2   Optimal contracts and working time

The above system is compatible with a variety of situations. In the following, we will focus on an interesting case, where some workers of the more demanding type 1 are unemployed. The availability constraint is not binding, implying $\varphi_1 = 0$. It can be checked that the hourly wage rate is necessarily higher for this type, since from equations (7.8) and (7.9),
$$\frac{c_1}{h_1} = \lambda - \frac{\theta}{h_1} \text{ and } \frac{c_2}{h_2} = \lambda + \frac{\varphi_2 - \theta}{h_1} \text{ with } \varphi_2 < 0.$$
The decision problem of the firm must be considered in two different situations according to the feasibility or impossibility of discrimination among workers.

7.2.1   The discriminating case

We can first consider the basic subproblem in which the firm is able to assign different contracts to different workers. Incentive compatibility constraints do not apply and participation constraints are necessarily both binding.[2] In this case, equations (7.8) to (7.19) hold with $\psi_1 = \psi_2 = x_1 = x_2 = 0$.

---

[2] In the event of a positive surplus for one type, cost could be reduced by the employer in decreasing compensation for this type in keeping with all the constraints.

From (7.12) and (7.13), $n_1 = \mu_1$ and $n_2 = \mu_2$; therefore (7.10) and (7.11) imply:

$$v_1'(h_1) = v_2'(h_2) = \lambda \qquad (7.20)$$

Finally, (7.8) and (7.9) may be written:

$$\begin{aligned} c_1 &= h_1 v_1'(h_1) + \varphi_1 - \theta \qquad (7.21) \\ &= h_1 v_1'(h_1) - \theta \end{aligned}$$

$$c_2 = h_2 v_2'(h_2) + \varphi_2 - \theta, \text{ with } \varphi_2 < 0 \qquad (7.22)$$

This solution is depicted in Figure 7.1 where points F_1 and F_2 illustrate the cost minimizing contracts. The contract F_1 is equivalent to labor cost minimization of labor services obtained from type 1 workers, a problem that has been analyzed at length in Chapter 6.

As in this analysis, the minimum cost per type 1 worker is obtained at the tangency point between the indifference curve at the reservation level and the lower isocost line. Unlike the former analysis, the quantity of labor services demanded is endogenous.

Let us denote the solution to the general problem h_1^*, h_2^*, n_1^* and $n_2^* = \bar{n}_2$, with $L_1^* = n_1^* h_1^*$ and $L_2^* = n_2^* h_1^*$. Whatever L_1^*, the cost of these labor services has been minimized. Constant costs for type 1 workers imply $n_1(c_1 + \theta) = \bar{E}_1$, entailing isocost lines of equation: $c_1 = -\theta + \dfrac{\bar{E}_1}{L_1^*} h_1$. The firm seeks to minimize $\bar{E}_1$ under the constraint $c_1 - v(h_1) > s_1$. The lowest cost is obtained at the tangency point F_1 between the indifference curve at the reservation level and the less abrupt isocost line (the slope at the isocost lines increases with costs).

We know from condition (7.20) that at the optimum, the slopes of the indifference curves are identical. Then, the other point F_2 is obtained by shifting this isocost line to the right, until it reaches the tangency point with the indifference curve of the type 2 workers. Notice that with discrimination, no worker retains any surplus from work.

The multiplier λ coincides with the wage rate c_i/h_i only for a type of worker in excess supply ($\varphi_i = 0$) and in the special case where the firm incurs no fixed labor costs $\theta = 0$. In such a case, the employer pays the reservation wage rate of this type and working time coincides with its Walrasian supply.

7.2.2 Non-discriminating contracts

When discrimination is ruled out, workers choose among the proposed contracts so as to maximize their satisfaction and the incentive compatibility

consumption

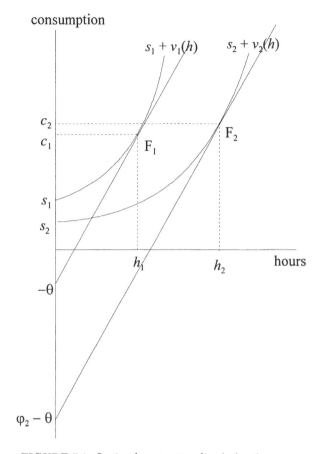

FIGURE 7.1. Optimal contracts: discrimination case

constraints cannot generally be ignored. In order to provide more explicit interpretations of the solution, we first introduce more assumptions about the preferences of the two types. We suppose that workers of type 1 may obtain more satisfaction in outside opportunities than workers of type 2, and demand more compensation for any increase in working time. We have therefore:

$$s_1 > s_2 \tag{7.23}$$

$$v_1'(h) > v_2'(h) \ \forall h > 0 \tag{7.24}$$

Clearly, workers of the second type are "cheaper" and will be hired first; the first type will be hired only in the event of a binding availability constraint on the second type.

With the supplementary assumptions (7.23) and (7.24), we can show that participation constraint P_2 and incentive constraint IC_1 are not binding.

To show that P_2 is not binding, we note that from (7.5) $c_2 - v_2(h_2) \geq c_1 - v_2(h_1)$, since $v_1(0) = v_2(0) = 0$, (7.24) $\Rightarrow v_1(h) > v_2(h)$ $\forall h > 0$, therefore $c_1 - v_2(h_1) > c_1 - v_1(h_1)$. Then, (7.3) $\Rightarrow c_1 - v_1(h_1) \geq s_1$ and from (7.23), $s_1 > s_2$. Therefore $c_2 - v_2(h_2) > s_2$. In the absence of discrimination, one category of workers may reap a surplus from work.

Since P_2 is not binding, IC_2 is necessarily binding (otherwise the firm could reduce labor cost by reducing c_2). Suppose that the two incentive compatibility constraints are simultaneously binding, (7.5) and (7.6) with $y_1 = y_2 = 0$ would imply: $v_1(h_2) - v_1(h_1) = v_2(h_2) - v_2(h_1)$, in contradiction to (7.24). IC_1 is therefore not binding and P_1 is binding.

On this set of assumptions, Kuhn and Tucker conditions (7.8) to (7.19) hold with: $x_1 = 0, \mu_1 > 0$; $x_2 > 0, \mu_2 = 0$; $y_2 = 0, \psi_2 > 0$; $y_1 > 0, \psi_1 = 0$.

In such a case, the following equations obtain:

$$\mu_1 = n_1 + n_2 \tag{7.25}$$

$$\lambda = v_2'(h_2) \tag{7.26}$$

$$n_2 = v_2 \tag{7.27}$$

Under these assumptions, we can state several interesting propositions.

Proposition 6 *Type 1 workers are requested to work fewer hours than type 2.*

Proof. Introducing equations (7.25), (7.26) and (7.27) in (7.10) yields:

$$v_1'(h_1) = \frac{n_1 v_2'(h_2) + n_2 v_2'(h_1)}{n_1 + n_2} \tag{7.28}$$

This last equation shows that either $v_2'(h_1) < v_1'(h_1) < v_2'(h_2)$ or $v_2'(h_1) > v_1'(h_1) > v_2'(h_2)$ but (7.24)$\Rightarrow v_2'(h_1) < v_1'(h_1)$ and the second case must be rejected. We have therefore:

$$v_2'(h_1) < v_1'(h_1) < v_2'(h_2) \tag{7.29}$$

Since $v_2'(h_1) < v_2'(h_2)$,

$$h_1 < h_2 \tag{7.30}$$

∎

Proposition 7 *When some workers of type 1 are unemployed, ruling out discrimination entails a shorter working time for incumbent workers of this type.*

Proof. In this case, $\varphi_1 = 0$, and condition (7.8) holds under the form:

$$c_1 = \lambda h_1 - \theta \qquad (7.31)$$

The binding participation constraint is:

$$c_1 = s_1 + v_1(h_1) \qquad (7.32)$$

Then, equations (7.31) and (7.32) imply:

$$v_1(h_1) = \lambda h_1 - (\theta + s_1) \qquad (7.33)$$

In the discriminating case, equation (7.33) is satisfied with $\lambda = v_1'(h_1)$. In the non-discriminating case, it is satisfied with $\lambda = v_2'(h_2)$. From (7.29) $v_2'(h_2) > v_1'(h_1)$ or $v_2'(h_2) = v_1'(h_1) + \alpha$, where $\alpha > 0$. Noting by h_1^d the discriminating solution and by h_1^{nd} the non-discriminating solution, we can write:

$$v_1(h_1^d) = h_1^d v_1'(h_1^d) - (\theta + s_1) \qquad (7.34)$$

and

$$v_1(h_1^{nd}) = h_1^{nd} \left[v_1'(h_1^{nd}) + \alpha \right] - (\theta + s_1) \qquad (7.35)$$

The last two equations, and $\alpha > 0$ imply:

$$v_1(h_1^{nd}) - h_1^{nd} v_1'(h_1^{nd}) > v_1(h_1^d) - h_1^d v_1'(h_1^d) \qquad (7.36)$$

The function $g_1(h) \equiv v_1(h) - hv_1'(h)$ is monotonously decreasing since its derivative is $g_1'(h) = -hv_1''(h) < 0$. In this case, condition $(7.36) \Rightarrow h_1^{nd} < h_1^d$
∎

We represent in Figure 7.2 the case in which the first type of worker is in excess supply ($\varphi_1 = 0$) and fixed costs are neglected ($\theta = 0$). Points F_1 and F_2 characterize the discriminating solution that has already been depicted in Figure 7.1; points F_1' and F_2' indicate the non-discriminating case; moving from F_1 to F_1' implies increasing the cost of labor services obtained from type 1, this increase being offset by a reduced incentive compatibility constraint applying to the contract designed for type 2. Consequently, $c_1^{nd} = h_1^{nd} v_2'(h_2^{nd})$ and $c_2^{nd} = h_2^{nd} v_2'(h_2^{nd}) + \varphi_2$ with $\varphi_2 < 0$.

It may be seen that in F_1', the type 1 worker would like to work more at a constant wage rate, and in F_2' workers of type 2 would like to work less.

7.2.3 The case of non-binding incentive compatibility constraints

When discrimination is feasible, constraints IC_1 and IC_2 do not apply. Ruling out discrimination however does not imply that incentive compatibility constraints are necessarily binding. In some instances, the firm is able

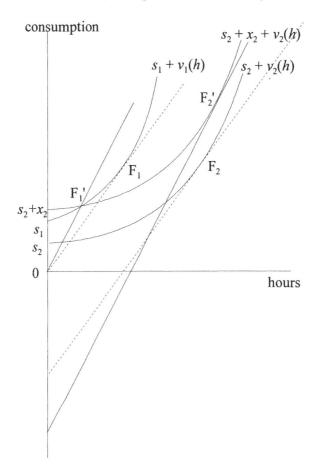

FIGURE 7.2. Optimal contracts: non-discrimination case

to capture the surplus of both categories of worker and discrimination has no value for the firm as a cost minimizing policy. In such a case, each type strictly prefers its own contract and there are positive relative surpluses; participation constraints are necessarily both binding and Kuhn and Tucker conditions apply with the following singularities: $y_1 > 0$, $\psi_1 = 0$; $y_2 > 0$, $\psi_2 = 0$; $\mu_1 = n_1 > 0$, $x_1 = 0$; $\mu_2 = n_2 > 0$, $x_2 = 0$.

We have therefore:

$$c_1 = s_1 + v_1(h_1) \tag{7.37}$$

$$c_2 = s_2 + v_2(h_2) \tag{7.38}$$

Non-binding IC_1 and IC_2 imply:

$$c_1 - v_1(h_1) > c_2 - v_1(h_2) \tag{7.39}$$

$$c_1 - v_1(h_1) > c_2 - v_1(h_2) \qquad (7.40)$$

Substituting c_1 and c_2 in (7.39) and (7.40) with their expressions in (7.37) and (7.38) yields the following inequalities:

$$s_1 + v_1(h_1) < s_2 + v_2(h_1) \qquad (7.41)$$

$$s_1 + v_1(h_2) > s_2 + v_2(h_2) \qquad (7.42)$$

These two inequalities are compatible only with crossing indifference curves, as represented in Figure 7.3.

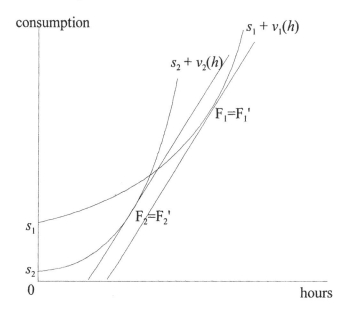

FIGURE 7.3. Non-binding incentive constraints

Crossing indifference curves may therefore explain optimality and feasibility of different wage rates for workers having the same productive abilities but different preferences, and not submitted to any discriminating pressure.

In the case depicted in this subsection, the cost minimizing policy set up by the employer is compatible with a working time structure of the wage rate which looks like a premium pay for overtime scheme. This may provide a theoretical background for the empirical analysis by Hart and Ruffel (1993) who have analyzed the highly deregulated labor market in the United Kingdom and put forward the emergence of spontaneously negotiated contracts with an overtime structure.[3]

---

[3] Premium schemes for long hours are investigated in Chapter 8.

7.3   Legal interference on working time

As put forward in subsection 7.2.2, in the absence of discrimination, the cost minimizing design links the contracts offered to the two different types of workers. In this section we consider the consequences of a superimposed undifferentiated legal limit to working hours, denoted $\bar{h}$. Legal reduction $(d\bar{h} < 0)$ cannot change employment of type 2 workers who are all employed, but is intended to foster employment of the first type who are in excess supply. We have seen in Proposition 6 that $h_1 < h_2$. In such a case, a (not too strong) legal constraint may be directly binding only for type 2.

We know that employment and working time of the two types are therefore related by the labor services constraint:

$$n_1 h_1 + \bar{n}_2 \bar{h} = \bar{L} \tag{7.43}$$

In differentiating (7.43), the elasticity of employment n_1 with respect to $\bar{h}$ may be decomposed in the following way:

$$\eta_{\bar{h}}^{n_1} = -\frac{L_2}{L_1} - \eta_{\bar{h}}^{h_1} \tag{7.44}$$

where $L_1 = n_1 h_1$ and $L_2 = \bar{n}_2 \bar{h}$. The policy of working time reduction would obviously contribute to increase employment (of type 1 workers) if the second term $\eta_{\bar{h}}^{h_1}$ were nil. Unfortunately, under a mandatory working time reduction the optimum working time exacted from type 1 workers may increase. The second term $\eta_{\bar{h}}^{h_1}$ is thus negative and tends to offset the man-hours substitution effect. If the ratio L_2/L_1 is small, this adverse effect would dominate the favorable substitution effect.

This may be established in the following terms. In the proximity of h_2, constraints P_1 and IC_2 remain binding, and the problem of the cost minimizing firm is in our set of assumptions (we assume away fixed costs for simplicity) equivalent to:

$$\min\{E = n_1 c_1 + \bar{n}_2 c_2\}$$

under constraints:

$n_1 h_1 + n_2 h_2 = \bar{L}$, $h_2 = \bar{h}$, $n_2 = \bar{n}_2$, $(IC_2) \Rightarrow c_2 - v_2(h_2) = c_1 - v_2(h_1)$ and $(P_1) \Rightarrow c_1 = v_1(h_1) + s_1$.

After substitutions, the objective may be expressed as a function of h_1 only:

$$E(h_1) = \frac{\bar{L} - \bar{n}_2 \bar{h}}{h_1} [v_1(h_1) + s_1] + \bar{n}_2 [v_1(h_1) + s_1 + v_2(\bar{h}) - v_2(h_1)] \tag{7.45}$$

First order condition on (7.45) implies:

$$\frac{\bar{L} - \bar{n}_2 \bar{h}}{h_1} \left[v_1'(h_1) - \frac{v_1(h_1) + s_1}{h_1} \right] + \bar{n}_2 [v_1'(h_1) - v_2'(h_1)] = 0 \tag{7.46}$$

The general comparative statics showing the effect of varying $\bar{h}$ on the optimal value h_1 solution of (7.45) is cumbersome. For a simpler treatment, we suggest introducing the quadratic proxies $v_1(h) = \alpha_1 h^2$ and $v_2(h) = \alpha_2 h^2$ with $\alpha_1 > \alpha_2$. In this case, it may be shown that (7.46) takes the form:

$$\left(\bar{L} - \bar{n}_2 \bar{h}\right)\left(s_1 - \alpha_1 h_1^2\right) = 2\bar{n}_2(\alpha_1 - \alpha_2)h_1^3 \qquad (7.47)$$

In Figure 7.4, the left hand side of this equation and the right hand side are represented as functions of h_1. Their intersection (point A) determines on the horizontal axis the cost minimizing value of h_1.

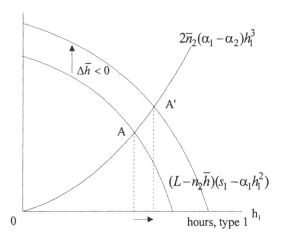

FIGURE 7.4. Hours constraint and the optimal duration

Decreasing $\bar{h}$ clearly shifts the curve representing the left hand side upwards, implying increasing working hours for the workers of the first type; the elasticity $\eta_{\bar{h}}^{h_1}$ is therefore negative.

7.4   Conclusion

Introducing diversity of preferences in cost minimization problems reveals new properties of optimal labor contracts. When firms do not know the true characteristics of the workers, or if the law precludes discriminatory attitudes, the employer's problem amounts to offering a cost minimizing set of labor contracts that motivates workers to freely reveal their preferences, by selecting the contract devised for their type. Moreover, in such a case, the response of the productive sector to a mandatory hours constraint applying to those most inclined to accept long hours may have disappointing effects on total employment, insofar as it implies an increased number of hours worked by the type of workers initially working fewer hours.

The next chapter introduces the analysis of legal overtime payment schemes often superseding the individual participation constraint.

8
Premium pay for overtime

8.1 Institutional schemes and possible supply response

In many countries, legislated schemes interfere with labor contracts by imposing a well-defined working time structure on the wage rate. In the United States, for instance, the Fair Labor Standard Act requires applying a 50% premium on hours worked each week beyond a threshold of 40 hours. In many other instances, working time regulations also impose a two-part compensating system, in which hours exceeding some statutory level are paid at a premium wage rate.

Such regulated paying schemes may be represented by the following form:

$$\text{wage rate} = \left\{ \begin{array}{l} w, \ \text{for } h \leq h_0 \\ aw, \ \text{for } h > h_0 \end{array} \right. \tag{8.1}$$

i.e., a normal wage rate applies to hours up to a threshold h_0, firms having to pay a times this normal wage for hours exceeding this threshold. In some countries, two successive thresholds are defined and determine the application of different (increasing) premium rates. In some cases, upper bounds on absolute durations of work have also been adopted. Hours payment schemes often include many other elements of complexity, described in detail in OECD, *Employment Outlook*, 1998.

Worker coverage by these schemes varies from one country to another (see Table 8.1).

	Percentage of workers accepting overtime	Overtime (hours per week)
Australia	32.1	2.7
Canada	17.0[c]	1.4
Finland	10.6	0.9
France	14.0	...
Germany[a]	...	1.2
Italy	...	5.0
Japan	...	3.4
UK[b]	53.3	5.3
US	...	4.2

TABLE 8.1. Overtime in manufacturing, selected countries, 1996. (a) all sectors; (b) male employment. Sources: OECD, *Employment Outlook*, 1998. For France: DARES, *Monthly Labor Survey*, 1996. For the US: Bureau of Labor Statistics. (c) from Duchesne (1997)

Table 8.2 at the end of the chapter describes the basic elements of such regulations in various countries.

What rationale lies behind such a widespread intervention of public authority? Mandatory overtime payment schemes are most often vindicated by different arguments:

– An overtime premium increases the relative cost of supplementary hours obtained from insiders compared with hours supplied by outside workers. When the firm faces peak demand on the goods market, it is therefore encouraged to hire new workers, reducing unemployment. This argument clearly resorts to the work-sharing paradigm in a dynamic context. For transitory activity increases, specific costs incurred by the firm in relation to changing numbers of workers creates an incentive to require the needed hours from the insiders. The overtime payment premium applying to them tends to counterpoise such cost of change, shifting the labor cost minimizing policy of the firm in favor of outsiders.

– In pure statics, mandatory overtime premium may be understood as protecting workers against the consequences of contracts they might accept, but deemed individually or socially detrimental by the authorities themselves. Too many hours of work may slowly ruin individuals' health or prevent them from investing in education or child rearing. Such behavior may be considered as detrimental to the development of the society in the long run and this form of market failure would appear if workers have a shorter planning horizon (life-time) than policy makers (several generations). In such a case, the law on working time pursues its own welfare objectives and aims at protecting workers against themselves.

An interesting question consists in conjecturing what would happen in the absence of such regulations. As we have seen in Chapter 6, competition among firms compels them to design contracts providing workers with a minimum utility level. If workers have neoclassical preferences, the feasible working contracts would exhibit a time increasing wage rate structure. The compensatory wage function $c(h)$ being convex, the effective compensatory wage rate $w(h) = c(h)/h$ would be increasing. The mandatory overtime premium scheme could therefore be interpreted as an institutional arrangement which approximates workers' preferences while economizing on the complexity and transaction costs of private negotiations.

The study by Hart and Ruffel (1993) would corroborate this hypothesis. They found that in the highly deregulated British economy where contracts and pay for overtime are freely negotiated between employers and workers in many sectors, the observed schemes are consistent with an overtime premium proportional to the basic wage rate. "In general however, while complicated non-monotonic relationships are possible, the marginal overtime premium of the individual worker may be typified either as a constant or as a rising step function of overtime hours" (Hart and Ruffel, 1993, p.184). Their estimations of the negotiated premium are close to 1.5. It turns out that the working time structure of the wage rate negotiated in the free labor market of the United Kingdom is close to the a priori legislated scheme in the United States. In Japan, regulation is more permissive, requiring a 1.25 times premium; Hart et al. (1996) showed that for very long working weeks, the negotiated marginal premium in this country rises to 1.32.[1]

Another possible interpretation for such freely negotiated premium pay for overtime agreements may be suggested by our analysis in Chapter 7: when the firm must recruit heterogeneous workers in terms of preferences, but does not have the right or practical possibility to discriminate among them, in some cases the incentive constraints may not be binding and the resulting optimal agreements coincide with a two-part wage rate.

As a first important consequence, overtime premium rules should affect the hours supply behavior. If we represent the worker's decision as the solution of the problem:

$$
\left\{
\begin{array}{l}
\max\left\{u(c,h)\right\} \\
\text{with} \left\{
\begin{array}{ll}
c = wh, & \text{if } h \leq h_0 \\
c = wh_0 + aw(h - h_0), & \text{if } h > h_0
\end{array}
\right.
\end{array}
\right.
\tag{8.2}
$$

it is easily checked that the feasible set in the space (Oh, Oc) is no longer convex. In this case, the solution of problem (8.2) may not be unique and the comparative statics on h_0 or a reveal individual discontinuity in the supply behavior

It must be noticed, however, that the overtime premium scheme may also be interpreted as restoring a Walrasian equilibrium when the contract

---

[1] See also Bell and Hart (1998) for a detailed observation of overtime patterns in the UK.

devised by the firm minimizes the cost of labor under the worker's utility
constraint. As has been shown in Chapter 6, with fixed cost of labor θ, the
cost minimizing labor contract F is not compatible with Walrasian supply
W for the effective wage rate (Figure 8.1). But point F as a worker's equilibrium may be supported by an infinity of overtime premium rules as in
(8.2) corresponding with varied w and h_0, provided that $aw = c'(h)$. Such
wage structures do not change the cost minimizing contract, but make it
possible to decentralize efficient transactions under the form of equilibri-
ums.

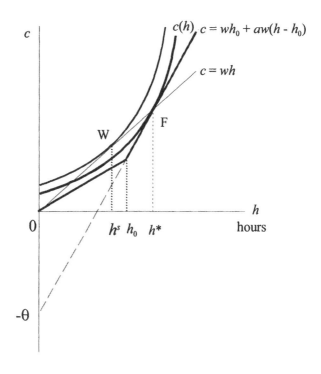

FIGURE 8.1. Premium wage for overtime and the hours supply

Comparative statics on a for given values of w and h_0 may be understood
statistically, for a given population. For different values of a, individual
supply may switch from $h < h_0$ to positive overtime $h > h_0$. Empirical
estimates have been attempted from US cross-sectional data by Idson and
Robins (1991). They find that an increase of a from 1.5 to 2 will only
increase the probability that a worker will offer to work overtime from
0.2999 to 0.3032, implying a negligible impact of this increment on the
supply side.

In the following developments of this chapter, we take a closer look at the
employment effect of this regulation on the demand for workers. The anal-

ysis will be carried out in the cost minimization framework where output is taken as given by the firm.

8.2 Premium pay for overtime in a cost minimization set-up

In this chapter we analyze the employment and hours decision of a firm whose output is predetermined, an economic context that has already been introduced in Chapter 6.[2] The firm is a "price taker" in a broad sense, since it considers the wage rate as predetermined, either determined by a trade union or resulting from some form of equilibrium in the labor market. Technology is represented by some production function $F(L)$, where labor services L take the multiplicative form $L = ng(h)$, n being the number of workers and $g(h)$ an effectiveness function.

The legal daily compensation schedule is represented by a piecewise linear function in worked hours. Then, allowing for a premium pay for overtime, it takes the form:

$$\chi(h) = \left\{ \begin{array}{l} wh, \text{ if } h \leq h_0 \\ wh_0 + aw(h - h_0), \text{ if } h > h_0 \end{array} \right.$$

with $a > 1$. The function $\chi(h)$ is therefore convex, presenting a kink for $h = h_0$. Although this expression describes daily compensation as an increasing function in hours of work, it should be clearly distinguished from the compensating consumption function $c(h)$ introduced in Chapters 4 and 6, and utilized throughout this text. The compensation function $c(h)$ is a pure consequence of workers' consumption/leisure preferences and of a minimum demanded utility level; the function $\chi(h)$ is an exogenous rule only representing a legal constraint, given a predetermined "normal" wage rate w. In the following, we consider that the legal premium rule only is binding, the participation constraint being not binding.

The basic labor cost function is therefore:

$$E(n, h) = n[\chi(h) + \theta]$$

where and θ are the fixed costs per worker.

If output is predetermined, then the required labor input is also exogenous, $L = \bar{L}$. In this case, using $ng(h) = \bar{L}$, the cost function takes the form: $E(h) = \dfrac{\bar{L}}{g(h)}[\chi(h) + \theta]$.

The first order condition $E'(h) = 0$ necessarily applies to the cost minimizing duration h^* if $h^* \neq h_0$. It can easily be shown that this optimal

---

[2] Alternative analyses of this subject are available in texts by Hart (1987) or Cahuc and Zylberberg (1996).

number of hours verifies:

$$\frac{\chi'(h)}{\chi(h) + \theta} = \frac{g'(h)}{g(h)} \tag{8.3}$$

A graphic solution may also be suggested, after introducing the auxiliary concept of isocost curve (defined in Chapter 6). In space (Oh, Oc), the pairs (h, c) implying a constant cost E_0 verify $E_0 = \dfrac{\bar{L}}{g(h)}[c + \theta]$. Then, an isocost curve is explicitly defined by $c = \dfrac{E_0}{\bar{L}}g(h) - \theta$ (previous equation 6.10). Its shape is easily derived from $g(h)$; since $g(0) = 0$, it intersects the vertical axis in $-\theta$. Lower constant cost levels define lower isocost curves on the graph. The solution (h^*, c^*) to the cost minimization problem is depicted in Figure 8.2. It represents the case where supplied working time exceeds the statutory hours, but, of course, the corner where solution $h^* = h_0$ may also obtain. It is worth noticing that in the traditional neoclassical case, the efficiency function being linear, $g(h) = h$, isocosts are straight lines and this corner solution $h^* = h_0$ necessarily obtains.

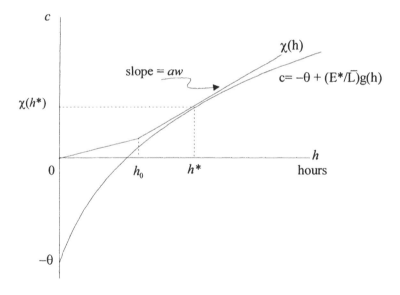

FIGURE 8.2. Cost minimizing hours

Explicit solutions may be obtained for specific effectiveness functions. We suggest considering the efficiency function introduced by Hart (1987): for $h > \tau$, $g(h) = (h - \tau)^\beta$, with $\beta < 1$ to account for some exertion effect, and $\tau \geq 0$ being interpreted as a set-up time. Then equation (8.3) takes the form:

$$\frac{aw}{[wh_0 + aw(h - h_0)] + \theta} = \frac{\beta}{h - \tau}$$

and implies a cost minimizing working time:

$$h^* = \frac{\beta\theta + aw\tau - wh_0\beta(a - 1)}{aw(1 - \beta)} \tag{8.4}$$

It must be kept in mind that the cost minimizing solution explains demand determined working time. It may not be feasible if it does not provide workers with a sufficient utility level; in other words if the participation constraint is not satisfied by the solution $(h^*, \chi(h^*))$. In some cases, the participation function and the legal constraint may be simultaneously binding. It may be checked graphically that the solution may not be efficient, i.e. may not minimize labor costs for constant workers' satisfaction.

8.3   Comparative statics on hours

We are now able to analyze the impact of varying the premium coefficient a and the statutory duration h_0 on the optimal working time.

In the standard neoclassical case $g(h) = h$ and with fixed costs of labor, the cost minimizing working time coincides with the threshold $h^* = h_0$. In this case, a reduction of the threshold obviously reduces the hours demanded, while increases in a have no effect on h^*.

We have shown that in the case of the concave efficiency function $g(h) = (h - \tau)^\beta$ for $h > \tau$, $(\beta < 1)$, the worker may undertake overtime hours. From equation (8.4), we have:

$$\frac{\partial h^*}{\partial a} = -\frac{\beta(\theta + wh_0)}{wa^2(1 - \beta)} < 0 \tag{8.5}$$

or, in equivalent elasticity terms,

$$\frac{a}{h^*}\frac{\partial h^*}{\partial a} = -\frac{(\theta + wh_0)}{(\theta + wh_0) + aw(\tau/\beta - h_0)} < 0$$

As expected, an increase in the wage premium should reduce the optimal number of demanded hours.

This sort of reaction has been empirically confirmed by Hamermesh and Trejo (1999). We have seen that under the Fair Labor Standards Act, the federal law in the United States requires that hours of work beyond 40 hours per week should be paid time and a half. California was one of the few states having imposed additional restrictions. In local regulations, California has required for many years that most women receive an overtime premium of 50% of the normal wage, for time exceeding eight hours a day. Starting from 1980, the same regulation has been extended to men, creating favorable circumstances to test the impact of this measure on worked hours. According to the estimates by the authors, a 1% increase in the overtime premium is responsible for a 0.5% reduction in overtime hours.

On the other hand, keeping the same assumptions in the form of the effectiveness function, it may be shown that reducing the statutory threshold h_0, for constant wage rate and premium ratio, would increase demanded working hours, since from (8.4):

$$\frac{\partial h^*}{\partial h_0} = -\frac{\beta(a-1)}{a(1-\beta)} < 0 \tag{8.6}$$

Such a response is not especially intuitive, but can easily be illustrated by means of Figure 8.3.

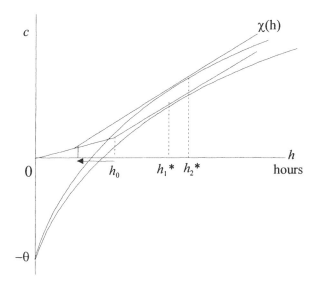

FIGURE 8.3. Impact of reducing statutory hours

8.4   Conclusion

For a constant activity level, supposing for instance price rigidities and Keynesian equilibrium, the cost minimizing models could provide some clues from which can be inferred the response of the productive sector in terms of employment to changing parameters of the wage scheme. Such changes modify the cost minimizing working time h^* and have an opposite effect on employment.

Indeed, the relationship between working time and employment is easily obtained by differentiating the labor services constraint $\bar{L} = ng(h)$. For a constant level of labor services, we can write:

$$d\bar{L} = g(h)dn + ng'(h)dh = 0$$

which implies the following negative elasticity of the demand for workers with respect to working hours:

$$\eta_h^n \equiv \frac{h}{n}\frac{dn}{dh} = -\frac{hg'(h)}{g(h)} \equiv -\eta_h^g < 0 \qquad (8.7)$$

General a priori predictions should be avoided since assumptions about the form of the efficiency function play a dominant role. The models may only help determine which relevant parameters in particular should be estimated in order to obtain the conditional predictions of comparative statics. Cost minimization models give some insights into more general settings since any profit maximization policy requires cost minimization; more dependable comparative statics should however be claimed from models in which activity levels are endogenous, i.e. under the assumption of profit maximization.

	Statutory weekly hours	Premium wage for overtime (in excess of normal hours)	Maximum weekly hours
Australia	38–40	50% the first 4 hours then 100%	void
Austria	40	50%	50
Belgium	40	50% (100% during the weekend)	60
Canada	40–48	50%	void
Czech Rep.	40.5	25%	51
Denmark	37	50% the first hour, then increasing	48
Finland	40	50% the first 2 hours, then 100%	45
France	39	25% the first 8 hours, then 50%	48
Germany	48	25%	60
Greece	40	25% the first 60 hours per year 50% the other 60 hours	48
Hungary	40	50%	52
Ireland	48	25%	60
Italy	48	25%	60
Japan	40	25%	void
Korea	44	50%	56
Luxemburg	40	25% blue collars, 50% white collars	48
Mexico	48	100%	57
Netherlands	45	no regulation	60
New Zealand	40	no regulation	48
Norway	40	40%	void
Portugal	40	50% the first hour, then 75%	50
Spain	40	...	54
Sweden	40	no regulation	47
Switzerland	45 (50)	25%	48 (52)
Turkey	45	50%	61 (66)
UK	...	collectively bargained	void
US	40	50%	void

TABLE 8.2. Overtime regulation in selected countries, 1996. Source: OECD, *Employment Outlook*, 1998

9
Working time in a profit maximization framework

9.1 Introduction

We have so far obtained general results by describing and interpreting the terms of labor contracts, using detailed descriptions pertaining to labor cost structures or working efficiency functions in the general framework of cost minimization. All these results necessarily hold in the case of profit maximization, for the profit maximizing output level.

The productive sector, however, may be considered either as working under an output constraint justified by some form of price rigidity as assumed in conventional Keynesian economics, or as optimally adjusting the activity to its profit maximizing value. This second point of view is often considered as more representative of long run reactions in the productive sector where rigidities may be overcome.

In this new chapter, as in the cost minimization approach (Chapter 6), the production function is generalized to account for imperfect substitution between workers and hours. We consider that firms must provide the representative worker with a minimum utility level to be obtained from a two-dimensional labor contract, determining simultaneously his or her consumption and leisure time. This utility constraint level is first considered in an unemployment context as predetermined, either by some unspecified institutional force, or by the utility level obtained out of work – depending mainly on the prevailing terms of the unemployment benefits. The situation in which the minimum requirements are flexible and decrease in the presence of outside unemployment is then considered; in this pure market economy, the minimum utility level is endogenous. This approach may be viewed as an attempt to generalize the endogenous equilibrium wage rate of standard textbook analysis.[1]

Under our assumptions, it is shown how the terms of the labor contract, (hours and wage rate) as well as the employment level, are jointly determined. Different configurations are possible from the worker's point of view, ranging from overwork (working more than desired for the going wage), to insider's underemployment (working less than desired). Comparative statics makes it possible to infer the impact of varying labor effectiveness, fixed costs of labor, or an exogenous utility level on the explained variables. Finally, the effect of mandatory working time reductions on the employment level is examined. While pointing out the complex relationship between labor effectiveness, fixed costs of labor, and demand for workers when the hours of work are constrained, the model developed here shows that if a limit on the duration of work is imposed on an initially free system, a first favorable effect on employment might be achieved for a constant utility level of workers. For a particular production function, it is shown by means of a numerical simulation that further applications of the constraint may decrease the employment level after reaching a maximum value. Consequently, only a too "strong" working-time constraint would have a perverse effect on the demand for workers.

Since unemployment is usually compensated with resources levied on the firm's wage bill, we finally introduce an elementary small size version of the equilibrium model in which a government operates under a balanced budget constraint. The authorities determine the level of unemployment benefits. For given consumption/leisure preferences, this welfare level of the unemployed determines the terms of the participation constraint of the workers. The tax rate to be applied on paid wages in order to exactly finance unemployment benefits results from this welfare objective and from the actual unemployment level; it is therefore an endogenous variable.

The chapter is organized as follows. Section 9.2 reformulates the basic assumptions about workers' consumption/leisure preferences, cost structure and the productive process, which have already been developed in general terms in previous chapters. Equilibrium working time, wage rate and employment are analyzed in section 9.3. The impact on employment of a cut in the legal working time is investigated in section 9.4. Section 9.5 sketches the role of endogenous payroll taxes in a simple general equilibrium framework.

---

[1] This chapter is a modified version of "A model of working time under utility competition in the labor market" published in the *Journal of Economics* (*Zeitschrift für Nationalöekonomie*), vol. 67, 1998, by the authors.

9.2   Main assumptions

9.2.1   The workers' consent to work

The workers' utility function is neoclassical: $u = u(c, l)$, where c stands for the daily consumption flow and l for the daily leisure time. Moreover, $c = wh$, where h is the daily working time and w the real wage rate. Then, $h + l = 1$ (using the day as time unit) and the utility function can be rewritten as: $u = u(wh, 1 - h)$.

The following axioms describe the preferences of workers:

Axiom 8 *Strong non-satiation and strict quasi-concavity implying respectively:* $u_1 = \partial u / \partial c > 0$ $u_2 = \partial u / \partial (1 - h) > 0$ *and convexity of any set in the* (Oc, Ol) *space such that* $u(c, l) \geq u_0$.

Axiom 9 *Workers accept only the contracts providing them with at least a utility level noted* s.

The condition $u(wh, 1 - h) \geq s$ defines thus in the (Oh, Ow) space an *acceptance region*, bounded by a frontier represented by the function: $w = w(h, s)$. That is $w(h, s)$ is implicitly defined by:

$$u(wh, 1 - h) = s \qquad (9.1)$$

We call $w(h, s)$ the *hours compensating wage rate function*; for any predetermined s, it represents the minimum wage rate firms must pay in order to determine workers to accept an h-hours contract (while granting them the utility level s). In the following, s being explicitly assumed constant, we note $w(h) = w(h, s)$. (This concept is related to the concept of "hours compensating consumption function", such as defined in Chapter 6, where $c(h) \equiv hw(h)$.)

Axiom 10 *Individual preferences are consistent with* a convex acceptance region, *implying* $w''(h) > 0$.

Notice that the quasi-concavity assumption on $u(c, l)$ is not sufficient for a convex acceptance region in (Oh, Ow) space.

Axiom 11 *We also assume that extreme values of the daily working time imply infinite values of* $w'(h)$, *i.e.:* $h \to 0 \Rightarrow w'(h) \to -\infty$ *and* $h \to 1 \Rightarrow$ $w'(h) \to \infty$.

All these assumptions are consistent with many neoclassical utility functions, for instance the multiplicative form: $u(wh, 1 - h) = wh(1 - h)$. It should be noticed that such utility functions embody relevant features of consumption/leisure preferences since any increase in resources due to a longer working day should compensate not only the direct nuisance induced by the extra work but also the reduction in leisure time which prevents the individual from enjoying his consumption possibilities.

One may remark that for any w, the utility function $u(,)$ allows us to define the individual *Walrasian labor supply*, i.e. the optimal working time from the worker's point of view for a given wage rate:

$$h^s(w) = \arg\max_h \left\{ u(wh, 1-h) \right\} \qquad (9.2)$$

Under the former set of assumptions, it is possible to state the following rule in terms of the compensating wage rate function:

Proposition 12 *The contract* $\{w(h), h\}$ *proposed by the firm coincides with workers' Walrasian labor supply* $h^s(w)$ *if* $w'(h) = \left(\dfrac{dw}{dh} \right)_{u=s} = 0$; *it involves* overwork *if the contract implies longer hours than the Walrasian supply* $h > h^s(w)$ *if* $w'(h) = \left(\dfrac{dw}{dh} \right)_{u=s} > 0$ *and* insider underemployment $h < h^s(w)$ *if* $w'(h) = \left(\dfrac{dw}{dh} \right)_{u=s} < 0$.

Proof. Differentiating $u(wh, 1-h) = s$ yields the slope of the compensatory wage function $w'(h) = \left(\dfrac{dw}{dh} \right)_{u=s} = \dfrac{u_2 - wu_1}{hu_1}$. The first order consequence of any variation dh of worked hours for a *constant* w is: $du = (u_1 w - u_2)dh$. Workers' Walrasian supply requires $\left(\dfrac{du}{dh} \right)_{w=Cst} = 0$ and consequently $w'(h) = \left(\dfrac{dw}{dh} \right)_{u=s} = 0$. For $w'(h) \neq 0$ two cases may arise. Since $hu_1 > 0$, $w'(h) = \left(\dfrac{dw}{dh} \right)_{u=s} > 0 \Rightarrow (wu_1 - u_2) < 0$, implying $\left(\dfrac{du}{dh} \right)_{w=Cst} < 0$: the utility of the worker would be increased by a reduced working time at the going wage (overwork prevails). Conversely, $w'(h) = \left(\dfrac{dw}{dh} \right)_{u=s} < 0 \Rightarrow (wu_1 - u_2) > 0$, implying $\left(\dfrac{du}{dh} \right)_{w=Cst} > 0$: the worker would welcome increased working hours (insider underemployment prevails). ∎

Figure 9.1 suggests an intuitive explanation in the case $w'(\hat{h}) > 0$. Two first curves are represented: $w(h, s)$ is the compensatory wage function for the competitive utility level s and $w'(h) = \left(\dfrac{dw}{dh} \right)_{u=s}$ is the subsequent marginal utility with respect to hours. The latter is an increasing function, given the assumption on the convexity of the compensatory wage curve. Let us consider a working time $\hat{h}$ such that $w'(\hat{h}) \neq 0$. In order to motivate workers to accept this duration, the firm should pay them the wage rate $w(\hat{h}, s)$. But for this wage rate workers would like to work only $h^s[w(\hat{h}, s)]$, and get a higher utility level $\tilde{s}$. The third upper curve represents the compensatory wage function for this *desired* utility level, $w(h, \tilde{s})$. As $h^s[w(\hat{h}, s)] < \hat{h}$, overwork prevails.

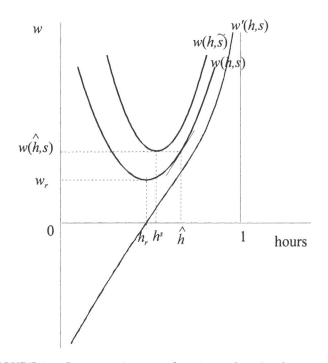

FIGURE 9.1. Compensating wage function and workers' rationing

We also represented the reservation wage w_r; the worker would not supply positive hours if the wage rate falls below this threshold. Of course, if $w'(\hat{h}) = \left(\dfrac{dw}{dh}\right)_{u=s} < 0$, the opposite situation of insider underemployment occurs, i.e. $h^s[w(\hat{h}, s)] > \hat{h}$.

9.2.2 Generalized technology

Generalizing the neoclassical paradigm, we consider technologies in which, due to fatigue or other factors, workers and hours (in logarithms) are not perfect substitutes. This can be done by integrating a production function $y = F(L)$ – where y stands for output and L for labor input, with standard properties $F(0) = 0, F'(\ ) > 0, F''(\ ) < 0$, but defining the labor input as a flow of labor services: $L = ng(h)$ where n is the number of people at work and $g(h)$ is the labor effectiveness function (see Chapter 5). We consider increasing functions $g'(h) > 0, \forall h$. A local property of the effectiveness function is its elasticity with respect to working hours, i.e.: $\eta_h^g = hg'/g$.

We also consider a generalized cost (or expenditure) function taking by assumption the two-part simplified form:

$$E = (wh + \theta)n, \text{ with } \theta > 0, \tag{9.3}$$

where wnh is the linear part of the wage bill and θn captures the various costs depending only on the number of people at work.

9.3   The optimal contract: wages and hours

9.3.1   Profit maximizing under the workers' utility constraint

By assumption, enterprises maximize profits in a goods market in full competitive equilibrium. In the labor market, firms are "utility-takers", the labor contract (wage, hours) providing workers with a minimum utility level denoted s.

The firm decision problem is thus:

$$\left\{ \begin{array}{c} \max_{w,n,h} \{\pi(w,n,h) = F[ng(h)] - wnh - \theta n\} \\ \text{with: } u(wh, 1 - h) \geq s \end{array} \right.$$

Using alternatively the former concept of compensatory wage function, $w = w(h, s)$ denoted for simplicity $w = w(h)$, the problem can be reconsidered as an unconstrained maximization in only two variables, the utility inequality constraint being obviously saturated:

$$\max_{n,h} \{\pi(n,h) = F[ng(h)] - w(h)nh - \theta n\} \tag{9.4}$$

First order conditions are expressed in terms of extensive (π_n) and intensive profit margins (π_h):

$$\pi_n = g(h)F'[ng(h)] - hw(h) - \theta = 0 \tag{9.5}$$

$$\pi_h = ng'(h)F'[ng(h)] - nhw'(h) - nw(h) = 0 \tag{9.6}$$

A solution of problem (9.4) is a labor contract $\{h^*, w(h^*)\}$ and an optimum employment level n^* as implicitly determined by (9.5):[2]

$$g(h^*)F'[n^*g(h^*)] - h^*w(h^*) - \theta = 0$$

---

[2] For a predetermined utility level, n^* may be consistent with the existence of unemployed persons. The case where unemployment pushes the utility constraint down to the point of external equilibrium will be analyzed later on.

To gain additional insight into the solution, we introduce the already defined elasticity of the labor effectiveness function η_h^g and eliminate $F'(\ )$ in equations (9.5) and (9.6):

$$w'(h^*) = \eta_h^g \frac{\theta}{(h^*)^2} - (1 - \eta_h^g)\frac{w(h^*)}{h^*} \qquad (9.7)$$

(Second order conditions are scrutinized in Appendix I.)

According to Proposition 12, if $w'(h) > 0$, overwork prevails; if $w'(h) = 0$ workers provide the Walrasian supply; if $w'(h) < 0$ insiders are submitted to underemployment.

According to equation (9.7), $\eta_h^g \geq 1 \Rightarrow w'(h) > 0$ and overwork is the only configuration possible.

The absence of worker rationing requires $w'(h) = 0$, implying:

$$\eta_h^g \frac{\theta}{h^2} - (1 - \eta_h^g)\frac{w(h)}{h} = 0 \qquad (9.8)$$

This condition can only be satisfied for $\eta_h^g < 1$ since (9.8) implies:

$$\eta_h^g = \frac{h^* w(h^*)}{\theta + h^* w(h^*)} < 1 \qquad (9.9)$$

It must be noticed that for $\eta_h^g < 1$ the three situations (overwork, Walrasian supply, insider underemployment) are possible, insiders' underemployment being the likely outcome of small values of η_h^g.

To bring out more clearly the determinants of the labor contract, we can write equation (9.7) in a slightly different form:

$$w'(h^*) = \eta_h^g \frac{\theta}{(h^*)^2} + (1 - \eta_h^g)\left[-\frac{w(h^*)}{h^*}\right] \qquad (9.10)$$

Equation (9.10) reveals a basic feature of the profit maximizing contract derived from the first order conditions: the first derivative of the compensatory wage function must coincide with a weighted average of the two well-defined functions θ/h^2 and $-w(h)/h$. It applies to fixed or variable labor effectiveness elasticities and lends itself to a graphic illustration helping to bring out clear comparative statics. Drawing in Figure 9.2 the two curves θ/h^2 and $-w(h)/h$ in the (Oh, Ow) space, we represent the right hand side of equation (9.10) as a combination of the two curves respectively weighted by η_h^g and $(1 - \eta_h^g)$ named ZZ. The case of a constant elasticity $\eta_h^g = \eta \in \ ]0,1[$ yielding a convex combination is used in the suggested curve.

The solution is observed at the intersection A of ZZ and $w'(h)$.[3]

---

[3] We cannot rule out another intersection between ZZ and $w'(h)$, indicating a possible multiplicity of solutions especially for small values of η and θ. Contrary to FitzRoy (1993), this multiplicity is not general. As shown in Appendix II, in the domain where $g''(h) < 0$ the profit function is concave and therefore can admit only one maximum.

The situation of overwork would prevail for high fixed costs and/or η_h^g close to (or higher than) one, as the curve ZZ would cross the $w'(h)$ curve in its positive region. The reverse situation, of insider underemployment, would emerge for low fixed costs and/or low η_h^g.

It must be noticed that the wage rate in this model is entirely determined by the labor effectiveness function, the worker's preferences and fixed costs of labor. As in most efficiency wage models, this wage rate appears disconnected from the marginal productivity, or more generally from the form of the production function (Solow, 1979). Of course, this last result stems from our assumption in which the services of labor L are multiplicatively separable in workers and hours.

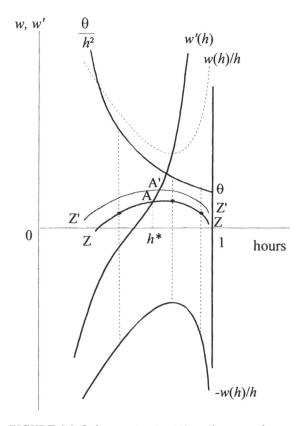

FIGURE 9.2. Labor contract setting: the general case

Some comparative statics can be sketched in Figure 9.2. An increase in η is represented by an upward shift of ZZ towards $Z'Z'$ unambiguously increasing working time and the wage rate.

An increase in fixed cost θ also shifts the ZZ curve upwards and therefore increases h^*. Appendix II shows in analytical terms that the sign of the sensitivities of employment and working time to variations of the fixed costs is well defined: $dn^*/d\theta < 0$ and $dh^*/d\theta > 0$.

9.3.2   The special case of perfect man-hours substitution

When $\eta = 1$, as implicitly assumed in the neoclassical standard case, equation (9.10) takes the simple form $w'(h) = \theta/h^2$. In this case, the ZZ curve and θ/h^2 coalesce, yielding the situation depicted in Figure 9.3, where overwork would prevail.

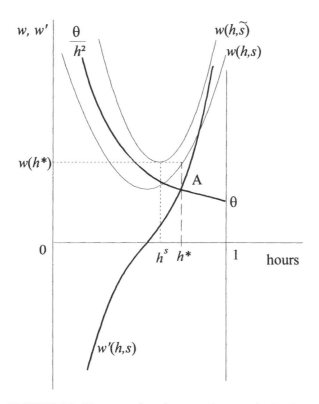

FIGURE 9.3. The case of perfect man-hours substitution

The segment $BC = h^* - h^s(w^*)$ measures an unavoidable gap between the optimal working time in the workers' view and the optimal working time in the firm's view. Only in the elementary version of the neoclassical case when $\theta = 0$ and $w'(h) = 0$ does the firm's optimal duration match the workers' Walrasian supply.

Overtime work at a premium wage rate could be introduced at this stage. The cost of a worker being only related to its consumption claim $c(h) = hw(h)$, the firm determines the optimal working time h^* and has to pay the compensating consumption $c(h^*) = h^*w(h^*)$. As mentioned in Chapter 8, this consumption can be achieved by a family of non linear wages of the form:

$$c(h^*) = w_0 h_0 + a w_0 (h^* - h_0), \text{ if } h^* > h_0 \qquad (9.11)$$

where h_0 separates regular and premium hours and $a w_0$ (with $a > 1$) is the premium wage rate. With more parameters under its control, the firm is able for instance to eliminate overwork in choosing a particular value for $w_0 = \dfrac{u_1 [c(h^*), 1 - h^*]}{a u_2 [c(h^*), 1 - h^*]}$, h_0 being fixed in accordance with (9.11). When legal constraints impose h_0 and a, the firm may not generally be able to fully eliminate the insider rationing. It is important to notice that optimum working time from the firm's point of view and the compensating consumption associated with this duration are independent of the payment scheme. In the following, we limit ourselves to the linear wage rate specification.

9.3.3   The full-employment utility level

The former analysis can be extended to the situation where the worker's requirements are flexible, unemployed outsiders being able to bid down the utility constraint level. In this case, outside equilibrium between the demand and the supply for workers determines the constraining utility level denoted u_E compatible with full employment.

This type of situation may be analyzed by the simulation of a simplified case with $g(h) = h^\beta$ (implying $\eta_h^g = \beta$). The computations use a particular neoclassical production function $F(n, h) = Q \left(n h^\beta \right)^\alpha$ and a particular utility function which entails the above mentioned property of a convex acceptance region: $u(wh, 1 - h) = wh(1 - h)$. This utility function implies a compensatory wage function: $w(h) = s/(h - h^2)$.

Figure 9.4 depicts two isoprofit networks in the plane (Oh, On) of equation $\pi(n, h) = constant$, the first obtained for $s = 1$, the second for $s' = 0.65$. The other parameters have been assigned the following values: $Q = 100, \alpha = 0.75, \beta = 0.9, \theta = 30$. Points A and A' indicate the profit maximizing demand for workers and hours corresponding respectively to s and s'.

When considering variations in the utility constraint level, the point A which describes the labor contract offered by the unconstrained firm slides along a positively sloped curve denoted qq'. For instance, a reduction in the utility level shifts the point A to A'.

This exercise makes it possible to infer some interesting properties of the external (full-employment) equilibrium. Consider a constant labor force,

workers

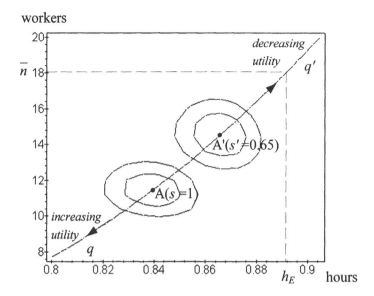

FIGURE 9.4. Flexible utility level and outside equilibrium

$\bar{n}$. Without a legal hour constraint, full-employment will be obtained at point E when workers' utility demands u_E are weak enough to fulfill the condition: $n^* = \bar{n}$. At this point, the full-employment working time h_E is indicated by the qq' curve.

The full-employment real wage rate is implicitly determined by first order conditions. For instance, we can write from (9.5):

$$w_E = \frac{g(h_E)}{h_E} F' \left[\bar{n} g \left(h_E \right) \right] - \frac{\theta}{h_E} \qquad (9.12)$$

This expression encompasses as a special case the standard rule $w = F'(L)$ when $g(h) = h$ and $\theta = 0$. The labor contract is compatible with overwork or insider partial unemployment along the terms indicated by equation (9.10).

9.4   Effect of a mandatory reduction of working time

The model makes it possible to analyze the effects on employment of a mandatory reduction in working hours. We first study the sensitiveness of employment to infinitesimal working time reductions, then we investigate the employment path for any value of the working time constraint.

9.4.1 Sensitivity of employment to small variations of the constraint

Let us consider that an upper limit $\bar{h}$ is set on the duration of work, with $\bar{h} < h^*$. The firm must pay the wage $w(\bar{h})$ and its decision is limited to the choice of the optimal value of n, denoted n.

The first order condition (9.5) implicitly defines n:

$$\pi_n = g(\bar{h})F'\left[ng(\bar{h})\right] - \bar{h}w(\bar{h}) - \theta = 0 \tag{9.13}$$

By differentiating (9.13) one can determine the sensitivity of the demand for workers with respect to $\bar{h}$:

$$\frac{dn}{d\bar{h}} = -\frac{ngg'F'' + g'F' - (w + \bar{h}w')}{g^2 F''} = -\frac{\pi_{nh}}{\pi_{nn}} \tag{9.14}$$

The sign and size of this expression indicate the local efficiency of mandatorily reducing the working time. From (9.6), we know that $g'F' - (w + \bar{h}w') = \frac{\pi_h}{n} = 0$ when h coincides with its profit maximizing value h^*, but $g'F' - (w + \bar{h}w') > 0$ when the constraint is binding and the sign of (9.14) is therefore indeterminate.

However, when the mandatory reduction applies to an initially free system, the effect of the measure is easily determined. Since $g'F' - (w + \bar{h}w') = 0$, equation (9.14) $\Rightarrow \dfrac{dn}{d\bar{h}} = -\dfrac{ng'}{g}$, the elasticity of the demand for workers with respect to $\bar{h}$ is:

$$\eta_h^n = -\eta_h^g$$

This incipient value coincides with the sensitiveness already obtained in the context of output constrained behavior (Chapter 6).

When working time is already constrained, $g'F' - (w + \bar{h}w') > 0$, thus the terms of the man-hours substitution indicated by equation (9.14) may be less favorable to employment.

In the light of the former analysis, the legal reduction of working time in an unconstrained system leads first to an increase in employment.

9.4.2 Employment as a function of the working time constraint

Equation (9.13) implies $F'[ng(\bar{h})] = [\bar{h}w(\bar{h}) + \theta]/g(\bar{h})$, leading to:

$$n(\bar{h}) = \frac{1}{g(\bar{h})}F'^{-1}\left\{\frac{\bar{h}w(\bar{h}) + \theta}{g(\bar{h})}\right\} \tag{9.15}$$

Equation (9.15) brings out an important structural feature of the economy, i.e. the relationship between the working time constraint and employment, under constant worker utility. The precise shape of this function depends on $g(h)$, $F(L)$ and $w(h)$. A thorough global analysis would therefore require precise knowledge of these three relevant functions. Consequently, $n(\bar{h})$ could, a priori, have local or global extrema for $\bar{h} \in\,]0,1[$.

From equation (9.14) it appears that maximizing employment n by a working time constraint implies, for an interior solution, the first order condition:

$$\frac{dn}{d\bar{h}} = 0 \Rightarrow ngg'F'' + g'F' = (w + \bar{h}w') \qquad (9.16)$$

Denoting the elasticity of the marginal productivity with respect to labor services $\eta_L^{F'} = LF''/F'$, the elasticity of the compensating wage with respect to hours $\eta_h^w = hw'/w$, the elasticity of output with respect to hours $\eta_h^F = \dfrac{dF}{dh}\dfrac{h}{F} = hng'F'/F$ and labor's share of output $\psi = wnh/F(ng(h))$, equation (9.16) takes the form:

$$\psi\,(1 + \eta_h^w) = \eta_h^F\left(1 + \eta_L^{F'}\right) \qquad (9.17)$$

This first order condition is not sufficient and one cannot rule out the possibility of the multiplicity of extrema of the function (9.15), in the general case.

9.4.3   A simple simulation

The existence of an interior global maximum of the former function is illustrated by a simple simulation using the already mentioned particular neoclassical production function: $F(n,h) = Q\left(nh^\beta\right)^\alpha$ and the particular utility function: $u(wh, 1 - h) = wh(1 - h)$. In order to analyze the impact of the hours constraint, in Figure 9.5 we draw first the isoprofit network in the plane (Oh, On) of equation $\pi(n,h) = constant$. Parameters were assigned the same values as before, $Q = 100, \beta = 0.9, \alpha = 0.75, \theta = 30$. In particular, the utility constraint is set to $s = 1$.

The slope of a given isoprofit curve is $dn/dh = -\pi_h/\pi_n$. It is indeterminate (takes the form $0/0$) at the point A where the profit is maximized without constraint. When the time constraint is binding, the firm chooses the number of workers which maximizes profits (in keeping with the first order condition (9.13): $\pi_n = 0$).

In Figure 9.5, the time constraint is represented by a vertical line and the employment constrained choice is the point where this vertical is tangent to an isoprofit curve. For various levels of the constraint the employment choice follows the curve denoted mm'. This last curve represents the graph of $n(\bar{h})$. Of course, the point A belongs to mm' since $n(h^*) = n^*$.

workers

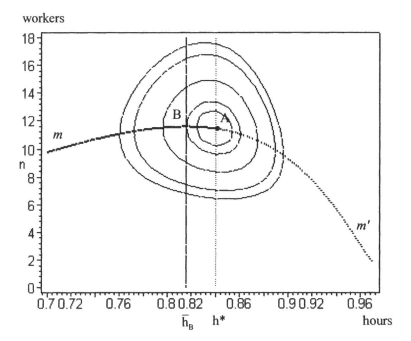

FIGURE 9.5. Working time constraints and the employment path

It can be checked that, as indicated by equation (9.14), in the neighborhood of A the mandatory reduction in working hours implies an increase in the demand for workers and a decrease in profits; in addition, for "low" durations of work, the terms of the substitution man/hours worsen and the relationship is inverted. Consequently, maximum employment is reached for a particular value of the working time constraint. In the simulation, this maximum employment level, denoted B on Figure 9.5, is equal to 11.59 for a duration of work $\bar{h}_B = 0.81$, which can be compared with the unconstrained choice (point A), where $n^* = 11.45$ and $h^* = 0.84$.

9.5 Working time reduction under predetermined unemployment benefits

It is worth considering a situation in which the authorities simultaneously control the unemployment benefits and working time. Interesting investigations pertaining to the multiplicity of solutions of similar systems may be found in FitzRoy et al. (1999). We restrict our analysis to a very simple model in which the productive sector comprises f identical competitive firms. Technology is still represented by $y = F[ng(h)]$.

The government determines a working time constraint $h \leq \bar{h}$.

The workers (in number $\bar{N}$) are identical. They accept working contracts (c, h) if $u(c, h) \geq u(b, 0)$ where b stands for the unemployment benefits in consumption units. This participation constraint defines a working time compensatory wage rate $w(h, b)$ such that $u\{hw(h, b), h\} = u(b, 0)$. This compensatory wage function is increasing in b.

The government determines the unemployment benefit level $b = \bar{b}$, and applies a flat tax rate τ on the cost of labor service to levy the corresponding resources. Unemployment is $U = \bar{N} - fn$, and the government budget constraint implies:

$$\bar{b}(\bar{N} - fn) = \tau fnhw(h, \bar{b}) \tag{9.18}$$

Under the participation constraint, each firm maximizes its profit $\pi = F[ng(h)] - nhw(h, b)(1 + \tau)$; we suppose that in the solution, the intensive margin is positive $ng'(h)F'[ng(h)] - n(w + hw_h)(1 + \tau) > 0$; the working time constraint is therefore binding, and $h = \bar{h}$. The only control variable for the firm is employment n; the competitive hypothesis entails that the firm individually considers τ as fixed.

The general equilibrium of this system is therefore represented by equation (9.18) and elimination of the extensive margin, i.e. the first order condition:

$$\pi_n = g(\bar{h})F'[ng(\bar{h})] - \bar{h}w(\bar{h}, \bar{b})(1 + \tau) = 0 \tag{9.19}$$

In this simple context, the government is in fact responsible for the endogenous variables n, U, w and τ.

Generous unemployment compensation $\bar{b}$ may induce a high unemployment level. In what terms is a policy of working time reduction able to reduce joblessness?

For a given value of $\bar{b}$, a smaller value of $\bar{h}$ should (in comparative statics) reduce the individual compensation; but no simple rule can be inferred since the reaction of the endogenous variables depends on unspecified characteristics of the G.P.F.

For small variations of $\bar{h}$, theoretical predictions of comparative statics may be obtained by differentiating the system of equations (9.18) and (9.19). Variations of endogenous variables are related to $d\bar{h}$ by:

$$\begin{pmatrix} g^2 F'' & -\bar{h}w \\ \bar{b} + \tau\bar{h}w & n\bar{h}w \end{pmatrix} \begin{pmatrix} dn \\ d\tau \end{pmatrix} = d\bar{h} \begin{pmatrix} (1 + \tau)(w + \bar{h}w_h) - g'F' - ng'gF'' \\ -n\tau(w + \bar{h}w_h) \end{pmatrix} \tag{9.20}$$

After inversion of (9.20), the sensitivity of the firm's individual employment to the imposed working time may be calculated:

$$\frac{dn}{d\bar{h}} = -\frac{ngg'F'' + g'F' - (w + \bar{h}w_h)}{g^2 F'' + (\bar{b} + \tau\bar{h}w)/n} \tag{9.21}$$

The order of magnitude and even the sign of this sensitivity cannot be readily inferred without the specification of the compensatory wage function – itself depending upon the worker's preferences – and of working efficiency functions.

We have to note that the sensitivity expressed by (9.21) applies locally to any solution of (9.18) and (9.19). It clearly encompasses the relationship (9.14) as a special case with no government; it includes as a special and trivial case the elementary neoclassical result in which production is constant and the employment reaction is reduced to a pure substitution effect with $\frac{dn}{dh} = -\frac{n}{h}$. This may be obtained by considering in (9.21) $F' = w$, $g = h$, $g\prime = 1$, $w_h = \bar{b} = \tau = 0$.

9.6   Conclusion

The first steps taken in generalizing the neoclassical paradigm, i.e. introducing fixed costs of labor, generalizing the representation of the productive process and submitting competitive labor contracts to the workers' utility constraint enabled us to draw a more flexible and comprehensive picture of the labor market than the standard neoclassical view. In Chapter 6, labor contracts were explained in a cost minimization perspective; in the present chapter, we introduced additional complexity, considering the situation in which profit maximizing firms also hold the flow of output under control.

In such conditions, a linear wage rate (the only price in our two commodities economy) is not generally able to eliminate simultaneously internal and external rationing; insider rationing is a natural outcome, with or without competing outsiders. The model makes it possible to analyze the structural factors influencing the rationing, by means of two central parameters: θ – related to the fixed costs of labor and η_h^g – related to the notion of labor effectiveness. If – as the empirical studies surveyed in Chapter 5 would suggest – the labor effectiveness elasticity is higher than one, fixed costs of labor entail higher wages, longer hours and overwork. In such industries where low fixed costs or low effectiveness elasticities prevail, the opposite insiders' rationing would occur. If the minimum utility requirements are rigid, insider overwork and unemployment are unfortunately compatible.

In spite of its drastic simplifications, the predictions of this model seem to be consistent with observed covariations of wages, employment and working time, especially if we refer to the stylized facts recorded by Layard et al. (1991) or Elmeskov (1993). These authors revealed that over a long period of time (10 to 20 years), countries where the duration of work has gone down have simultaneously recorded an increase in the unemployment level. Although other alternative explanations could be proposed, such a paradoxical evolution is consistent with this model: an increase in the minimum level of utility claimed by the workers would shift the equilibrium downwards on the qq' curve in Figure 9.4.

Insider satisfaction being assumed constant, a reduction in the legal working time may entail an increase in employment within a limited domain at the expense of profits. It must be noted that this favorable result resting on constant workers' utility implies an hourly wage rate reduction. More appealing, a decrease in fixed costs of labor would simultaneously reduce working time, increase employment and profits.

The view adopted here fits best economies with highly deregulated labor markets, like the British one. Most economies in continental Europe have more structured labor markets, where legal constraints and collective bargaining between unions and firms play a central role in the formation of the equilibrium contract. The model may anyway provide an elementary interpretation for this set-up by considering the role played by unions or state regulation in granting insiders a minimum utility level. The next chapter builds on an alternative explanation, which explicitly models the objectives of the trade unions and the bargaining process.

9.7 Appendix I: Second order conditions

A local maximum of the profit function is reached when conditions (9.5) and (9.6) are fulfilled, and if the Hessian of the profit function is negative definite.

The Hessian is obtained in calculating the second derivatives:

$$
\begin{aligned}
H &= \begin{pmatrix} \pi_{nn} & \pi_{nh} \\ \pi_{hn} & \pi_{hh} \end{pmatrix} \\
&= \begin{pmatrix} g^2 F'' & g'F'+gg'nF''-w-hw' \\ g'F'+gg'nF''-w-hw' & n\left[(g')^2 nF'' + g''F' - (2w'+hw'')\right] \end{pmatrix}
\end{aligned}
$$

H is definite negative iff $Tr(H) > 0$ and $\det(H) > 0$; this requires $\pi_{nn} < 0$, $\pi_{hh} < 0$ and $\pi_{nn}\pi_{hh} > (\pi_{hn})^2$.

In a point where first order conditions prevail, $g'F' = w + hw'$ and we can write:

$$
H = \begin{pmatrix} g^2 F'' & gg'nF'' \\ gg'nF'' & n\left[(g')^2 nF'' + g''F' - (2w'+hw'')\right] \end{pmatrix}
$$

The condition $\pi_{nn} < 0$ is always fulfilled; $\pi_{hh} < 0$ iff:

$$
g''F' < (2w'+hw'') - (g')^2 nF'' \tag{9.22}
$$

The condition $\det(H) > 0$ is fulfilled iff:

$$
g''F' < (2w'+hw'') \tag{9.23}
$$

Since $(g')^2 nF'' < 0$, $(9.23) \Rightarrow (9.22)$.

The only second order condition is therefore $g''F' < (2w' + hw'')$. The second member of this inequality is the second derivative of $c(h) = hw(h)$ where $u\,[c(h), 1-h] = s$. Decreasing marginal rates of substitution between consumption and leisure imply therefore $c''(h) = 2w' + hw'' > 0$.

In particular, *if $g'' \leq 0$, first order conditions are sufficient.* The domain where $g'' \leq 0$ is included in the concavity domain of the profit function.

9.8   Appendix II: Comparative statics of fixed costs

We show that in our assumptions, an increase $d\theta$ of the fixed cost of labor always implies a positive variation dh^* of hours and a negative variation dn^* of employment for profit maximizing contracts.

Differentiating equation (9.5), we obtain:

$$g'F'dh^* + gF''\left(gdn^* + n^*g'dh^*\right) - c'dh^* - d\theta = 0$$

which can be simplified, since $(9.6) \Rightarrow g'F' - c' = 0$, into the form:

$$g^2 F''dn^* + n^* gg'F''dh^* = d\theta \tag{9.24}$$

Differentiating (9.6), we obtain:

$$gg'F''dn^* + \left(g''F' + n^*(g')^2 F'' - c''\right)dh^* = 0 \tag{9.25}$$

Solving the system (9.24) and (9.25), and after noticing that:

$$\left(g''F' + n^*(g')^2 F'' - c''\right) = \pi_{hh}/n^*$$

We obtain:

$$\frac{dn^*}{d\theta} = \frac{\pi_{hh}}{n^* g^2 F'' \left(g''F' - c''\right)} \tag{9.26}$$

$$\frac{dh^*}{d\theta} = -\frac{g'}{g\left(g''F' - c''\right)} \tag{9.27}$$

The signs of the two sensitivities are unambiguous: $dn^*/d\theta < 0$ and $dh^*/d\theta > 0$ since $F'' < 0$ and second order conditions imply (Appendix I) $\pi_{hh} < 0$ and, in keeping with condition (9.23), $g''F' - c'' < 0$. In the special case $g(h) = h$, $g' = 1$, $g'' = 0$, yielding: $\dfrac{dn^*}{d\theta} = -\dfrac{\pi_{hh}}{nh^2 F''c''}$ and $\dfrac{dh^*}{d\theta} = \dfrac{1}{hc''}$.

10
Working time in a trade union model

10.1 Trade unions and hours negotiation

Modern working time analysis builds on a host of generalizations of the standard neoclassical paradigm. Labor economists have generalized production functions, doing away with the assumption of perfect substitution between hours and workers. They have also introduced two-part cost structures, where fixed costs of labor and non-linear wages are explicitly dealt with. In this more detailed context, demand for labor services evolves into a two-dimensional magnitude: optimum (profit maximizing) number of workers and optimal working time. As far as the structure of the labor market is concerned, we argued in former chapters why firms would not compete any longer for workers in pure wage terms. In more realistic terms, the participation constraint imposed on firms by labor market competition is a minimum satisfaction level derived by the worker from a labor contract specifying working time and its wage compensation. In the former chapters, several models have explained equilibrium working hours, wages and employment in this more adequate set-up and provided different interpretations for the observed insider rationing.

In many countries, however, in particular in continental Europe, trade unions play a central role in the labor market as they hold the right to negotiate the collective labor contract on behalf of the workers. In this case, the problem of working time determination is substantially modified, since unions may not only transpose the goals of the individual worker, but also have specific objectives, like membership building and employment protection. Table 10.1 presents the main characteristics of the union systems in the OECD countries in 1994. The first column indicates the estimated membership rate, and the second column the coverage rate, that is the proportion of employed persons that are covered by a collective agreement.

	Unionization rate	Coverage rate
Australia	35	80
Austria	42	98
Belgium	54	90
Canada	38	36
Denmark	76	69
Finland	81	95
France	9	95
Germany	29	92
Italy	39	82
Japan	24	21
Netherlands	26	81
New Zealand	30	31
Norway	58	74
Portugal	32	71
Spain	19	78
Sweden	91	89
Switzerland	27	50
United Kingdom	34	47
United States	16	18

TABLE 10.1. Extent of unionization in the OECD. Source: OECD, *Employment Outlook*, 1997

Since the pioneering work by Dunlop (1944) and Ross (1948) , an impressive literature has investigated the economics of trade unions, focusing on employment and wage determination. Working time was paid relatively less attention as a theoretical matter. Among the notable exceptions, Calmfors (1985), Booth and Schiantarelli (1987, 1988), FitzRoy et al. (1999) worked out monopoly union models, where the union unilaterally sets wages (and sometimes hours), the firms finally setting employment to maximize profits. Although this framework helps emphasize some results usefully contrasted with the purely competitive labor market approach, it is, however, a limit case, since in modern industrial practice, unions seldom impose anything; in general, they bargain over a set of variables in order to achieve their objectives (Layard et al., 1991). This point of view is confirmed by the ILO (1997) *World Labor Report* on contemporary industrial relations in an international comparison, which points at the significant emphasis placed on working time issues in the collective bargaining process observed in Europe.

More general than the monopoly case, another approach using Nash (1950) negotiation theory has been introduced by McDonald and Solow (1981) to the bargaining process in the labor market.[1] This method has also been used by Booth and Schiantarelli (1987, 1988), D'Autume and Cahuc (1997) or Cahuc and Granier (1997) to analyze the determination of employment and wages under the influence of predetermined working time. In these analyses, wages are negotiated between the firm and the union, employment is set by the firm in the right to manage tradition (Nickell, 1982), and working time is either chosen by the individual on his supply curve or settled at a different negotiation level.

A further generalization is due to Booth and Ravallion (1993) who explicitly include working time in the set of negotiated variables, as suggested by the way collective negotiations occur in most continental European countries, to mention only France, Germany and Italy as outstanding examples. They still consider a two-tier process in which employment is decided by the firm in a second stage. The labor contract resulting from the negotiation reflects the trade union decision to maximize a utilitarian objective function, subject to an isoprofit constraint. This analytical framework enables them to study the marginal impact of politically controlled hours on equilibrium employment. It must be noticed, however, that the proposed model rests on a limited concept of union rationality: the suggested objective function of the union includes employment as an argument, but this variable, although controlled by the firm in a second stage, is considered as constant by the union in the first stage. In other words, during the labor contract bargaining phase, the union does not take into account the ex post employment response of the firm.

In this chapter, we attempt to carry a step further the analysis by Booth and Ravallion (1993). As assumed in their text, both working time and wages are brought to the negotiation table, while employment only is kept under the firm's control. At variance with them, we apply the Nash solution to the bargaining problem: this enables us to work out a well-defined solution for equilibrium working time, wages and employment. We also consider a more flexible union objective, allowing for variable relative weight of employment and individual utility in the union's objective. Last, but not least, we consider that the value of employment is not considered as predetermined in the first stage of negotiation, the union fully anticipating the consequences of the negotiated wage rate and working time on the demand for workers as a consequence of the right to manage.

---

[1] The Nash (1950) axiomatic approach builds on a set of "natural" properties of the solution. Critics have put forward the fact that replacing one natural property by another one, as plausible as the original, entails a different solution. However, in the eighties, analyses of dynamic strategic games came to support Nash's solution. See Rubinstein (1982), Binmore et al. (1986) or Sutton (1986).

The model does not include the possible link between employment and the tax burden related to unemployment benefits, an important feature in the monopoly union model by FitzRoy et al. (1999). Our approach is therefore relevant if negotiations take place at a highly decentralized level (the case of Canada, Japan, New Zealand, United States, but also, to a lesser extent, of continental Europe; see OECD (1997)). In this institutional context, it may reasonably be assumed that unions and firms take tax rates as given.

In section 10.3 we focus on the contract terms obtained without any legislated constraint on working time. Comparative statics about the terms of the labor contract are possible in relation to varying parameters like fixed costs, worker effectiveness in time, bargaining power or relative weights of insiders and unemployed in the unions' objective. Section 10.4 analyzes the impact of a mandatory reduction in working time on employment and wages. After computing negotiated values of the wage rate, we finally bring out an important structural feature of the economy through a function relating employment to the level of the legal working time. A relatively simple condition for a favorable effect of the law on the employment level is derived analytically; numerical simulation is used to show that a first favorable effect may be achieved by a relatively weak constraint, but that further enforcement of the constraint would generate perverse results. Given that most policies of working time reductions consider significant variations in the hours constraint, the possibility of bringing out a global relationship between hours and employment seems to be a useful feature of our model.

10.2   Main assumptions

10.2.1   The productive sector and the profit function

We introduce a production function in which the number of workers and working time are separate arguments represented respectively by (continuous) variables n, and h. By suitable choice of unit, $h \in [0, 1]$.

If y stands for output in real terms, the technology is represented by $y = F(L)$ where $F(\ )$ is a concave production function and L a measure of the flow of labor services. It is further assumed that $L = ng(h)$ where $g(h)$ is an effectiveness function. In this case, elasticities involving y, L, h are related by the equation $\eta_h^y = \eta_L^y \eta_h^L$.

Our assumptions will be conveyed in a simple form by constant elasticity functions $F(L) = L^\alpha$ and $g(h) = h^\beta$ and finally:

$$y = A \left(nh^\beta \right)^\alpha$$

with $A > 0, \alpha \in \,]0, 1[\,, \beta > 0$.

As in former chapters, we denote by β the elasticity of labor services with respect to hours, thus $L = nh^\beta$. Our model does not impose any restriction on this parameter; one may adopt the view held by the advocates of the reduction of working time and assume that $\beta < 1$. In this case, $\alpha\beta < \alpha$: due to exertion effects or other factors, the hours elasticity of output is supposed to be smaller than the elasticity with respect to the number of workers, and productivity (y/nh) is a decreasing function of working time.

The cost structure is kept very simple, including only labor expenses of the form:

$$E = (wh + \theta)n$$

w being the wage rate and θ representing the individual cost of incumbent workers. For more compact notation, we often use alternatively the notion of per period compensation $c = wh$; in this case $E = (c + \theta)n$.

Booth (1995) notices that trade unions contribute to higher fixed costs, given their claims for fringe benefits like health insurance, pensions, vacations, supplementary unemployment insurance, in general computed on a per head basis.

Capital is kept implicit, insofar as it represents collective equipment; some of the individual equipment expenses (computers, office space) can however be considered as included in the fixed cost.

Consequently, the firm profit function is:

$$\pi(n, h, w) = An^\alpha h^{\alpha\beta} - (wh + \theta)n \tag{10.1}$$

In fact, $\pi(n, h, w)$ represents economic profit if capital costs can be neglected; it represents surplus from work in the opposite case.

10.2.2   The union's objective function

The objective of the union is supposed to be equivalent to maximizing a simple function V of two arguments: the insider's satisfaction S and the number of employed people n.

The individual satisfaction of the insider S is explained by a neoclassical utility function of real consumption and leisure time available each day $S = u(c, 1 - h)$ (the length of the day is normalized). For simplicity, we use the following multiplicative form:

$$S = c(1 - h) \tag{10.2}$$

Since $c = wh$, this function entails a rigid individual Walrasian labor supply $h^s = 0.5 \ \forall w$.[2]

Following Pemberton (1988), the suggested union's objective function is:

$$V = (S - S_0)^\nu \, n^{1-\nu} \tag{10.3}$$

---

[2] A more general form could be: $u = wh^\epsilon (1 - h)^{1-\epsilon}$, leading to $h^s = \epsilon \ \forall w$. The simplified version used in this text for parsimony does not alter the main conclusions.

with $\nu \in [0, 1]$ and where S_0 is the individual satisfaction attainable out of employment. The relative weight of the insiders in the objective function is indicated by ν; in the limit (unlikely) case where $\nu = 0$, the union is only interested in expanding employment; when $\nu = 1$, the union is purely upholding the incumbent workers' interest.

10.3   Wage rate and working time are simultaneously negotiated

We consider that the wage rate w as well as the working time h are negotiated between the firm and the trade union, and that the firm keeps employment n under its control in the "right to manage" tradition. More precisely, the firm sets employment after the negotiation, being only able to eliminate the extensive margin. In this case, it can be checked that a unique solution to the profit maximization problem exists whatever $w > 0$ and $h > 0$, if $\alpha \in \,]0, 1[$. The employment chosen by the firm verifies the first order condition $\pi_n = 0 \Leftrightarrow \alpha A n^{\alpha-1} h^{\alpha\beta} = wh + \theta$. The firm's demand for workers is thus:

$$\hat{n}(w, h) = \left(\frac{\alpha A h^{\alpha\beta}}{wh + \theta} \right)^{\frac{1}{1-\alpha}} \tag{10.4}$$

Introducing in equation (10.1) this optimal employment value, we get the maximum profit function:

$$\hat{\pi}(w, h) = A\hat{n}^{\alpha} h^{\alpha\beta} - (wh + \theta)\hat{n} \tag{10.5}$$

We adopt the Nash (1950) solution to the bargaining problem, in considering that the result of the negotiation maximizes the weighted product of union's utility and firm's profit (the fall-back payoffs are assumed to be nil):

$$\widehat{T}(w, h) = \left[(S(w, h) - S_0)^{\nu} \, (\hat{n}(w, h))^{1-\nu} \right]^{1-\lambda} [\hat{\pi}(w, h)]^{\lambda}, \quad \lambda \in [0, 1] \tag{10.6}$$

where λ and $1 - \lambda$ are the respective unknown but predetermined negotiation powers of the firm and of the union (Roth, 1979).

Taking logarithms of equation (10.6), the Nash maximand becomes:

$$\ln\left\{\widehat{T}(w, h)\right\} = \nu(1 - \lambda) \ln\left\{S(w, h) - S_0\right\} \tag{10.7}$$
$$+ (1 - \nu)(1 - \lambda) \ln\left\{\hat{n}(w, h)\right\} + \lambda \ln\left\{\hat{\pi}(w, h)\right\}$$

The first order conditions related to this problem are (in terms of partial elasticities with respect to w and h):

$$\nu(1 - \lambda)\eta_w^{S-S_0} + (1 - \nu)(1 - \lambda)\eta_w^{\hat{n}} + \lambda\eta_w^{\hat{\pi}} = 0 \tag{10.8}$$

$$\nu(1 - \lambda)\eta_h^{S-S_0} + (1 - \nu)(1 - \lambda)\eta_h^{\hat{n}} + \lambda\eta_h^{\hat{\pi}} = 0 \qquad (10.9)$$

The system formed by equations (10.8) and (10.9) can be simplified in introducing relations between elasticities shown in the Appendix to this chapter. More precisely, from equation (10.38) in the Appendix, $\eta_h^{\hat{n}} = \delta + \eta_w^{\hat{n}}$, where $\delta = \alpha\beta/(1-\alpha)$. According to equation (10.39), $\eta_w^{\hat{\pi}} = \alpha\eta_w^{\hat{n}}$. From equation (10.41), $\eta_h^{\hat{\pi}} = \delta + \eta_w^{\hat{\pi}}$, thus $\eta_h^{\hat{\pi}} = \delta + \alpha\eta_w^{\hat{n}}$.

The system of first order conditions can therefore be rewritten:

$$\nu(1 - \lambda)\eta_w^{S-S_0} + [(1 - \nu)(1 - \lambda) + \alpha\lambda]\,\eta_w^{\hat{n}} = 0 \qquad (10.10)$$

$$\nu(1 - \lambda)\eta_h^{S-S_0} + [(1 - \nu)(1 - \lambda) + \alpha\lambda]\,\eta_w^{\hat{n}} + \delta[(1 - \nu)(1 - \lambda) + \lambda] = 0 \qquad (10.11)$$

Substracting equation (10.11) from equation (10.10) yields:

$$\eta_w^{S-S_0} - \eta_h^{S-S_0} = \delta\frac{(1 - \nu)(1 - \lambda) + \lambda}{\nu(1 - \lambda)} \qquad (10.12)$$

From definition (10.2): $\eta_w^{S-S_0} - \eta_h^{S-S_0} = \dfrac{ch}{S - S_0}$, and equation (10.12) becomes:

$$\frac{ch}{S - S_0} = \delta\frac{(1 - \nu)(1 - \lambda) + \lambda}{\nu(1 - \lambda)}$$

Defining

$$\Phi \equiv \delta\frac{(1 - \nu)(1 - \lambda) + \lambda}{\nu(1 - \lambda)}$$

we write equation (10.12) $\dfrac{ch}{S - S_0} = \Phi$ and since $S = c(1 - h)$, worker daily compensation c may be considered as an explicit function of h:

$$c = \frac{S_0\Phi}{\Phi - (1 + \Phi)\,h} \qquad (10.13)$$

After introducing the explicit values of elasticities $\eta_w^{S-S_0} = \dfrac{S}{S - S_0}$, $\eta_w^{\hat{n}} = -\left(\dfrac{1}{1 - \alpha}\right)\dfrac{c}{c + \theta}$ (equation 10.36), and $\eta_w^{\hat{\pi}} = \alpha\eta_w^{\hat{n}}$ (equation 10.39), equation (10.10) takes the form:

$$\frac{S}{S - S_0} = \frac{(1 - \nu)(1 - \lambda) + \alpha\lambda}{\nu(1 - \lambda)(1 - \alpha)}\left(\frac{c}{c + \theta}\right) \qquad (10.14)$$

or, after defining $\Psi \equiv \dfrac{\nu(1-\lambda)(1-\alpha)}{(1-\nu)(1-\lambda)+\alpha\lambda}$,

$$\frac{S-S_0}{S} = \Psi\left(\frac{c+\theta}{c}\right) \tag{10.15}$$

This equation relates two interpretable magnitudes: $(S-S_0)/S$ is the relative welfare loss an insider would undergo having to quit; $(c+\theta)/c$ is the ratio of the labor cost to labor income.

Since $S = c(1-h)$, equation (10.15) makes it possible to represent the negotiated value of c as another explicit function of h:

$$c = \frac{\Psi\theta}{1-\Psi} + \frac{S_0}{(1-\Psi)(1-h)} \tag{10.16}$$

The negotiated value of working time $\tilde{h}$ is therefore a solution of the nonlinear equation formed by equation (10.13) and equation (10.16).

$$\frac{S_0\Phi}{\Phi-(1+\Phi)h} = \frac{\Psi\theta}{1-\Psi} + \left(\frac{1}{1-\Psi}\right)\left(\frac{S_0}{1-h}\right) \tag{10.17}$$

Representing graphically in Figure 10.1 the left hand side of equation (10.17) as $L(h)$ and the right hand side as $R(h)$, the equilibrium working time $\tilde{h}$ is given by the intersection of the two curves. The ordinate of the intersection indicates the equilibrium compensation of the insiders, $\tilde{c} = \tilde{w}\tilde{h}$. Employment can be inferred from equation (10.4), $\tilde{n} = \hat{n}(\tilde{w},\tilde{h})$.

The comparative statics of the negotiated equilibrium in relation to fixed costs is easily determined, Ψ and Φ being both independent of θ : an increase in θ shifts $R(h)$ upwards, which entails longer hours and higher compensation. The general comparative statics of the solution $\tilde{w}$ and $\tilde{h}$ is cumbersome, and further information at this stage should be gained through numerical simulation.

The existence of an interior solution requires $L(0) < R(0)$. A sufficient condition is: $\Psi < 1 \iff \dfrac{\nu(1-\lambda)(1-\alpha)}{(1-\nu)(1-\lambda)+\alpha\lambda} < 1$. This condition is obviously fulfilled when $\nu \to 0$ or if $\alpha \to 1$; more generally, the condition on ν for given α and λ is:

$$\nu < \frac{1-\lambda(1-\alpha)}{1+(1-\alpha)(1-\lambda)} \tag{10.18}$$

The evolution of the solution when $\Psi \to 1$ is worth closer analysis. In Figure 10.1, the intersection of $L(h)$ and $R(h)$ shifts upwards, suggesting infinitely increasing compensation. From equation (10.17) it is possible to check that when $\Psi \to 1$, the limit of the negotiated working time is $\tilde{h}_1 =$

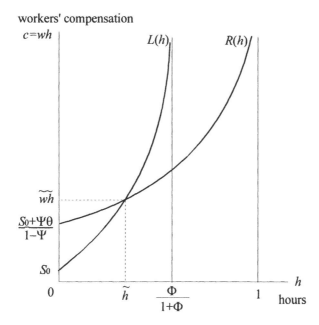

FIGURE 10.1. Equilibrium working time and workers' compensation

$\dfrac{\Phi}{1+\Phi}$ (of course, generally changes in parameters influencing Ψ have also an impact on Φ).

The existence sufficient condition (10.18) may be interpreted in a more intuitive way in *the case of privileged insiders,* i.e. when the union is unaffected by the employment level ($\nu = 1$). In this case,

$$\Psi = \left(\frac{1-\lambda}{\lambda}\right)\left(\frac{1-\alpha}{\alpha}\right) \text{ and } \Phi = \delta\frac{\lambda}{1-\lambda}$$

Then,

$$\Psi < 1 \Longleftrightarrow \frac{\lambda}{1-\lambda} > \frac{1-\alpha}{\alpha}$$

There is a negotiated solution if the relative weight of the firm in the negotiation is sufficient.

When this relative weight tends to the limit $\dfrac{\lambda}{1-\lambda} \to \dfrac{1-\alpha}{\alpha}$, $\Psi \to 1$,

compensation c increases indefinitely and simultaneously, since $\delta = \dfrac{\alpha\beta}{1-\alpha}$,

$\Phi \to \beta$ and $\tilde{h}_1 \to \dfrac{\beta}{1+\beta}$.[3] In the perfect man-hours substitution special case, $\beta = 1$, and this limit coincides with the Walrasian supply.

---

[3] This unrealistic feature of the model in a limit case is clearly an idiosyncratic property related to our basic constant elasticity assumption of the production function, mak-

10.4   Introducing a binding working time constraint

10.4.1   Analytical considerations

Let us consider now the macroeconomic impact of a mandatory reduction in working hours. We consider that the regulation imposes $\bar{h} \leq \tilde{h}$; (i.e., the constraint is binding). As before, the decision of the firm after negotiation consists in eliminating the extensive margin by the choice of n. Therefore $\widehat{\pi}_n = 0$ makes it possible to define:

$$\hat{n}(w) = \left[\frac{\alpha A \bar{h}^{\alpha\beta}}{w\bar{h} + \theta} \right]^{\frac{1}{1-\alpha}} \tag{10.19}$$

Then profits $\widehat{\pi}(w)$ are defined for a given $\bar{h}$ by:

$$\widehat{\pi}(w) \equiv A \left[\widehat{N}(w) \right]^{\alpha} \bar{h}^{\alpha\beta} - w\bar{h}\hat{n}(w) - \theta\hat{n}(w) \tag{10.20}$$

As the individual utility can be written $S(w) = w(\bar{h} - \bar{h}^2)$, the negotiated wage rate is expected to maximize the Nash bargaining product:

$$\widehat{T}(w) = \left[(S(w) - S_0)^{\nu} \left(\widehat{N}(w) \right)^{1-\nu} \right]^{1-\lambda} [\widehat{\pi}(w)]^{\lambda} \tag{10.21}$$

Maximizing $\ln \left[\widehat{T}(w) \right]$ implies:

$$\nu(1 - \lambda)\eta_w^{S-S_0} + (1 - \nu)(1 - \lambda)\eta_w^{\hat{n}} + \lambda\eta_w^{\widehat{\pi}} = 0 \tag{10.22}$$

As shown in the Appendix, $\eta_w^{\widehat{\pi}} = \alpha\eta_w^{\hat{n}}$, and equation (10.22) yields:

$$\eta_w^{S-S_0} + \frac{(1 - \lambda)(1 - \nu) + \alpha\lambda}{\nu(1 - \lambda)}\eta_w^{\hat{n}} = 0$$

Substituting elasticities with their values computed in the Appendix, i.e. $\eta_w^{S-S_0} = \dfrac{S}{S - S_0}$ and $\eta_w^{\hat{n}} = -\left(\dfrac{1}{1 - \alpha} \right)\dfrac{w\bar{h}}{w\bar{h} + \theta}$, equation (10.22) can be written:

$$\frac{S - S_0}{S} = \Psi \left(\frac{c + \theta}{c} \right) \tag{10.23}$$

where we recall that $\Psi \equiv \dfrac{\nu(1 - \lambda)(1 - \alpha)}{(1 - \nu)(1 - \lambda) + \alpha\lambda}$.

---

ing positive profits compatible with any wage rate for a sufficiently small scale of production, but does not generally impair its validity.

Since $S = c(1 - h)$, the negotiated compensation for a given $\bar{h}$ is:

$$c(\bar{h}) = \frac{\theta\Psi}{(1 - \Psi)} + \frac{S_0}{(1 - \Psi)(1 - \bar{h})} \qquad (10.24)$$

Employment chosen by the firm as a function of $\bar{h}$ is then given by:

$$\hat{n}(\bar{h}) = \left[\frac{\alpha A \bar{h}^{\alpha\beta}}{c(\bar{h}) + \theta} \right]^{\frac{1}{1-\alpha}} \qquad (10.25)$$

Or in terms of the predetermined parameters:

$$\hat{n}(\bar{h}) = \left[\frac{\alpha A(1 - \Psi)\bar{h}^{\alpha\beta}(1 - \bar{h})}{\theta(1 - \bar{h}) + S_0} \right]^{\frac{1}{1-\alpha}} \qquad (10.26)$$

This expression describes an important structural feature of our economy, employment being an explicit function of the imposed working time and of relevant parameters.

It is now possible to scrutinize the response of negotiated employment with respect to the working time constraint. From (10.25), we write:

$$\ln(\hat{n}) = \frac{1}{1 - \alpha} \left\{ \ln(\alpha A) + \alpha\beta \ln(\bar{h}) - \ln \left[c(\bar{h}) + \theta \right] \right\} \qquad (10.27)$$

implying:

$$\frac{\hat{n}'(\bar{h})}{\hat{n}(\bar{h})} = \frac{1}{1 - \alpha} \left\{ \frac{\alpha\beta}{\bar{h}} - \frac{c'(\bar{h})}{c(\bar{h}) + \theta} \right\} \qquad (10.28)$$

The condition for a favorable impact on employment of an imposed working time reduction is $\hat{n}'(\bar{h}) < 0$ or:

$$\alpha\beta < \frac{\bar{h}c'(\bar{h})}{c(\bar{h}) + \theta} \qquad (10.29)$$

It must be noted that this condition has an expression in elasticity terms: $\eta_h^y < \eta_h^c \sigma(\bar{h})$, where σ stands for the proportion $\dfrac{c(\bar{h})}{c(\bar{h}) + \theta}$, i.e. the ratio of compensation over total labor cost of a worker.

Introducing equation (10.24) in equation (10.29) yields after some simplifications the following condition:

$$\alpha\beta < \frac{S_0\bar{h}}{\theta(1 - \bar{h})^2 + S_0(1 - \bar{h})} \qquad (10.30)$$

Clearly, the right hand side of equation (10.30) is monotonously increasing in $\bar{h}$ in the relevant interval and is nil for $\bar{h} = 0$. We thus cannot rule out the possibility that the condition is fulfilled for durations of work above a threshold denoted by $\bar{h}_c$.

A remarkable feature of this condition is that all the parameters related to the negotiation terms vanish; the switching point between favorable effect and perverse effect of the mandatory time reduction is determined by S_0 and θ only. When there are no fixed costs, $\theta = 0$ and the condition is simply:

$$\alpha\beta < \frac{\bar{h}}{(1 - \bar{h})} \tag{10.31}$$

In this case, the threshold is $\bar{h}_c = \dfrac{\alpha\beta}{1 + \alpha\beta}$. The policy of working time reduction contributes to increasing employment if the initial duration was larger then this critical value. (When $\bar{h}$ coincides with the Walrasian labor supply, $\bar{h} = 0.5$ and the condition on hours elasticity is $\alpha\beta = \eta_h^y < 1$.)

10.4.2   A numerical simulation

A numerical simulation is useful at this stage to illustrate in detail the response of the economy to the legislated working time constraint.

Parameter $\lambda = 0.5$, implying equal bargaining power between the union and the firm; parameter $\nu = 0.5$, i.e. the union's objective takes the traditional utilitarian form; output elasticity with respect to labor services is $\alpha = 0.75$, and labor services elasticity with respect to hours is $\beta = 0.9$, as envisaged by proponents of working time reductions. The other parameters are: $A = 1$, $\theta = 0.15$ and $S_0 = 0.05$.

Solving equation (10.17), the free equilibrium duration of work is $\tilde{h} = 0.61$. Then we solve for employment $\tilde{n} = 0.95$, worker compensation $c = 0.16$, firm's profits $\tilde{\Pi} = 0.39$ and union utility $\tilde{V} = 0.11$.

Then we use equation (10.26) to plot employment as a function of the constrained working time, i.e. for $\bar{h} < \tilde{h} = 0.61$. Of course, if $\bar{h} > \tilde{h}$, the constraint is not binding and the free equilibrium prevails. Figure 10.2 represents employment, profits, compensation and union's utility as functions of the working time constraint.

Computations show that firm's profits are maximized for $\bar{h} = 0.53$, employment is maximized for $\bar{h}_c = 0.41$ and union utility is maximized for $\bar{h} = 0.38$.

In this example, a mandatory reduction in the working hours imposed on a free system might cause first a favorable employment effect.[4] In a first interval, both firm's profits and union's utility increase. This seemingly paradoxical result is a natural consequence of the hypothesized negotiation

---

[4]Simulations performed for varying β, λ and ν indicate that this result is robust.

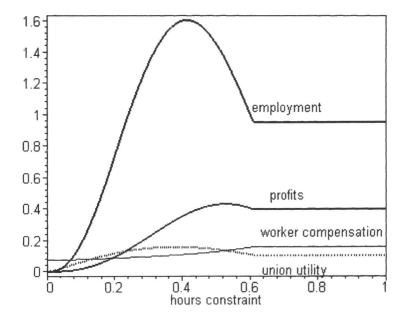

FIGURE 10.2. Impact of the hours constraint on employment and other variables

framework, wherein employment is not brought explicitly to the bargaining table, and is not efficiently determined. The hours constraint helps reduce the inefficiency. It must be noted however that a necessary condition for a favorable employment effect is a reduction of negotiated insiders' compensation, as implied by equation (10.25) and visible in Figure 10.2.

Further enforcement of the hours constraint would contribute to increasing employment and union utility, but will be opposed by employers, insofar as their profits decrease. In this second interval, there is a manifest conflict about working time. In this simulation, the unions would demand a drastic reduction in hours, the duration providing them with the highest utility implying low profits, but also reduced employment.

10.5 Conclusion

Actual working time must be explained with due consideration to the institutional features of the labor market in which it is observed. Continental Europe, for instance, is still characterized by the weight of influential trade unions in the bargaining process. Empirical surveys (ILO 1997, OECD 1997) confirm that along with wages, working hours are a sensitive bargaining issue.

Our analysis has consisted in handling the complexity of the negotiating situation in introducing only the most relevant features of the problem in a tractable form. Taking into account labor efficiency effects and fixed costs, the model captures the main elements of the profit structure of the firm. The union has a rather general objective, allowing for variable weight assigned to individual and collective interests. The Nash approach to the negotiation problem makes it possible to compound the conflicting objectives of the parties and to determine employment and the final terms of the labor contract.

It must be acknowledged, however, that this model cannot claim to be a full general equilibrium construction and should be seen as a first step towards a more complete treatment. The fixed costs have been considered as full dissipation of value. In fact, they represent resources for a second omitted sector supplying the corresponding services and whose activity is proportional to these costs. While the model fully takes into consideration the relation between the negotiated variables and the employment level, it does not take into consideration the link between employment and the tax burden related to unemployment benefits. Thus, our model is relevant if negotiations take place at a highly decentralized level, the union taking as given global unemployment; in the opposite case of centralized bargaining, the tax impact on the demand for workers should be brought into the picture.

The analysis in this chapter finally reveals an important structural feature of the unionized economy, i.e. the relationship between exogenously imposed maximum working time and the employment level obtaining when the parties have expressed their bargaining powers. By numerical simulation, it has been shown that if a limit on the duration of work is imposed on an initially unconstrained system, decentralized negotiation may, at first, induce reduced compensation for the incumbent workers and therefore a favorable effect on employment might be expected. Further enforcement of the constraint would entail perverse employment consequences.

10.6   Appendix: Main elasticities and their relationships

When working time is predetermined either by legal constraint or by negotiated commitments, the demand for workers by the firm eliminates only the extensive margin, and the following equations hold:

$$\pi_N = 0 \Leftrightarrow \alpha A \hat{n}^{\alpha-1} h^{\alpha\beta} = wh + \theta \tag{10.32}$$

$$\widehat{y} = F(\hat{n}, h) = A \hat{n}^\alpha h^{\alpha\beta} \tag{10.33}$$

Multiplying equation (10.32) by $\hat{n}$ gives $\alpha \widehat{y} = w \hat{n} h + \theta \hat{n} = \hat{E}$ (labor expenses) and therefore profit is related to output by:

$$\widehat{\pi} = (1 - \alpha)\widehat{y} \tag{10.34}$$

Employment elasticities with respect to wages and hours
Taking logarithms of equation (10.32) yields:

$$\ln\{\alpha A\} + (\alpha - 1)\ln\{\hat{n}\} + \alpha\beta\ln\{h\} = \ln\{wh + \theta\} \qquad (10.35)$$

Taking the partial derivative of equation (10.35) with respect to w:

$$\frac{(\alpha - 1)}{\hat{n}}\frac{\partial\hat{n}}{\partial w} = \frac{h}{wh + \theta}$$

and finally:

$$\eta^{\hat{n}}_w = -\left(\frac{1}{1 - \alpha}\right)\frac{wh}{wh + \theta} \qquad (10.36)$$

Taking the partial derivative of (10.35) with respect to h:

$$\frac{(\alpha - 1)}{\hat{n}}\frac{\partial\hat{n}}{\partial h} + \frac{\alpha\beta}{h} = \frac{w}{wh + \theta}$$

and multiplying the two sides by h :

$$\eta^{\hat{n}}_h = \frac{\alpha\beta}{1 - \alpha} - \left(\frac{1}{1 - \alpha}\right)\frac{wh}{wh + \theta} \qquad (10.37)$$

Defining $\dfrac{\alpha\beta}{1 - \alpha} = \delta$, equation (10.37) and equation (10.36) are related by:

$$\eta^{\hat{n}}_h = \delta + \eta^{\hat{n}}_w \qquad (10.38)$$

Profit elasticities with respect to wages and hours
Profit elasticities with respect to w and h can be related to $\eta^{\hat{n}}_w$ in the following way:
From equation (10.34), $\eta^{\hat{\pi}}_w = \eta^{\hat{y}}_w$ and $\eta^{\hat{\pi}}_h = \eta^{\hat{y}}_h$.
From equation (10.33), $\eta^{\hat{y}}_w = \alpha\eta^{\hat{n}}_w$ and we can write:

$$\eta^{\hat{\pi}}_w = \alpha\eta^{\hat{n}}_w \qquad (10.39)$$

From (10.33), $\eta^{\hat{y}}_h = \alpha\eta^{\hat{n}}_h + \alpha\beta$ and therefore:

$$\eta^{\hat{\pi}}_h = \alpha\eta^{\hat{n}}_h + \alpha\beta \qquad (10.40)$$

To show the relation between $\eta^{\hat{\pi}}_h$ and $\eta^{\hat{\pi}}_w$, it is possible either directly to calculate the elasticities at a point where equation (10.32) holds, or equivalently to combine equations (10.38), (10.39) and (10.40). The value of $\eta^{\hat{n}}_h$ from equation (10.38) is introduced in equation (10.40), giving $\eta^{\hat{\pi}}_h = \alpha\delta + \alpha\eta^{\hat{n}}_w + \alpha\beta$.
From equation (10.39), $\eta^{\hat{n}}_w = \alpha^{-1}\eta^{\hat{\pi}}_w$, therefore:

$$\eta^{\hat{\pi}}_h = \delta + \eta^{\hat{\pi}}_w \qquad (10.41)$$

11
Complementary labor services and working time regulation

11.1 Introduction

The preceding chapters analyzed how working time is determined in the absence of hours regulations, then examined the impact of binding hours constraints on the main endogenous economic variables, in particular, on the level of employment. This chapter and the next one will analyze the impact of a mandatory reduction in working hours on employment under more detailed assumptions concerning the structure of the productive process.

As mentioned in Chapter 3, the main objective of the working time policy in periods of high unemployment is to prompt firms to hire more workers and most work-sharing policies finally call for a uniform reduction in the working day for all activity sectors, qualifications and occupations. Such simple forms of the work-sharing paradigm are undoubtedly based on a special technological case in which workers are perfect substitutes for one another.

However, as previously reported in Table 2.6, observable working hours are the highest for qualified workers and the lowest for the less qualified ones. For instance, in the European Union, in 1997, managers worked in average 43.9 hours a week, while less qualified workers spent only 32.4 hours a week at the workplace (Eurostat, 1998).

A model with globally substitutable labor services could indirectly account for this stylized and pervasive fact. The elementary neoclassical model detailed in Chapter 4 is able to explain the diversity of work durations, by considering segmented labor markets and differences in preferences; yet, such an explanation cannot account for workers' internal rationing reported in different surveys (Chapter 2). As put forward in other chapters, the fixed cost of labor and varying effectiveness in time may explain the wedge between the optimal duration of work from the firm's point of view and the hours desired by the workers. These models are also based on the assumption of substitutable labor services.

In this chapter, we explore the consequences of the special case in which two types of work are considered. The two types will be interpreted in relation to the qualification level. There is perfect substitution within each type: an assembly line worker may be replaced by another or a salesman by another salesman, and perfect complementarity is assumed between the two types of labor services. Working time may be set independently for the two types. Workers of both groups may have different effectiveness in time, in keeping with the nature of their jobs. It will be seen in particular that if the effectiveness of the less qualified workers is more affected by fatigue than it is for the qualified, a shorter working time may be imposed on them by the cost minimizing firms.

In this case of basic complementarity between two forms of labor services related to two types of different workers, a policy of working time reduction actually binding only for the qualified staff may entail quite paradoxical effects. As the unit cost of the labor service increases, the total demand for those services is depressed; the direct consequence is a reduction in the demand for non-qualified workers. This is clearly an undesirable consequence, insofar as the less qualified workers are more exposed to unemployment than the qualified. As Table 11.1 shows, this pattern is stable throughout the Western world. For instance, in 1995, the EU-15 unemployment rate of those having an education level inferior to secondary level is 13.7%, while the unemployment rate of those having a university degree is only 5.8%.

Below, we present a formal model of working time determination within a profit-maximization framework, a context that has been analyzed at length in Chapter 9, but with two complementary forms of labor services. We still consider that labor market competition compels firms to design labor contracts compatible with the participation constraint, i.e. implying a minimum utility level attainable by workers. After specifying the main assumptions, we analyze the decision problem of the firm, then we study the influence of an hours constraint on the demand for each type of workers.

	Minimum education level:		
	Lower than secondary	Secondary	Higher education
Belgium	13.4	7.5	3.6
France	14.0	8.9	6.5
Germany	13.3	7.9	4.9
Ireland	16.4	7.6	4.2
Italy	9.1	7.9	7.3
Spain	20.6	18.5	14.5
The Netherlands	7.9	4.8	4.1
Sweden	10.1	8.7	4.5
UK	12.2	7.4	3.7
EU-15	13.7	8.2	5.8
OECD	12.3	6.5	4.2

TABLE 11.1. Unemployment rate with respect to education level, 1995. Source: OECD, *Employment Outlook*, 1998.

11.2   Main assumptions

11.2.1   The production function and the structure of labor services

We consider that the firm uses a homogeneous flow of labor input measured by L. One unit of this input is obtained by combining one unit of labor services of type 1 (non-qualified) and λ units of labor services of type 2 (qualified). Qualified and less qualified workers are therefore strictly complementary. The parameter λ is a fixed ratio related to the applied technology. The composite labor input may be combined with existing equipment to produce the final good. For a constant stock of capital, output is a concave function in the labor input, $y = F(L)$, with $F' > 0$, $F'' < 0$.

The flow of non-qualified labor services (index 1) is supplied by n_1 employees working h_1 hours in terms described by a constant elasticity function: $g_1(n_1, h_1) = n_1 h_1^{\beta_1}$; the flow of qualified labor services (index 2) is supplied by n_2 employees working h_2 hours and is indicated by $g_2(n_2, h_2) = n_2 h_2^{\beta_2}$.

We assume that the working times of qualified and less qualified workers are set independently. We further assume that, due to exertion, output elasticity with respect to hours is lower than unity. This fatigue effect is assumed to be stronger in the case of less qualified workers. Formally, $0 < \beta_1 < \beta_2 \leq 1$.

11.2.2   Worker compensating wage

Workers have neoclassical preferences, represented by the utility function $u(wh, 1-h)$, where w is the hourly wage rate, and $1-h$ is the available leisure time. As in the previous chapters, the representative firm has to provide workers with a minimum satisfaction level, denoted by s. The producers' constraint is thus $u(wh, 1-h) \geq s$, and for well-behaved utility functions, the constraint should be saturated in the labor cost minimization problem. The compensating wage rate $w(h)$ conditional for the utility requirement s is then implicitly defined by: $u[hw(h), 1-h] = s$.

In the case of segmented labor markets for qualified and non-qualified workers, this minimum utility level might not be the same. In purely competitive labor markets, this satisfaction level should be consistent with full employment; but our approach is also compatible with positive unemployment if the satisfaction requirement is subject to downward rigidity. This last interpretation yields the framework in which work-sharing policies in the form of working time limits may be analyzed.

For simplicity, we introduce an analytically convenient form of utility function:

$$u(wh, 1-h) = [wh]^{\gamma} [1-h]^{(1-\gamma)} \qquad (11.1)$$

where $\gamma \in [0, 1]$. The resulting compensating wage function is then: $w(h) = s^{\frac{1}{\gamma}} [1-h]^{\frac{\gamma-1}{\gamma}} h^{-1}$, implying a compensated wage-hours elasticity:

$$\eta_h^w = \frac{hw'(h)}{w(h)} = \frac{h-\gamma}{\gamma(1-h)} \qquad (11.2)$$

For a predetermined wage rate w, the corresponding Walrasian hours supply is:

$$h^s(w) = \arg\max_h \{u(wh, 1-h)\}$$

It can be verified that with the particular utility function defined in (11.1), $h^s(w) = \gamma \quad \forall w$.

11.3   The unconstrained hours decision of the firm

The profit function of the firm is $\pi = F(L) - mL$, where m is the cost of one unit of the composite labor input. On our assumptions, m does not depend on L and profit maximization may be divided for analytical purposes into two stages.

In the first stage, the cost of the labor input must be minimized. The cost incurred by the firm for each unit of labor services is the sum of the costs of the two types of labor services; it takes the form:

$$m(n_1, n_2, h_1, h_2) = n_1 h_1 w_1(h_1) + n_2 h_2 w_2(h_2) \qquad (11.3)$$

where $w_1(h_1)$ and $w_2(h_2)$ are the relevant compensating wage functions.[1] The first problem consists in determining $\hat{m} = \min \{m(n_1, n_2, h_1, h_2)\}$, the control variables of the firm being n_1, n_2, h_1, h_2. In the second stage, the firm determines $L^* = \arg \max_L \{F(L) - \hat{m}L\}$.

11.3.1 The cost minimization problem

There is no constraint on available workers, but one unit of labor input requires one unit of less qualified labor services and λ units of qualified ones; consequently, the constraints $n_1 h_1^{\beta_1} = 1$ and $n_2 h_2^{\beta_2} = \lambda$ apply. Therefore, we substitute in (11.3) n_1 with $h_1^{-\beta_1}$ and n_2 with $\lambda h_2^{-\beta_2}$ obtaining a new form of the objective function with only two independent arguments:

$$m(h_1, h_2) = h_1^{1-\beta_1} w_1(h_1) + \lambda h_2^{1-\beta_2} w_2(h_2) \qquad (11.4)$$

First order conditions are thus:

$$\frac{\partial m}{\partial h_1} = (1 - \beta_1)h_1^{-\beta_1} w_1(h_1) + h_1^{1-\beta_1} w_1'(h_1) = 0$$

$$\frac{\partial m}{\partial h_2} = \lambda(1 - \beta_2)h_2^{-\beta_2} w_2(h_2) + \lambda h_2^{1-\beta_2} w_2'(h_2) = 0$$

In terms of the hours-elasticity concept applied to the compensating wage functions $w(h)$, the two first order conditions may be written:

$$\eta_{h_1}^{w_1} = -(1 - \beta_1) \qquad (11.5)$$

$$\eta_{h_2}^{w_2} = -(1 - \beta_2) \qquad (11.6)$$

But according to equation (11.2), $\eta_{h_1}^{w_1} = \dfrac{h_1 - \gamma_1}{\gamma_1(1 - h_1)}$ and $\eta_{h_2}^{w_2} = \dfrac{h_2 - \gamma_2}{\gamma_2(1 - h_2)}$. Optimal hours from the firm's point of view are therefore:

$$\hat{h}_1 = \frac{\gamma_1 \beta_1}{1 - \gamma_1 + \gamma_1 \beta_1} \qquad (11.7)$$

$$\hat{h}_2 = \frac{\gamma_2 \beta_2}{1 - \gamma_2 + \gamma_2 \beta_2} \qquad (11.8)$$

---

[1] We omit for the purpose of parsimony the fixed costs of labor.

Cost minimizing hours increase in both parameters, i.e. increase when workers assign higher importance to consumption or when worker effectiveness decreases less strongly in the duration of work.

It can be noticed that $\beta < 1$ and $\gamma \in]0,1[\Rightarrow \hat{h} = \dfrac{\beta\gamma}{1 - \gamma + \gamma\beta} < \gamma = h^s$, indicating that rationing prevails: the hours laid down in the labor contract do not satisfy the individual supply (workers are in a situation of inside underemployment).

In this framework, the longer hours of work of the qualified (type 2) can be explained by considering the respective values of γ and β for the two types. Since $\hat{h}$ increases in the two parameters, it can be said that for identical consumption/leisure preferences, longer hours are explained by less time dependent effectiveness $\beta_2 > \beta_1$ (due to more significant physical exertion during the working day for type 1). If effectiveness follows the same time pattern for both types ($\beta_1 = \beta_2$) longer working time for type 2 is explained by differences in consumption/leisure preferences: more exhausting and monotonous tasks for the less qualified are expressed by $\gamma_1 < \gamma_2$, implying $\hat{h}_1 < \hat{h}_2$.

The minimum cost of the labor unit is obtained by introducing in equation (11.4) the durations indicated by equations (11.7) and (11.8).

In the following, in order to keep the analysis as simple as possible, we only consider the case of identical preferences, $\gamma_1 = \gamma_2 = 1/2$, and where the satisfaction level s is the same in the two markets. The compensated-wage functions are therefore identical and take the special form: $w(h) = s^2/h(1 - h)$. In this case, optimal working times are respectively $\hat{h}_1 = \beta_1/(1 + \beta_1)$ and $\hat{h}_2 = \beta_2/(1 + \beta_2)$, the differences in the effectiveness function alone being responsible for the hours wedge.

The minimum unit cost is:

$$\hat{m} = s^2 \left[\frac{(1 + \beta_1)^{1+\beta_1}}{(\beta_1)^{\beta_1}} + \lambda\frac{(1 + \beta_2)^{1+\beta_2}}{(\beta_2)^{\beta_2}} \right] \qquad (11.9)$$

11.3.2 Optimal employment

Then, the total demand for labor input can be obtained by considering the profit function of the productive sector:

$$\pi = F(L) - \hat{m}L \qquad (11.10)$$

The first order condition is: $F'(L^*) = \hat{m}$, which determines the demand for labor input $L^* = F'^{-1}(\hat{m})$. By differentiating this condition, we get the sensitivity of the demand for labor input with respect to cost:

$$\frac{dL^*}{d\hat{m}} = \frac{1}{F''(L^*)} < 0 \qquad (11.11)$$

The demand for non-qualified workers is then: $n_1^* = L^* \hat{h}_1^{-\beta_1}$, and the demand for qualified workers is: $n_2^* = \lambda L^* \hat{h}_2^{-\beta_2}$.

Finally, the activity level is $F(L^*)$.

11.4 Employment under the hours constraint

11.4.1 The analytical approach

This model makes it possible to analyze the employment impact of a mandatory constraint on working time. If the maximal duration of work is limited by a legal constraint, $h \leq \bar{h}$, two situations may be considered:

a) the hours constraint applies only to those workers who perform the longer hours, i.e. the qualified: $\hat{h}_1 < \bar{h} < \hat{h}_2$. Introducing $\bar{h}$ in the wage-compensating function of type 2 workers yields the new expression for the unit cost:

$$\hat{m}(\hat{h}_1, \bar{h}) = s^2 \left[\frac{(1+\beta_1)^{1+\beta_1}}{(\beta_1)^{\beta_1}} + \lambda \frac{\bar{h}^{(-\beta_2)}}{1-\bar{h}} \right] \qquad (11.12)$$

The unit cost can only increase with reduced hours. In this case, the demand for total labor input will diminish ($dL^* < 0$). As working time of the non-qualified ($\hat{h}_1$) is unchanged, this implies a reduced demand for this type of worker ($dn_1^* < 0$).

As to the qualified workers, the cost-increase effect can be offset by a substitution effect; the total impact on the demand for qualified workers is undetermined.

b) the hours constraint applies to both sets of workers: $0 < \bar{h} < \hat{h}_1$. The unit cost is:

$$\hat{m}(\bar{h}) = s^2 \left[\frac{\bar{h}^{(-\beta_1)}}{1-\bar{h}} + \lambda \frac{\bar{h}^{(-\beta_2)}}{1-\bar{h}} \right] \qquad (11.13)$$

Two opposing effects are at work: while the unit cost increase entails a reduced demand for labor services, the man-hours substitution tends to increase the demand for workers.

11.4.2 A numerical example

In order to better represent the impact of the hours constraint on the demand for workers, we will carry out a numerical analysis. We consider the technology represented by the production function $F(L) = L^\alpha$. Parameters are assigned: $\alpha = 0.75$, $\lambda = 0.5$, $\beta_1 = 0.5$, $\beta_2 = 0.85$ and $s^2 = 0.1$.

Figure 11.1 depicts employment of the non-qualified (n_1), Figure 11.2 represents employment of the qualified (n_2), and Figure 11.3 represents total employment $n_1 + n_2$ (qualified and non-qualified) in the three regions.

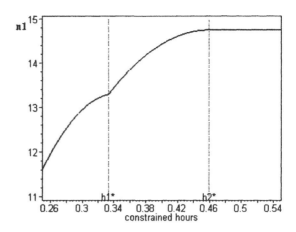

FIGURE 11.1. Demand for less qualified workers

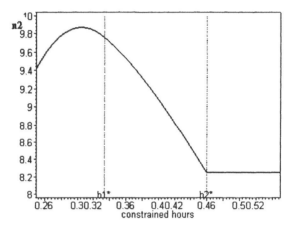

FIGURE 11.2. Demand for highly qualified workers

Without constraint (or if the constraint is not binding, $\hat{h}_2 < \bar{h}$), the optimal free durations are $\hat{h}_1 = 1/3$ and $\hat{h}_2 = 0.46$. Optimal demand for labor services is $L^* = 8.52$; these services are provided by $n_1^* = 14.76$ non-qualified workers and $n_2^* = 8.25$ qualified workers.

If $\hat{h}_1 < \bar{h} < \hat{h}_2$, the unit cost (11.12) increases, L^* diminishes, $\hat{h}_1 = 1/3$ is constant, thus n_1^* decreases. On the other hand, n_2^* increases initially in keeping with a strong man-hours substitution effect. Total employment increases, reaches a maximum, then decreases.

If $0 < \bar{h} < \hat{h}_1$, the unit cost is given by (11.13). The two opposite effects are at work, but the effect of reduced demand for labor services dominates.

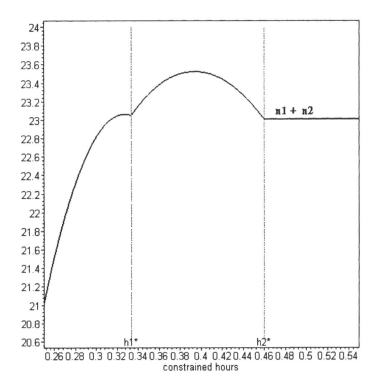

FIGURE 11.3. Total demand for workers

11.5   Conclusion

Most models of working time determination, including those presented in earlier chapters of this text, are based on a simplifying assumption of homogeneous workers, substitutable in particular in the supply of labor services. This chapter offers a countervailing example of an economy in which a strict complementarity is assumed between two types of labor, made necessary by the technology currently applied to produce the representative commodity. We have seen that heterogeneous individual preferences and effectiveness in time explain the observed differences in working hours between two complementary groups, which may be interpreted as highly qualified and less qualified workers.

When working time limits are superimposed on such a system, it is shown that the impact of a moderate value of the constraint on working time may be favorable to global employment. The structure of employment is however modified, with the creation of qualified jobs and destruction of non-qualified jobs: the policy is not neutral and, unfortunately, would harm those who are the most exposed to unemployment in the present situation faced by most countries in the Western world, i.e. the less qualified workers. Obviously, if joblessness only affects the non-qualified, such a policy would apply under a shortage of qualified workers; in this case, the adverse effect on unqualified jobs would be more significant than suggested by our simulation and would be the only outcome of the mandatory working time reduction.

12
Working time reduction in a vertically integrated two-sector model

12.1 Introduction

In a context of massive unemployment, a mandatory reduction in working hours is intended to increase the demand for workers and improve the distribution of rationing in the labor market, more people being needed to supply a constant flow of working hours. In practice, governments have sometimes proved themselves reluctant to impose working hours reductions on industries producing tradable commodities exposed to foreign competition. Some of them have enforced or inspired such constraints in the sectors mainly producing non-tradable commodities. For instance, in France, the state-owned company producing and distributing electricity (EDF) adopted a shortened working week by January 1997 (35 hours as compared with the standard 39 hours) and claimed to alleviate the burden of joblessness through the process of man-hours substitution. A similar working time configuration is reported in Italy. According to CNEL, the Italian national center for economic and labor research, in 1998, the ENEL state-owned electricity monopoly operated under a negotiated 38 hour week, while the predominant model in the other manufacturing sectors was of 40 hours per week.

  In this chapter, we set out to examine in general quantitative terms how a working time constraint imposed on a first sector producing a factor of production impinges on the total number of jobs supplied in a closed economy, when insiders in the job market are able to defend a predetermined satisfaction level. The model combines a simple submodel explaining working time and labor cost with conventional equilibrium competitive analysis. As in former chapters, we consider that fixed costs of labor and consumption/leisure preferences account for the observed working time in the two sectors. Departing from the line followed in the preceding chapters, we adopt a standard view about technology, in assuming that hours and workers are perfect substitutes in the production of labor services; this simplification permits us to focus on the vertical structure of the economy and to emphasize the sectorial interactions.[1]

The vertical structure of our economy is described in Figure 12.1. Sector 1 produces a *production commodity* (interpreted as energy, transportation, etc.) in quantity Z, with labor as sole input. To allow for public monopoly peculiarities, we consider first that the production commodity is produced in the public sector, with increasing returns to scale. State-owned monopolies often apply Ramsey–Boiteux pricing, when different subsets of users derive different surpluses. In our model, the consumer good industry being its only customer, we suppose that the public monopoly simply applies linear pricing and is constrained by a balanced budget.

In sector 2, the productive commodity is combined with labor to produce C units of a *consumption commodity*. The technology of the consumption commodity industry is described by a concave production function implying increasing cost curves. The firms of this second sector maximize profit in competitive terms.

In order to assess the global effect on employment of a working time constraint imposed on the first sector, the variations of the demand for workers in both sectors must be taken into account.

The *prima facie* consequence of an imposed working time reduction in the first sector is a process of person-hours substitution increasing the number of jobs supplied within this sector. But since it delivers a production commodity to the consumption goods industry, other less visible consequences can be expected to develop throughout the system. As an effect of the new constraint on labor contracts, the full cost of the production commodity and its price are bound to increase, reducing its demand by the consumption goods industry and therefore introducing an adverse effect on job creation and on scale economies in the first sector.

The second sector, i.e. the consumption goods industry, reacts to the increased price of the production commodity. According to standard microeconomic theory, its activity should decrease (if we rule out the case of an inferior factor), and its own demand for labor is affected through an activity effect and through effects related to the substitution/complementarity relationship between the two inputs.

---

[1] Hoel (1986) analyses the impact of hours reduction in a model with two parallel sectors, one producing a tradable good (manufacturing), the other a non-tradable good (services).

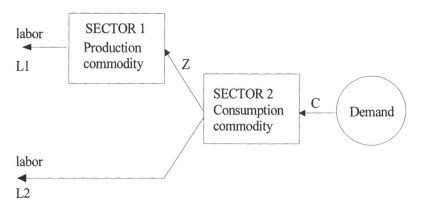

FIGURE 12.1. Vertical structure of the economy

The developments below aim at bringing out the relevant parameters related to preferences and technology enabling us to assess the final impact of the suggested constraint on the aggregate job supply in the economy. The validity of the results is limited to small variations of the working time constraint; more radical changes would require a different approach taking into account discontinuities in the labor cost functions.

The chapter is organized as follows: the spontaneously adopted working time in the two sectors is analyzed in the next section. Section 12.3 introduces with more precision the structure and decisions of the two sectors. The comparative statics of the model when a working time constraint is imposed on the first sector is studied in section 12.4. Section 12.5 introduces two special cases related to fixed proportions; in the second one, sector 1 is private and can be interpreted as road transport.

12.2 Explaining working time: a simple model of the labor contract

12.2.1 The compensating wage function

Workers have individual consumption/leisure preferences represented by a utility function $u(c, l)$ where c and l represent daily consumption and leisure. This function is assumed to have the standard neoclassical properties. The time unit being the day, the working time $h \in]0, 1[$ and with a linear real wage rate (in units of the consumption good) w, we can write:

$$u(c, l) = u(wh, 1 - h) \qquad (12.1)$$

The labor supply constraint is represented by a minimum utility level s obtained by the worker. The value of s could be endogenous in a competitive labor market and compatible with full employment. We are interested however in a situation with static unemployment and consider therefore that union power, insider privileges, or a generous unemployment compensation policy explain a level of s non-compatible with labor market static equilibrium (there is excess supply of workers). Provided that the utility constraint is satisfied, the firm determines wages and working time.

From equation (12.1), we derive the compensating wage function $w(h)$ defined by:

$$u(hw(h), 1 - h) = s$$

As in Chapter 9, we assume preferences such that: $w''(h) > 0$, $\forall h \in \,]0, 1[$.[2]

12.2.2 The optimal contract

The techniques applied in the two sectors share the neoclassical property according to which the labor input L can be measured by the product nh, where n is the number of workers. This means that workers and hours are perfect substitutes (in logarithms) and that our model does not take into account possible productivity effects of the working time variations.

The cost of the labor input L is explained by wages and fixed costs of labor, i.e. costs related to the number of workers n only (described in Chapter 5). We consider linear fixed costs of the form θn, implying that, for any labor input $L = nh$, the labor cost function can be written as:

$$\Psi(L, h) = w(h)L + \theta \frac{L}{h} \tag{12.2}$$

or, in an equivalent form, $\Psi(L, h) = LH(h)$, with:

$$H(h) = w(h) + \frac{\theta}{h} \tag{12.3}$$

$H(h)$ represents the *full cost of one unit of labor input*. Using our assumptions, it is easily checked that $H''(h) > 0$, and first order condition of cost minimization explains the optimal working time decided by the firm, h^*:

$$\Psi_h(L, h^*) = LH'(h) = 0 \Leftrightarrow w'(h^*) = \frac{\theta}{(h^*)^2}, \forall L \tag{12.4}$$

Some features of the labor cost minimizing contract are worth noticing:
 – The optimal contract $(h^*, w(h^*))$ is a separate choice (independent of the activity level determination and of the demand for L).
 – As shown in Chapter 9, the fixed cost of labor introduces a systematic conflict about working time since the optimum value for the firm h^* is

---

[2] As already mentioned, this property is not a general consequence of standard neoclassical assumptions on $u(,)$ but can be exemplified by very simple utility functions such as $u = wh(1 - h)$ yielding the compensating wage function $w(h) = s/h(1 - h)$.

higher than the individual labor supply $h^s[w(h^*)]$. Reduction of working time *for a constant wage rate* would improve the worker's utility.

– If there are two sectors $i = (1,2)$, the labor market can be considered either as homogeneous $(s_1 = s_2)$ or segmented $(s_1 \neq s_2)$. In each sector, it is therefore possible to define $H_i(h)$, the full cost of one unit of labor input, as a function of h, such that $H_i(h) = w_i(h) + \theta_i/h$. On our assumptions, this function admits a unique minimum value h_i^*, and $h_i < h_i^* \Rightarrow H_i'(h_i) < 0$ and $h_i > h_i^* \Rightarrow H_i'(h_i) > 0$.

12.3   The vertical structure of the economy

The economy comprises two vertically linked sectors. In sector 1, a productive commodity (interpreted as energy, transportation, etc.) is produced in quantity Z, with labor as sole input. In sector 2, the productive commodity is combined with labor in producing C units of the consumption commodity. Sector 2 is the only customer of sector 1.

12.3.1   Sector 1: Production of the productive service.

Technique is described by the production function: $Z = F(n_1 h_1) = F(L_1)$. Our increasing returns assumption implies $F''(L_1) > 0$ and explains public ownership or public control of a single firm. The activity Z of the sector 1 is explained by the demand from sector 2.

The profit in sector 1 may be written as:

$$\pi_1 = pF(n_1 h_1) - [w_1(h_1)n_1 h_1 + \theta_1 n_1] \tag{12.5}$$

where $w_1(h_1)$ is the compensating wage function associated with a predetermined utility level s_1 and p is the price of the productive commodity in terms of the consumption good. In more compact terms: $\pi_1 = pF(L_1) - L_1 H_1(h_1)$.

We assume that the price of the productive commodity or service is set in application of a zero profit rule:

$$pF(L_1) - L_1 H_1(h_1) = 0 \Rightarrow p = \frac{H_1(h_1)}{q(Z)} \tag{12.6}$$

where $q(Z) \equiv F(L_1)/L_1$ is the average productivity of labor in sector 1 $(q'(Z) > 0)$.

For a given activity Z, the minimum value of p obtains if the labor cost is minimized by the optimal contract $(h_1^*, w_1(h_1^*))$ and:

$$p = \frac{w_1(h_1^*) + \theta_1/h_1^*}{q(Z)} = \frac{H_1(h_1^*)}{q(Z)} \tag{12.7}$$

When a working time constraint $\bar{h}_1$ is imposed on sector 1, we can write more generally:

$$p(Z) = \frac{H_1(\bar{h}_1)}{q(Z)} \qquad (12.8)$$

12.3.2 Sector 2: Production of the consumption commodity

The technology applied in this sector is represented by a neoclassical (concave) production function relating the number of produced units C to factor consumption: $C = G(L_2, Z)$, where $L_2 = n_2 h_2$.

The profit function is:

$$\pi_2 = G(L_2, Z) - w_2(h_2)L_2 - \theta_2 \frac{L_2}{h_2} - pZ \qquad (12.9)$$

where $w_2(h_2)$ is the compensating wage function associated with a predetermined utility level s_2. Sector 2 is free in determining working time, which will constantly be set at its optimum value h_2^*. Therefore:

$$\pi_2 = G(L_2, Z) - L_2 H_2(h_2^*) - pZ \qquad (12.10)$$

Profit maximization in sector 2 determines explicitly the demand for labor L_2, and implicitly the demand for labor L_1, through its demand for Z. The representative firm of sector 2 is a price-taker (takes p as given) and maximizes its profit.

First order conditions applying to maximization of (12.10) are:

$$\begin{cases} \dfrac{\partial \pi_2}{\partial L_2} = G_L\left(L_2^*, Z^*\right) - H_2(h_2^*) = 0 \\ \dfrac{\partial \pi_2}{\partial Z} = G_Z\left(L_2^*, Z^*\right) - p = 0 \end{cases} \qquad (12.11)$$

where L_2^* and Z^* represent the demands for workers and productive services by sector 1. Obviously, they are both functions of the relative price of the productive commodity, p.

12.4 Equilibrium and comparative statics

12.4.1 A graphic introduction

First order conditions (12.11) and equation (12.8) determine together the endogenous variables for any value of $\bar{h}_1$.

Graphically (Figure 12.2), the solution can be illustrated in space (OZ, Op) in which it is possible to draw for a given value of $\bar{h}_1$:

– a balanced budget equilibrium locus BB of sector 1, representing $p(Z)$ according to equation (12.8); its negative slope results from our assumption that $q'(Z) > 0$;

– a curve representing the demand function for the production good $Z^*(p)$, denoted by DD. From the general theory of factor demand by competitive firms, we know that the slope of this curve is negative. (We consider the case where the slope of $Z^*(p)$ is steeper than the slope of BB assuming "small" values of $q'(Z)$.)

The intersection of the two curves noted (Z_E, p_E) shows the values of two endogenous variables in equilibrium.

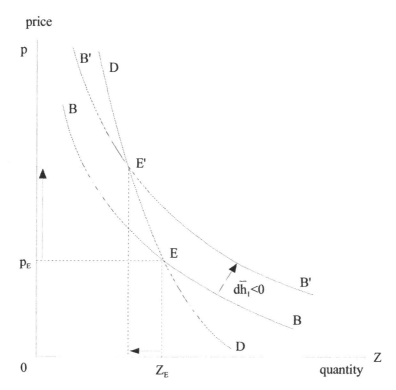

FIGURE 12.2. Equilibrium and comparative statics

Comparative statics can be sketched graphically: if we consider an imposed reduction of working time in the first sector, the labor cost increases in sector 1 and the BB locus shifts upwards; therefore, $d\bar{h}_1 < 0 \Rightarrow dp_E > 0$ and $dZ_E < 0$. The reduced demand for the productive service introduces a first offsetting effect on the demand for workers in sector 1.

The price variation $dp_E > 0$ entails variations of the activity and of the demand for labor in sector 2. If the productive factor is not an inferior factor, the output of the private sector may be expected to diminish. Its demand for labor is modified through an activity effect and through a substitution effect.

12.4.2 The analytical approach

Analytically, we have to determine the local impact of a variation $d\bar{h}$ on the total number of available jobs $(dN_1 + dN_2)$.

Equations (12.8) and (12.11) implicitly determine jointly equilibrium values of a set of principal endogenous variables (Z, p, L_2). Since a variation of p does not change the optimal labor contract in sector 2, a differentiating system (12.11) yields:

$$\begin{pmatrix} G_{LL} & G_{LZ} \\ G_{LZ} & G_{ZZ} \end{pmatrix} \begin{pmatrix} dL_2 \\ dZ \end{pmatrix} = \begin{pmatrix} 0 \\ dp \end{pmatrix}$$

Defining $\mathbb{D} = \det \begin{pmatrix} G_{LL} & G_{LZ} \\ G_{LZ} & G_{ZZ} \end{pmatrix} > 0$, we can write:

$$\begin{pmatrix} dL_2 \\ dZ \end{pmatrix} = \frac{1}{\mathbb{D}} \begin{pmatrix} G_{ZZ} & -G_{LZ} \\ -G_{LZ} & G_{LL} \end{pmatrix} \begin{pmatrix} 0 \\ dp \end{pmatrix} \tag{12.12}$$

thus:

$$dL_2 = -\frac{G_{LZ}}{\mathbb{D}} dp \tag{12.13}$$

$$dZ = \frac{G_{LL}}{\mathbb{D}} dp \tag{12.14}$$

Differentiating equation (12.8), we obtain:

$$q(Z)dp + pq'(Z)dZ = H_1'(\bar{h}_1)d\bar{h}_1 \tag{12.15}$$

Substituting (12.14) for dZ in (12.15), we obtain the sensitivity of the equilibrium value of p with respect to $\bar{h}_1$:

$$\frac{dp}{d\bar{h}_1} = \frac{\mathbb{D}H_1'(\bar{h}_1)}{\mathbb{D}q(Z) + pq'(Z)G_{LL}} \tag{12.16}$$

From (12.13) and (12.16), we obtain the sensitivity of the equilibrium value of L_2 with respect to $\bar{h}_1$:

$$\frac{dL_2}{d\bar{h}_1} = -\frac{G_{LZ}H_1'(\bar{h}_1)}{\mathbb{D}q(Z) + pq'(Z)G_{LL}} \tag{12.17}$$

Finally, (12.14) and (12.16) imply:

$$\frac{dZ}{d\bar{h}_1} = \frac{G_{LL}H_1'(\bar{h}_1)}{\mathbb{D}q(Z) + pq'(Z)G_{LL}} \tag{12.18}$$

The sign of the different sensitivities is ambiguous in the general case. We must notice that if the working time is initially free in the first sector $(\bar{h}_1 = h_1^*)$, we know from (12.4) that $H_1'(\bar{h}_1) = w_1'(\bar{h}_1) - \theta_1/\bar{h}_1^2 = 0$ and the numerator of the three last equations is nil in the first order. For $\bar{h}_1 < h_1^*$ however, i.e. if the working time is already suboptimal from the firm's point of view, $H_1'(\bar{h}_1) < 0$.

The sign of the denominator $\mathbb{D}q(Z) + pq'(Z)G_{LL}$ is clearly related to the differences of the slopes (Figure 12.2) of the locus BB and of the demand curve $Z^*(p)$ for the productive good. The first slope is $\left(\dfrac{dp}{dZ}\right)_{BB} = -\dfrac{pq'(Z)}{q(Z)}$ and the slope of the demand curve is (from 12.14) $\left(\dfrac{dp}{dZ}\right)_{DD} = \dfrac{\mathbb{D}}{G_{LL}}$ and since $G_{LL} < 0$, $\dfrac{\mathbb{D}}{G_{LL}} < -\dfrac{pq'(Z)}{q(Z)} \Rightarrow \mathbb{D}q(Z) + pq'(Z)G_{LL} > 0$. We consider in the following that the order of magnitude of scale economies is such that the denominator can be considered as positive. In this case, $dp > d\bar{h}_1 < 0$, $dZ/d\bar{h}_1 > 0$ and the sign of $dL_2/d\bar{h}_1$ is the same as the sign of $G_{LZ} \gtrless 0$.

The final impact of the working time constraint on the total number of available jobs is obtained by considering the sign and value of $(dn_1 + dn_2)/d\bar{h}_1$.

In the first sector, we have $Z = F(n_1 h_1)$ and therefore:

$$\frac{dn_1}{d\bar{h}_1} = \frac{1}{\bar{h}_1 F'(L_1)} \frac{dZ}{d\bar{h}_1} - \frac{n_1}{\bar{h}_1}$$

or in elasticity terms:

$$\eta_{\bar{h}_1}^{n_1} = -1 + \frac{\eta_{\bar{h}_1}^Z}{\eta_{L_1}^Z}$$

The first term can be interpreted as representing the "substitution effect" between workers and hours of the constraint variation, the second term being the "activity effect".

In sector 2, the working time is constant and therefore:

$$\frac{dn_2}{d\bar{h}_1} = \frac{1}{h_2^*} \frac{dL_2}{d\bar{h}_1}$$

The sensitivity of the total number of jobs with respect to the working time constraint is explained by three additive terms:

$$\frac{dn_1 + dn_2}{d\bar{h}_1} = -\frac{n_1}{\bar{h}_1} + \frac{1}{\bar{h}_1 F'(L_1)} \frac{dZ}{d\bar{h}_1} + \frac{1}{h_2^*} \frac{dL_2}{d\bar{h}_1} \tag{12.19}$$

On our assumptions, the favorable substitution effect might be partially offset or more than offset by two other effects. The worst case would take place when $G_{LZ} > 0$ since $G_{LZ} > 0 \Rightarrow dL_2/d\bar{h}_1 > 0$; reducing the working time in sector 1 implies job destruction in sector 2.

Values of $dL_2/d\bar{h}_1$ and $dZ/d\bar{h}_1$ being taken from (12.17) and (12.18), we can write as a final form:

$$\frac{dn_1 + dn_2}{d\bar{h}_1} = -\frac{n_1}{h_1} + \frac{H_1'}{\mathbb{D}q(Z) + pq'(Z)G_{LL}} \left[\frac{G_{LL}}{\bar{h}_1 F'(L_1)} - \frac{G_{LZ}}{h_2^*} \right] \quad (12.20)$$

where $H' < 0$, $G_{LL} < 0$, $G_{LZ} \lesseqgtr 0$.

For sufficiently small values of $q'(Z)$ or G_{LL}, the second term of the right hand side of equation (12.20) is positive iff $G_{LZ} > \dfrac{h_2^* G_{LL}}{\bar{h}_1 F'(L_1)}$ (a negative number). We have to keep in mind that any technology in which the marginal productivity of labor is increasing with the consumption of the productive commodity implies $G_{LZ} > 0$ and therefore satisfies this condition.

12.5   Special cases of fixed proportions

Our former representation allows for technical substitution between labor and the productive commodity in sector 2. We suggest considering hereafter two different special cases of complementarity: in the first case, the production commodity is used in a fixed proportion α of labor, $Z = \alpha L_2$ (perfect complementarity between the two inputs); in the second case, the production commodity is used in a fixed proportion of output, $Z = \gamma C$. This second case applies in particular when the sector 1 commodity is interpreted as a transport service from a predetermined production place to a predetermined consumption area. In both cases, the technology of sector 2 is represented by a neoclassical function of a single variable

$$C = G(L_2)$$

12.5.1   Fixed proportion of labor

In this case, $Z = \alpha L_2$, and the profit function of sector 2 is:

$$\pi_2 = G(L_2) - H_2(h_2^*)L_2 - \alpha p L_2$$

The first order condition is:

$$\frac{d\pi_2}{dL_2} = G'(L_2) - [H_2(h_2^*) + \alpha p] = 0 \quad (12.21)$$

Differentiating (12.21) yields

$$\frac{dL_2}{dp} = \frac{\alpha}{G''(L_2)} \quad (12.22)$$

and

$$\frac{dZ}{dp} = \frac{dZ}{dL_2}\frac{dL_2}{dp} = \frac{\alpha^2}{G''(L_2)} \tag{12.23}$$

Using (12.16), we obtain the sensitivities

$$\frac{dL_2}{d\bar{h}_1} = \frac{\alpha H'(\bar{h}_1)}{q(Z)G''(L_2) + \alpha^2 pq'(Z)} \tag{12.24}$$

$$\frac{dZ}{d\bar{h}_1} = \frac{\alpha^2 H'(\bar{h}_1)}{q(Z)G''(L_2) + \alpha^2 pq'(Z)} \tag{12.25}$$

The sensitivity of the total amount of jobs available $(dn_1 + dn_2)/d\bar{h}_1$ is obtained by substituting $dL_2/d\bar{h}_1$ and $dZ/d\bar{h}_1$ in (12.19) with the right hand side of (12.24) and (12.25).

We obtain the following final form:

$$\frac{(dn_1 + dn_2)}{d\bar{h}_1} = -\frac{n_1}{\bar{h}_1} + \frac{\alpha H'(\bar{h}_1)}{q(Z)G''(L_2) + \alpha^2 pq'(Z)} \left[\frac{\alpha}{\bar{h}_1 F'(L_1)} + \frac{1}{h_2^*}\right] \tag{12.26}$$

For "small" values of $q'(Z)$, the sign of the second term in (12.26) is positive. Two effects offset the man-hours substitution in sector 1; if $G''(L_2)$ also takes small values, the order of magnitude of this second term might explain the overall job destruction when $\bar{h}_1$ is reduced.

12.5.2   Fixed proportion of output: the trucking case

In France, the threat of strikes and traffic blockades has imposed on firms a reduced working time in the service activity of road transport (November 1997). The model may shed some light on the employment impact of this measure.

If we interpret sector 1 as supplying transport services to the consumption goods industry, we cannot keep a natural monopoly assumption; we consider sector 1 as private, working with constant productivity $q(Z) = \bar{q}$ and under a competitive zero-profit equilibrium. In this case, the BB locus in Figure 12.2 is horizontal and equation (12.8) takes the form:

$$p = \frac{H_1(\bar{h}_1)}{\bar{q}} \tag{12.27}$$

As mentioned, the production function indicates $C = G(L_2)$. The demand for the productive factor is $Z = \gamma G(L_2)$. The profit function becomes:

$$\pi_2 = G(L_2) - H_2(h_2^*)L_2 - \gamma p G(L_2)$$

where γ is related to the average mileage of the output and p is a per-unit flat tariff.

The first order condition is:

$$G'(L_2)(1 - \gamma p) - H_2(h_2^*) = 0 \qquad (12.28)$$

Differentiating (12.27) and (12.28) yields:

$$\frac{dL_2}{d\bar{h}_1} = \frac{\gamma G'(L_2)H_1'(\bar{h}_1)}{\bar{q}G''(L_2)(1 - \gamma p)} \qquad (12.29)$$

and

$$\frac{dZ}{d\bar{h}_1} = \frac{[\gamma G'(L_2)]^2 H_1'(\bar{h}_1)}{\bar{q}G''(L_2)(1 - \gamma p)} \qquad (12.30)$$

The sensitivity of the total amount of available jobs $(dn_1 + dn_2)/d\bar{h}_1$ is again obtained by substituting $dL_2/d\bar{h}_1$ and $dZ/d\bar{h}_1$ in (12.19) with the right hand side of (12.29) and (12.30). The final form in this special case is:

$$\frac{dn_1 + dn_2}{d\bar{h}_1} = -\frac{n_1}{\bar{h}_1} + \frac{\gamma G'(L_2)H_1'(\bar{h}_1)}{\bar{q}G''(L_2)(1 - \gamma p)}\left[\frac{\gamma G'(L_2)}{\bar{h}_1 F'(L_1)} + \frac{1}{h_2^*}\right] \qquad (12.31)$$

The sign of the second term of (12.31) is positive $(\gamma p < 1)$. For small values of $G''(L_2)$, working time reduction in the transport sector may imply job destruction at an aggregate level.

12.6   Conclusion

The suggested model is able to indicate the structural elements of the economy accounting for unsatisfactory or paradoxical variations in the number of available jobs, when working time constraints are applied to the sectors supplying productive factors or services, and when the workers (insiders) are generally able to defend a constant utility level.

In many cases, the perverse effects are negligible if the system is initially free, i.e. if the working time coincides with its optimum value from the firms' point of view, but can play a major role when firms are already constrained (working time of the truck drivers is obviously constrained by safety regulations).

It must be noticed, however, that joblessness may push down the minimum utility requirement. In this case the perverse effect of the applied working time constraint would be partially offset by lower compensating wages. But working time reductions usually seem to be linked to opening new negotiation rounds between unions and firms. Quite often, the resulting wage rate variations in the public monopoly do not follow the terms of a compensatory wage function but improve the utility level of the insiders, sometimes stimulating similar claims in the other sectors.[3] In such a case, the total impact on job supply variations is worse than indicated by the terms of our model.

---

[3] The French EDF agreement on the reduction of the working week from 38 to 32 hours reached in January 1997 is estimated to imply a 9% increase of the hourly wage rate.

13
Working hours and unemployment in a matching model

13.1 Introduction

Previous chapters provided several analyses of working time under various assumptions pertaining to the institutional set-up and the constraints imposed upon profit maximizing firms of the productive sector. They are all based on a static framework, firms and workers taking once and for all decisions concerning only one period. This simplifying design allowed us to emphasize the role played by fixed costs of labor and worker time effectiveness functions on the optimal duration of work, given various organizational contexts.

Recent advances in unemployment analysis build on a dynamic approach grounded in equilibrium search theory (see the survey by Mortensen and Pissarides, 1999). Some authors had provided founding contributions to this approach. One should mention the pioneering texts by Stigler (1961), Mc-Call (1970) and various texts collected in a famous book edited by Phelps (1970). More recently, Dale Mortensen and Christopher Pissarides developed this innovative approach in a significant way. These two authors introduced a macroeconomic notion of matching technology, explaining how all the firms are able at each point in time to convert vacancies into employment at a rate depending on an indicator of labor market tightness.

The standard search economy is subject to a sequence of exogenous shocks, entailing job destructions and job creations; there are large flows in and out of jobs, with unemployed persons searching for jobs and firms searching for workers. In search economies, the influence of costly information technology interfering with decentralized transactions in the labor market is explicitly modeled. Costly information explains why at any point in time, unemployed able workers and job vacancies coexist.

In this context, Walrasian equilibrium is substituted by search equilibrium. As clearly stated by Pissarides (1990, p.4):

> Equilibrium in the system is defined by a state in which firms and workers maximize their respective objective functions, subject to the matching and separation technologies, and in which the flow of workers into unemployment is equal to the flow of workers out of unemployment.

This chapter develops an introductory analysis of working time along this research path. This particular issue was extensively studied by Marimon and Zilibotti (1999) who analyzed the employment impact of a working hours constraint under various specifications of individual preferences and Rocheteau (1999) who worked out a matching model with moral hazard, carrying a step further the "shirking" approach once pioneered by Shapiro and Stiglitz (1984) and applied to the working time issue by Moselle (1996). We focus on the employment behavior of an economy made up of many firms, each of them taking the global state of vacancies and unemployment variables as given. In contrast to Marimon and Zilibotti (1999) who consider homogeneous labor services estimated by the men-hours product, or to Rocheteau (1999) who introduces a technology where output is linear in the number of workers, the generalized production function introduced in this text allows for different output elasticities with respect to hours and workers. Indeed, as mentioned in Chapter 5, many empirical studies have shown that hours and workers are not perfect substitutes (in logarithms) in the production of labor services. Our approach simplifies on the negotiation issues (developed in Chapter 10) and plainly considers a participation constraint expressed with the help of a working time compensating consumption function used in an intertemporal framework.

The first part of the chapter studies an unregulated labor market, where the firm is free to choose working time and employment so as to maximize intertemporal profits. We show that the steady state of this economy is fully described by three equations: the obtained system may be numerically solved for the relevant endogenous variables, i.e. hours of work, unemployment and probability of filling a vacancy. We put forward a solution in which unemployment and individual overwork coexist, an economic context which makes a policy of working time reduction particularly appealing

In the second part of the text, the model is used to study the unemployment effect of a binding constraint on working hours demanded by the firm. Numerical simulations show that a weak constraint may help to reduce unemployment down to a minimum value, but further enforcements of the constraint entail perverse effects. Particular focus is given to the special case where the hours constraint matches the worker supply.

13.2 Main assumptions

13.2.1 The firm and its technology

The productive sector is represented by a firm producing a homogeneous good to be sold at a predetermined unit price. Technology is summarized by a production function having as arguments the number of workers N and the daily hours per worker h:

$$F(N,h) = AN^{\alpha}h^{\beta}, \qquad \text{with: } 0 < \alpha < 1, 0 < \beta, A > 0 \qquad (13.1)$$

Such a function is compatible with different output elasticities with respect to hours and to workers, an empirical finding first put forward by the empirical studies mentioned in Chapter 5. For purpose of parsimony, $A = 1$. Setting the day as the relevant time period, and using the time index t, daily output is: $y_t = N_t^{\alpha}h_t^{\beta}$.

All the firms are identical and the number of firms is supposed constant;[1] N_t stands simultaneously for the firm's employment input and for global employment.

The total labor force is assumed to be constant and equal to L. Therefore global unemployment $U_t = L - N_t$.

13.2.2 Workers' consent to work and the labor contract

Firms retain workers with labor contracts indicating an hourly wage rate w_t and the daily hours of work h_t. The daily satisfaction of an employed person (or worker) increases with his consumption possibilities, which are themselves equal to the daily wage income $c_t = w_t h_t$, and decreases with hours of work, h_t. Formally, worker daily satisfaction is of the form $S(c_t, h_t)$, where t is the day index, with $S_1 > 0, S_2 < 0$. The daily satisfaction of the unemployed person is constant and will be denoted $\bar{S}$.[2]

Individuals would accept a contract $\{w_t, h_t\}$ if it provides them with an intertemporal utility level (denoted V^E) at least equal to the intertemporal utility of the unemployed person (denoted V^U). Such a participation constraint ties the hands of the firms, which must offer workers labor contracts such that $V^E \geq V^U$. In this elementary framework, the individual worker has no bargaining power and the employer is able to submit take-it or leave-it contracts.[3]

---

[1] If f is the number of firms, global employment should be denoted fN_t.

[2] This minimal satisfaction index may be written as $\bar{S} = S(b, 1)$, where b stands for unemployment benefits. Obviously, $\partial \bar{S}/\partial b > 0$.

[3] In Marimon and Zilibotti (1999) or Rocheteau (1999), workers and the firm split the surplus from the match under a Nash bargaining procedure.

Proposition 13 *The firm should provide workers with a wage compensation such that the daily satisfaction of the employed person equals the daily satisfaction of the unemployed* $S(c_t, h_t) = \bar{S}$.

Proof. Let us denote by q the probability of an employed person losing his job during the time period t, and by p the probability of an unemployed person finding a job during the period t. Given a psychological discount rate $\rho > 0$, the expected life-time utility of the employed person is:

$$V^E = S(c_t, h_t) + (1 + \rho)^{-1}[qV^U + (1 - q)V^E]$$

and the expected life-time utility of the unemployed person is:

$$V^U = \bar{S} + (1 + \rho)^{-1}[pV^E + (1 - p)V^U]$$

In an equivalent form, these two equations can be written as:

$$\rho V^E = (1 + \rho)S(c_t, h_t) + q(V^U - V^E) \tag{13.2}$$
$$\rho V^U = (1 + \rho)\bar{S} + p(V^E - V^U) \tag{13.3}$$

Substracting (13.3) from (13.2), we get:

$$(\rho + q + p)(V^E - V^U) = (1 + \rho)[S(c_t, h_t) - \bar{S}]$$

If the firm fixes wages such that $V^E = V^U$, then $S(c_t, h_t) = \bar{S}$ ∎

The intertemporal decision is thus reduced to the static case studied in preceding chapters where individuals would accept the terms of the contract if it provides them with a daily (or instantaneous) satisfaction equal to the daily satisfaction of the unemployed person.

Thus $c(h_t)$, the minimal daily compensation required by the person asked to work h_t hours, is implicitly defined by:

$$S(c(h_t), h_t) = \bar{S} \tag{13.4}$$

Notice that $c(h_t)$ is one particular indifference curve; it is therefore a convex function, in keeping with the standard neoclassical axioms on consumption/leisure preferences.

For instance, a particular utility function, able to convey in a straightforward way the neoclassical assumptions is:

$$S(c_t, h_t) = c_t^\varphi(1 - h_t)^{1-\varphi}, \qquad \varphi \in \,]0, 1[\tag{13.5}$$

where the length of the day has been set to one. It implies the compensation function:

$$c(h_t) = \left(\bar{S}_t\right)^{\frac{1}{\varphi}} (1 - h_t)^{\frac{\varphi-1}{\varphi}} \tag{13.6}$$

and a positive compensation-hours elasticity: $\eta_h^{c(h)} = \dfrac{h_t dc(h_t)}{c(h_t) dh_t} = \dfrac{(1-\varphi)h_t}{(1-h_t)\varphi}$.

It can be noticed that this elasticity increases in h_t.

Let us also introduce the concept of individual hours supply, i.e. worker desired daily hours for any wage rate, $h_t^s(w_t)$. Formally, the hours supply is defined by:

$$h_t^s = \arg\max_{h_t} S(w_t h_t, h_t) \qquad \forall w_t \tag{13.7}$$

Under the former definition of $c(h)$, actual hours coincide with the individual supply if $c'(h) = c(h)/h$ or $\eta_h^{c(h)} = 1$; overwork occurs if $c'(h) > c(h)/h$ or $\eta_h^{c(h)} > 1$. With the particular utility function indicated by equation (13.5), $h_t^s = \varphi, \forall w$.

13.2.3 The matching function

In an economy with decentralized trade, vacant jobs and unemployed job seekers take time to locate each other; information on vacant jobs is not immediately available to workers. Thus unemployed persons and vacancies coexist and only a fraction of the potential matches occurs during a given time period. Following the approach pioneered by Diamond (1982), Mortensen (1982) and Pissarides (1984), this complex process may be described by an *aggregate matching function*.[4]

Let us denote by U_t the number of unemployed persons and by V_t the number of vacancies. Also, let M_t denote the number of unemployed persons who find jobs during period t (i.e. the number of successful matches between vacancies and the unemployed). Given the frictions in the labor market, $M_t < \min\{U_t, V_t\}$. It is further assumed that M_t is an increasing function in both V_t and U_t, and is quasi-concave and homogeneous of degree one (Pissarides, 1990). It follows that:

$$M_t = M(V_t, U_t) \tag{13.8}$$

A convenient form for $M(,)$ is the constant elasticity specification: $M_t = V_t^{1-z} U_t^z$, with $z < 1$.

Denoting the relative number of traders in the market by $\zeta_t = V_t/U_t$, the probability of filling a vacancy is:

$$m(\zeta_t) = \frac{M(V_t, U_t)}{V_t} = \frac{V_t^{1-z} U_t^z}{V_t} = \left(\frac{V_t}{U_t}\right)^{-z} = (\zeta_t)^{-z} \tag{13.9}$$

---

[4] The main innovation of these papers consists in modelling market frictions by an exogenously given matching function relating the number of successful matches per period to the stock of vacancies and unemployed persons. There is an obvious likeness between the matching technology and a traditional production function which encompasses in a simple relationship the influence on output of two inputs.

In keeping with traditional literature, $\zeta = V/U$ will be interpreted as a proxy for the "tightness" of the labor market.

Under these assumptions, the *probability of an unemployed person finding a job* during the period t is:

$$\frac{M_t}{U_t} = \frac{V_t}{U_t}\frac{M_t}{V_t} = \zeta_t m(\zeta_t) \tag{13.10}$$

In the constant elasticity formulation of the matching function, $\zeta_t m(\zeta_t) = (\zeta_t)^{1-z}$, thus the probability of finding a job is increasing in ζ_t.

13.3 The free profit maximization

13.3.1 Profit function and the optimal decision

During each t period, a fraction q of the occupied jobs is destroyed as a consequence of various random shocks that disturb this economy. This separation rate is assumed to be structural. With previous notation, employment evolves according to:

$$N_{t+1} = (1-q)N_t + m_t V_t \tag{13.11}$$

where $m_t = m(\zeta_t)$. The number of vacancies can thus be written as: $V_t = [N_{t+1} - (1-q)N_t]/m_t$.

Let κ be the cost of maintaining one vacancy unoccupied. This can be seen either as an advertising cost or an opportunity cost related to idle capital. Firms also incur fixed costs of labor, proportional only to the number of employees and which have already been introduced in former chapters. These fixed costs per worker will be denoted by θ. Introducing a discount factor $\delta = (1+r)^{-1}$, the firm's objective consists in maximizing the present value $\mathcal{P}$ of a sequence of profits:

$$\begin{aligned}\mathcal{P} &= \sum_{t=0}^{\infty} \delta^t [N_t^\alpha h_t^\beta - N_t c(h_t) - \theta N_t - \kappa V_t] \\ &= \sum_{t=0}^{\infty} \delta^t \left[N_t^\alpha h_t^\beta - N_t c(h_t) - \theta N_t - \kappa \frac{N_{t+1} - (1-q)N_t}{m_t} \right] \end{aligned} \tag{13.12}$$

The firm controls vacancies and hours; employment is indirectly controlled following (13.11). In terms of employment and hours, first order conditions are:

$$\frac{\partial \mathcal{P}}{\partial N_t} = 0 \Rightarrow \alpha N_t^{\alpha-1} h_t^\beta = c(h_t) + \theta + \frac{\kappa}{\delta m_{t-1}} - \frac{\kappa(1-q)}{m_t} \tag{13.13}$$

$$\frac{\partial \mathcal{P}}{\partial h_t} = 0 \Rightarrow \beta N_t^{\alpha-1} h_t^{\beta-1} = c'(h_t) \tag{13.14}$$

In free equilibrium, the firm simultaneously adjusts vacancies (employment) and hours so as to maximize intertemporal profits. The steady state equilibrium may be characterized by three equations.

13.3.2   Three basic equations

The $m - h$ relationship

Let us first substitute $N_t^{\alpha-1} = c'(h_t)/\beta h_t^{\beta-1}$ in equation (13.13):

$$\frac{\alpha h_t c'(h_t)}{\beta} = c(h_t) + \theta + \frac{\kappa}{\delta m_{t-1}} - \frac{\kappa(1-q)}{m_t} \tag{13.15}$$

Denoting $\dfrac{\alpha}{\beta} = \epsilon$, with $\eta_h^c = \dfrac{h_t c'(h_t)}{c(h_t)}$ and $1/\delta = 1 + r$, then acknowledging that in the steady state $m(\zeta_t) = m(\zeta_{t-1}) = m(\zeta)$, the former equation becomes:

$$m(\zeta) = \frac{\kappa(q+r)}{(\epsilon\eta_h^c - 1)c(h_t) - \theta} \tag{13.16}$$

With the constant elasticity form of the matching function, $m(\zeta) = (\zeta)^{-z}$, $z < 1$; then $(\zeta_t)^{-z} = \dfrac{\kappa(q+r)}{(k\eta_h^c - 1)c(h_t) - \theta}$, and the probability of getting out of the unemployment pool is an increasing function of the hours of work:

$$\zeta m(\zeta) = \left[\frac{(\epsilon\eta_h^c - 1)c(h_t) - \theta}{\kappa(q+r)}\right]^{\frac{1-z}{z}} \tag{13.17}$$

The $u - h$ relationship

Condition (13.14) allows us to infer a relationship between hours and unemployment. Indeed, $N_t^{\alpha-1} = \beta^{-1}h_t^{1-\beta}c'(h_t)$. But for a constant labor force, $N_t = L - U_t$, it results that:

$$[L(1 - u_t)]^{\alpha-1} = \beta^{-1}h_t^{1-\beta}c'(h_t) \tag{13.18}$$

where $u_t = U_t/L$ is the unemployment rate. In the following, we consider the case in which due to exertion effect, $\beta < 1$, the right hand side of (13.18) is therefore an increasing function in h_t, thus the unemployment rate and hours are positively related.

The $u - m$ relationship

Unemployment dynamics are indicated by:

$$U_{t+1} = U_t + qN_t - M_t \tag{13.19}$$

As in the steady state $U_{t+1} = U_t$, then $qN = M$, i.e.: $q(L - U) = \zeta m(\zeta)U$. After some calculus, we reach the well-known equation:

$$u = \frac{q}{q + \zeta m(\zeta)} \tag{13.20}$$

In equation (13.20), the term $\zeta m(\zeta)$ measures the probability of finding a job for an unemployed worker. In the steady state, unemployment is a decreasing function in this probability (itself increasing in ζ). Expressing $\zeta m(\zeta)$ in terms of the unemployment rate u and the vacancy rate v would yield a Beveridge curve, i.e. a decreasing relationship between the two variables, such as revealed from data by the British economist in the forties.

13.3.3   Equilibrium unemployment and hours of work

Equations (13.16), (13.18) and (13.20) characterize a system with the unknowns h, u and $\zeta m(\zeta)$. As we consider only steady state values, the subscript t may be omitted. The solution of the system, if it exists, is denoted $\{h^*, u^*, \zeta^* m(\zeta^*)\}$.

Graphic solution

Figure 13.1 sketches a graphic solution in the plane (Oh, Ou). First, the relationship (13.18) is depicted as the increasing ZZ' curve. Then, according to equation (13.20), unemployment decreases in $\zeta m(\zeta)$, the probability of the unemployed person finding a job; this probability itself increases with working hours in keeping with equation (13.17); we may therefore draw a second decreasing curve YY' summarizing the two relationships. The steady state equilibrium is depicted at point E, and characterizes the steady state equilibrium values of unemployment and duration of work.

Comparative statics of the solution may be performed. For instance, increases in q, interpreted as higher economic turbulences, would shift the curve YY' upward: hours of work and unemployment increase simultaneously. Increases in fixed costs θ and κ would have a similar effect.

Numerical solution

The system (13.16), (13.18) and (13.20) may be numerically solved. We assign a standard figure for $\alpha = 0.64$; if an exertion effect is at work, one may reasonably assume that $\beta < \alpha \leq 1$, we thus set $\beta = 0.60$. The other parameters are $\bar{S} = 0.4$, $\varphi = 0.65$, $z = 0.25$, $\kappa = 0.25$, $\theta = 0.05$, $r = 0.06$, $q = 0.15$, $L = 1$. The solution is

$$
\begin{aligned}
h^* &= 0.68 \\
u^* &= 18.45\% \\
\zeta^* m(\zeta^*) &= 0.66
\end{aligned}
$$

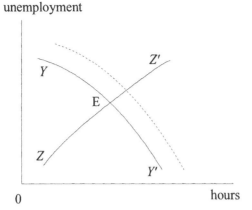

FIGURE 13.1. Steady state equilibrium

The daily compensation is equal to $c^* = 0.45$ and the firm's daily profits are positive, $\pi^* = 0.169$.

Notice that a reduction in the minimal satisfaction requirement would lead – as expected – to a lower unemployment rate (for instance, if $\bar{S} = 0.395$, $u^* = 16.10\%$). The impact of other changes in the parameter values may be analyzed in a similar way.

Finally, it can be seen that workers are in a situation of overwork, that is actual working time (h^*) exceeds their hours supply ($h^s = 0.65$).

13.4   The policy of working time reduction

13.4.1   The steady state solutions

The former section developed a simple model of working time and unemployment determination in a decentralized economy where the employer is free to choose the optimal mix of hours and workers. In a context of massive unemployment, a government may be tempted to impose a constraint on hours of work in order to push firms to substitute hours with workers. Let us denote by $\bar{h}$ the hours constraint.

Under this constraint the firm operates with a positive intensive margin $\partial \mathcal{P}/\partial \bar{h}_t > 0$, but is still able to optimize employment: the extensive margin is nil, $\partial \mathcal{P}/\partial N_t = 0$ whatever t. Remember that in order to attract workers, the firm must pay them a compensation $c(\bar{h}_t)$.

With $h = \bar{h}$, two basic equations characterize this economy. The first is based on the zero extensive margin condition (13.13), $\partial \mathcal{P}/\partial N_t = 0$:

$$\alpha N_t^{\alpha-1}\bar{h}_t^{\beta} = c(\bar{h}_t) + \theta + \frac{\kappa}{\delta m_{t-1}} - \frac{\kappa(1-q)}{m_t} \qquad (13.21)$$

which in the steady state becomes:

$$\alpha N^{\alpha-1} \bar{h}^{\beta} = c(\bar{h}) + \theta + \frac{\kappa(r+q)}{m(\zeta)}$$

Given that $N = L(1 - u)$, it can alternatively be written as:

$$\alpha \left[L(1 - u)\right]^{\alpha-1} \bar{h}^{\beta} = c(\bar{h}) + \theta + \frac{\kappa(r+q)}{m(\zeta)} \tag{13.22}$$

The second equation is (13.19), which in the steady state was written as:

$$u = \frac{q}{q + \zeta m(\zeta)} \tag{13.23}$$

Equations (13.22) and (13.23) have as a solution the constrained hours unemployment rate $u(\bar{h})$ and the constrained hours probability of obtaining a job, $\zeta m(\zeta)$.

Figure 13.2 is the plot of $u(\bar{h})$, the steady state unemployment value as a function of the hours constraint (dark line) against the free equilibrium unemployment u^* determined in the previous section (grey line). Parameters were assigned the same values as before while $\bar{h}$ is allowed to vary between the upper limit h^* and an arbitrarily chosen inferior limit.

Of course, $u(h^*) = u^*$. It can be seen in Figure 13.2 that a first favorable effect appears for an hours constraint in the neighborhood of the optimal time from the firm point of view (h^*). There exists a duration of work for which unemployment reaches a minimum. Further enforcements of the constraint would only increase unemployment.

While the former model is consistent with different working time configurations, realistic policy proposals would consider only situations where the hours constraint contributes to reducing overwork. Indeed, a policy aiming at bringing working time below the desired hours from the workers' point of view $(\bar{h} < h^s)$ would meet little political support, even if it would further reduce unemployment.

Given this remark, the most appealing policy in our numerical example would to be $\bar{h} = h^s$. Unemployment is $u(\bar{h} = h^s) = 16.6\%$ (1.8% less than in the unconstrained equilibrium), the probability of getting job increases to $\zeta m(\zeta) = 0.7537$, daily compensation is $c_1 = 0.43$ and firms' daily profits are $\pi_1 = 0.1475$ (lower than in the unconstrained case).

13.4.2   The adjustment dynamics

In the simulation above, we show that by imposing a constraint on working time, the steady state unemployment rate may be reduced. What can be said about the dynamics of the adjustment?

unemployment rate

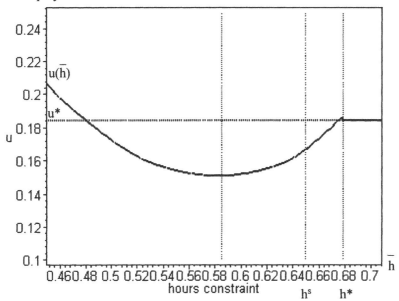

FIGURE 13.2. Steady state unemployment, constrained and unconstrained hours

To answer this question, it should be noticed that after a shock, firms may adjust vacancies immediately, while employment and unemployment will adjust only gradually. By inspection of equation (13.21), it can be observed that the variable ζ_t is "forward looking", i.e. the tension in the labor market at date t depends on the tension in the labor market at date $t+1$. Furthermore, there is only one constant value of ζ consistent with a finite expectation of ζ_{t+T} when $T \to \infty$.[5] In this case, after a shock on $\bar{h}$, ζ will instantaneously jump to its new steady state value $\hat{\zeta}$ (such as resulting from (13.22) and (13.23)), and equation (13.19) alone can characterize the unemployment time path.

More precisely, equation (13.19) can alternatively be written as:

$$u_{t+1} = u_t + q(1 - u_t) - u_t \hat{\zeta} m(\hat{\zeta})$$

or

$$u_{t+1} = u_t[1 - q - \hat{\zeta} m(\hat{\zeta})] + q \qquad (13.24)$$

Let us denote u_0 the initial unemployment value and $[1 - q - \hat{\zeta} m(\hat{\zeta})] = a$. Then, the unemployment time path is obtained by solving the recursive

---

[5] Cahuc and Zylberberg (1996, chapter 7.3.1) provide the formal proof for a related problem.

equation (13.24). The solution is:

$$u_t = u_0 a^t + \frac{1 - a^t}{1 - a} q \qquad (13.25)$$

As $|a| < 1$, the steady state value of unemployment is finite and equal to:

$$u(\bar{h}) = \lim_{t \to \infty} u_t = \frac{q}{q + \hat{\zeta} m(\hat{\zeta})} \qquad (13.26)$$

This solution also applies to the particular case provided by the numerical simulation. Initially, unconstrained hours unemployment is $u_0 = u^* = 18.44$. For a constraint, $\bar{h} = h^s$, the steady state unemployment is brought down to 16.60%. Immediately after the shock, unemployment becomes: $u_1 = au^* + q = u^*[1 - q - \hat{\zeta} m(\hat{\zeta})] + q = 16.77\%$, the rest of the unemployment reduction taking some more time to occur.

13.5   Conclusion

This chapter builds on a simple matching model *à la* Pissarides (1990) to analyze how unemployment and working time are determined in a decentralized labor market with trading frictions. The first part of the text investigates a free system, where employers hold the right to manage working time. It is shown that, in some cases, overwork and unemployment may unfortunately coexist. No doubt, in such an economic context a policy of working time reduction may be intuitively appealing.

In the second part, the matching model is used to study the macroeconomic impact of a mandatory reduction in working hours. It is shown that in the neighborhood of the optimal duration from the firm's point of view, the hours constraint may help diminish the unemployment rate (at the expense of firm profits); in particular, unemployment is reduced when the hours constraint is equal to the individual supply. The numerical simulation also shows that there is a working time for which unemployment reaches a minimum; below this threshold, further enforcements of the constraint bring about an increase in unemployment.

It must be noticed that introducing the flow vision of the labor market and the matching problem has not drastically changed the results of simulated working time constraints, as compared to already exposed results derived from the static models of previous chapters. The generalized model obtained with this more accurate representation of labor markets makes possible a better interpretation of the impact of working time policy. It must be kept in mind however that model tractability depends upon some supplementary assumptions, like a predetermined quit rate and independence of the matching function with respect to endogenous state variables. Simulations tend to show that the existence of consistent solutions of such models is critically confined to a narrow range of the parameter values.

14
Deregulation of overtime premium and employment dynamics

14.1 Introductory concepts: overtime and flexibility

Static cost structure of labor services in relation to working time has been mainly influenced for years by public regulation, since in most industrial countries, strict overtime premium rules have prevailed. The Fair Labor Standard Act fixing the determination of overtime premium rates is a simple and typical example of such legal interference. The consequences of mandatory overtime premium rules have been examined in comparative statics in Chapter 8.

In recent years, however, the role of legal constraints and of legally predetermined working time premium rates is tending to recede. In many instances, firms are granted more flexibility in adjusting their working hours to a changing environment. In many countries (to mention only France, Germany, Japan), the trend is in favor of so-called flexibility accords, as indicated in Bosch (1997), Takagi (1993), OECD (1998). Such collective agreements may take varied and complicated forms, including a whole set of contingent provisions related to various states of the world. However, they always embody in some form the terms of a trade-off negotiated between the employers' need for flexibility and the workers' preferences for some central values of working hours. The compensation of workers is usually commensurate with the whole working time profile over the year. This form of collective contract between employers and workers is clearly intended to give more leeway to working time fluctuations than the traditional legal framework.

But relaxing legal constraints on the duration of the working week or the working day does not mean that labor costs become flat in working time. In its attempt to change hours, the firm meets either market constraints on the price structure of labor services or union determined requirements. This would explain why in the United Kingdom, where overtime premiums are freely negotiated without legal interference, a positive correlation between the hourly wage and the duration of work has been clearly confirmed by Hart and Ruffel (1993). Along the same lines, Hart et al. (1996) point out that in Japan, where working hours regulation requires only a premium of 25% applying to hours beyond 40 hours per week, a negotiated premium of approximately 32% actually applies to late hours of work. The legal constraint appears to be less binding in this country than the observed conditions in the labor market.

This new situation also modifies the setting of dynamic analysis applied to labor demand. The mainstream of the dynamic approach of the demand for labor has placed emphasis on explaining the employment time path in relation to various assumptions pertaining to employment adjustment cost but for a predetermined fixed working time. The behavior of the firm is analyzed either in a profit maximizing context or under output constraint (Sargent, 1978; Nickell, 1986). An interesting result of this class of model in their deterministic versions is the fact that they account for anticipated labor hoarding around the upturn of the business cycle and give some predictions about the productivity cycle. As intuitively understood, increasing penalties for varying the number of persons at work induce the firm to dampen its response to activity fluctuations in terms of employment. But working time is considered as constant.

Treating working time as an endogenous variable in a dynamic model introduces a second control trajectory into the problem and calls for the complementary considerations:

– Effectiveness functions may be necessary if labor services are not homogeneous in time, in particular if the technology lends itself to the effects of warming-up or exertion.

– The participation constraint imposed on the firm is no longer determined by a competitive wage rate. A well-defined labor cost structure must be derived from the requirement of workers expressed either by the market in a laissez-faire context, or by the terms of the so-called flexibility accords, when the intermediation of unions is to be observed in labor relations.

The cost of changing the employment level is however not modified by the introduction of working time as a new control variable; such costs have already been analyzed in depth, particularly by Hamermesh (1995) and Nickell (1986).

In this chapter, we limit ourselves to examining the consequences of stylized working time effectiveness and labor cost structures on the optimal time paths of employment and working time for demand constrained firms producing services or non-storable commodities. As usually assumed in comparable models, the firm has point expectations about its future activity. We focus on the general conditions for existence or complete elimination of labor hoarding and point to some properties of the obtained paths for the two control variables, employment and hours.

The text is organized as follows. After introducing the main assumptions, we study the cost minimization problem and put forward the conditions for the emergence of labor hoarding. The case of periodic activity is then analyzed.

14.2 Main assumptions

We investigate the cost minimizing path of the number of employees n_t and of their working time h_t when the firm operates under the following conditions:

- The demand follows a continuous function of time noted y_t.

- Fluctuations of demand must be met by output without reducing stocks (as for services or perishable goods).

- Hoarded labor may appear and the number of non-working insiders (slack) is denoted s_t.

- Individual labor services are related to the number of worked hours by a continuous efficiency function $g = g(h_t)$, such that $g(0) = 0$, $g'(h_t) > 0$. the elasticity of this function is noted $\eta_h^g(h)$.

- Productivity of labor services is constant; it is equal to one by the choice of measurement unit, so that the following constraint must hold with $s_t \geq 0$ $\forall t$:

$$(n_t - s_t)\, g(h_t) = y_t \qquad (14.1)$$

- Labor cost is represented by simplified functions respectively standing for static costs and dynamic costs (costs of change apply to variations of the number n_t only; there is no cost intrinsically related to working time variations).

At each point in time, the participation of each worker induces a flow of cost represented by a stationary continuous function $c(h)$. This participation cost function $c(h)$ may be considered either as the consequence of negotiated flexibility accords holding throughout the analytical period, or as compensation of working time in a strictly competitive labor market. This function indicates the flow of cost paid for each choice by the firm of a definite working time. The elasticity of this function is denoted $\eta_h^c(h)$. In a first approach, we assume that $c(h)$ is a convex function of h admitting a global minimum $h^* = \arg\min\{c(h)\} > 0$. In this case, the function $c(h)$ is such that the hourly labor cost of a worker admits a global minimum $\hat{h} = \arg\min\{c(h)/h\}$; it may be checked that $\hat{h} > h^*$ and $\eta_h^c(\hat{h}) = 1$. (Interpretation of the participation cost function is further detailed in the Appendix.)

– The rate of change in the number of employees $\dot{n}_t$ generates another flow of expenses represented for simplification by the convex (quadratic) function: $e_t = (\gamma/2)\dot{n}_t^2$. In the terminology proposed by Hamermesh (1995) this function describes net costs of change; gross cost of change are neglected.

– Slack workers and active workers are paid at the same rate according to the same nominal working time.

– There is no cost of change incurred by the firm associated with variation rates $\dot{h}_t$.

14.3   The cost minimization problem

14.3.1   Euler necessary conditions

Under these assumptions, the firm's decision problem is:

$$
\left\{
\begin{array}{l}
\min \displaystyle\int_{t=0}^{T} e^{-\rho t}\left\{\dfrac{\gamma}{2}\dot{n}_t^2 + n_t c(h_t)\right\} dt \\[2mm]
\text{with } (n_t - s_t)\, g(h_t) = y_t \\[1mm]
\text{and } s_t \geq 0
\end{array}
\right.
\tag{14.2}
$$

where ρ is a constant continuous discounting rate, and the non-negativity of n_t and h_t is implied by (14.1).

Euler necessary conditions must hold at each point in time, relative to:

$$
\mathcal{L} = \int_{t=0}^{T} e^{-\rho t}\left\{\frac{\gamma}{2}\dot{n}_t^2 + n_t c(h_t)\right\} dt - \int_{t=0}^{T} \lambda_t\left[(n_t - s_t)\, g(h_t) - y_t\right] dt
\tag{14.3}
$$

with $s_t \geq 0$.

Therefore we can write this condition for each variable $(n_t, h_t, s_t, \lambda_t)$, i.e.:

$$
e^{-\rho t} c(h_t) - \lambda_t g(h_t) = e^{-\rho t} \gamma \ddot{n}_t - \rho e^{-\rho t} \gamma \dot{n}_t
\tag{14.4}
$$

$$
e^{-\rho t} n_t c'(h_t) - \lambda_t\left[(n_t - s_t)\right] g'(h_t) = 0
\tag{14.5}
$$

$$
\lambda_t \geq 0 \; ; \; s_t \lambda_t = 0
\tag{14.6}
$$

$$
y_t = (n_t - s_t)\, g(h_t)
\tag{14.7}
$$

Equations (14.4), (14.5), (14.6) and (14.7) are compatible with two different regimes.

14.3.2   First regime: the case with positive labor hoarding

If there is hoarding, $s_t > 0$, $\lambda_t = 0$, and equation (14.5)$\Rightarrow$ $c'(h_t) = 0$, implying a constant working time h^*, unique solution of $c'(h_t) = 0$.

This condition may be interpreted by noting that when there is positive labor hoarding, (14.1) is not binding and the firm simply imposes the working time which minimizes the direct participation cost of each worker.

Consequently, the time path of working time is $h_t = h^*$, and (14.4) takes the form:

$$\ddot{n}_t = \rho\dot{n}_t + \frac{c(h^*)}{\gamma} \tag{14.8}$$

The time path $n(t)$ within a labor hoarding interval is therefore of the general following form:

$$n(t) = \frac{\varphi}{\rho}e^{\rho t} - \frac{c(h^*)}{\rho\gamma}t + \mu$$

If we choose the time origin at the beginning of the hoarding interval, for given initial conditions $n(0) = n_0$ and $\dot{n}(0) = \dot{n}_0$, θ and μ may be determined:

$$\varphi = \dot{n}_0 + \frac{c(h^*)}{\rho\gamma} \text{ and } \mu = \rho^{-1}\left(\rho n_0 - \dot{n}_0 - \frac{c(h^*)}{\rho\gamma}\right)$$

The employment trajectory is:

$$n(t) = \rho^{-1}\left(\dot{n}_0 + \frac{c(h^*)}{\rho\gamma}\right)e^{\rho t} - \frac{c(h^*)}{\rho\gamma}t + n_0 - \rho^{-1}\left(\dot{n}_0 + \frac{c(h^*)}{\rho\gamma}\right) \tag{14.9}$$

Using the Taylor's expansion $e^{\rho t} = 1 + \rho t + \frac{\rho^2 t^2}{2} + ...$, it can be shown that

$$\lim_{\rho\to 0} n(t) = \frac{c(h^*)}{2\gamma}t^2 + \dot{n}_0 t + n_0 \tag{14.10}$$

14.3.3   Second regime: the production constraint is binding

In this case, $\lambda_t > 0$, $s_t = 0$, equation (14.5)$\Rightarrow$ $\lambda_t = \dfrac{e^{-\rho t}c'(h_t)}{e'(h_t)} > 0$ and therefore $c'(h_t) > 0$.

Substituting λ_t with this value in (14.4) yields:

$$c(h_t) - g(h_t)\frac{c'(h_t)}{g'(h_t)} = \gamma\ddot{n}_t - \rho\gamma\dot{n}_t \tag{14.11}$$

or in elasticity terms:

$$c(h_t)\left[1 - \frac{\eta^c(h_t)}{\eta^g(h_t)}\right] = \gamma\ddot{n}_t - \rho\gamma\dot{n}_t \tag{14.12}$$

In such an interval the two endogenous time paths are also related by the constraint (14.1) in its binding form:

$$n_t g(h_t) = y_t$$

When the constraint is binding, the time paths of working time and employment are finally related by the following system:

$$c(h_t) \left[1 - \frac{\eta_h^c(h_t)}{\eta_h^g(h_t)} \right] = \gamma \ddot{n}_t - \rho \gamma \dot{n}_t \tag{14.13}$$

$$n_t g(h_t) = y_t \tag{14.14}$$

(The first equation generalizes the standard neoclassical case in which the left hand side is nil since $\eta_h^c(h_t) = \eta_h^g(h_t) = 1$).

Equations (14.13) and (14.14) imply continuity of both trajectories within any interval in which the constraint is binding, since y_t and any optimal trajectory n_t (due to the cost of change function) are themselves continuous.

It may be assumed that the participation cost of the individual worker is the sum of a fixed cost θ and of a compensating wage rate determined by the flexibility accord. We suppose that the same instantaneous compensating wage rate applies to all workers, whatever the length of their participation period (see our discussion in the Appendix). Therefore, we can write $c(h_t) = \theta + h_t w(h_t)$. In this case, equation (14.11) may be rewritten for the special case where $\eta_h^g(h) = 1$:

$$\theta - h_t^2 w'(h_t) = \gamma \ddot{n}_t - \rho \gamma \dot{n}_t \tag{14.15}$$

generalizing in a dynamic setting the result obtained in Chapter 9.

14.4   A simplified dynamic submodel

In order to illustrate graphically the possible behavior of this type of system, we consider the simplified case where the discounting factor is nil, efficiency is linear implying $g(h) = h$.

In this case, when the constraint is not binding (in a hoarding interval), $h_t = h^* \ \forall t$ and (14.11) with $\rho = 0$ takes the form:

$$\ddot{n}_t = \frac{c(h^*)}{\gamma}$$

The acceleration of the employment time path is constant and positive in a hoarding interval and n_t is a convex function of time. Defining $n(0) = n_0$, $\dot{n}(0) = \dot{n}_0$, the evolution of employment follows:

$$n(t) = \frac{c(h^*)}{2\gamma} t^2 + \dot{n}_0 t + n_0 \tag{14.16}$$

This equation coincides with the limit trajectory already described by (14.10).

When the constraint is binding, (14.11) takes the simplified form:

$$\ddot{n}_t = \frac{c(h_t)\left[1 - \eta_h^c(h_t)\right]}{\gamma} \tag{14.17}$$

Since $c''(h) > 0$, we can deduce from (14.17) the following rule: *the time path of the number of hired workers is concave ($\ddot{n}_t < 0$) when $h_t > \hat{h}$, is convex ($\ddot{n}_t > 0$) if $h_t < \hat{h}$ and admits inflection points when $h_t = \hat{h}$.*

Figure 14.1 represents trajectories compatible with the obtained results.

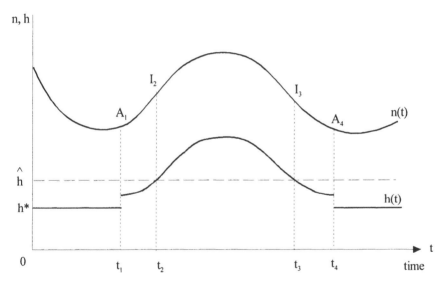

FIGURE 14.1. Employment and hours time paths

In the first interval, $t \in [0, t_1]$, existence of hoarding implies $h_t = h^*$ $\forall t$ and $\ddot{n}_t = c(h^*)/\gamma > 0$. In the second interval, $t \in [t_1, t_4]$, the output constraint is binding, the two represented trajectories are related by $n_t h_t = y_t$. Inflection points I_2 and I_3 of trajectory n_t are observed for $t = t_2$ and $t = t_3$, when the working time trajectory h_t crosses the dashed horizontal line $h = \hat{h}$. Discontinuity of the path $h(t)$ in points such as t_1 and t_4 are compatible with continuously varying output. In t_1, the slack $s(t)$ jumps to zero; in t_4 it jumps from zero to a positive value.

14.5   The labor cost functions and existence of labor hoarding intervals

We have seen that hoarding implies minimizing the participation cost of the worker. If the function $c(h)$ is such that $c'(h) > 0 \ \forall h \in \,]0,1[$, the first regime is ruled out and the constraint is constantly binding; flexibility of working time has eliminated labor hoarding.

For a better analysis of necessary conditions for hoarding, we suggest introducing simple particular cost functions. It may be assumed that the participation cost of the individual worker is the sum of a fixed cost θ and of a compensating wage rate determined by the flexibility accord. We suppose that the same instantaneous compensating wage rate applies to all workers, whatever the length of their participation period (see our discussion in the Appendix). Therefore, we can write $c(h_t) = \theta + h_t w(h_t)$.

A suggested simple compensating wage function could be of the form:

$$w(h) = \tilde{w} + \frac{\alpha}{2}(h - \tilde{h})^2 \tag{14.18}$$

where $\tilde{h} = \arg \min\{w(h)\}$ is the wage minimizing working time, and $\tilde{w}$ the corresponding minimum.

The advantage of this function is that the parameter α may be considered as reflecting (inversely) the degree of flexibility of the labor agreement: for $\alpha = 0$, there is no penalty cost related to unpleasant working time, the flexibility is infinite; the situation where $\alpha \to +\infty$ reflects as a limit case the strict rigidity of working time implicit in cost of change models mentioned above.

The associated participation cost function is a polynomial of the third degree:

$$c(h) = \theta + \tilde{w}h + \frac{\alpha h}{2}(h - \tilde{h})^2 \tag{14.19}$$

For $h \geq 0$, the global minimum of $c(h)$ is always θ, for $h = 0$. It can be shown that a local minimum exists for sufficiently large values of α.

A local minimum requires $c'(h) = 0$ and $c''(h) < 0$. From (14.19), this local minimum obtains for:

$$h = \frac{2}{3}\tilde{h} + \frac{1}{3}\sqrt{\tilde{h}^2 - 6\tilde{w}/\alpha} \tag{14.20}$$

This solution is real for $\alpha > 6\hat{w}/\hat{h}^2$, i.e. a minimum rigidity level. This is not however a sufficient condition for hoarding. Since it is only a local minimum of the participation cost function, idle workers may be retained only if a supplementary constraint is added to the problem, ruling out too short working time. Figure 14.2 illustrates how sufficiently high values of α

give rise to a local maximum and minimum of the participation cost as a function of working time. Function $c(h)$ is plotted for $\hat{w} = 1$, $\hat{h} = 1/3$ and increasing values of α.

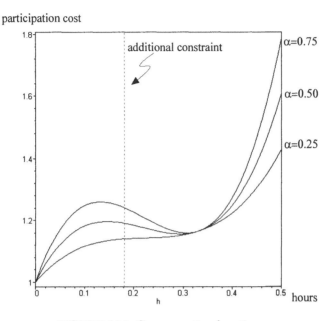

FIGURE 14.2. Compensation function

14.6   The case of a periodic activity constraint

Minimizing production cost on a one-period horizon implies the above Euler conditions on the time interval $[0, T]$. If the activity fluctuation is seasonal, $y_{(t+T)} = y_t$ $\forall t$, and optimal values of n_t, $\dot{n}_t$ and h_t are also periodic, when the system is stationary.

$$\int_{t=0}^{T} \ddot{n}_t dt = \dot{n}(T) - \dot{n}(0) = 0 = \int_{t=0}^{T} \dot{n}_t dt = n(T) - n(0)$$

If there is no labor hoarding in this whole interval, equation (14.15) applies and we can write:

$$\int_{t=0}^{T} h_t^2 w'(h_t) dt = \theta T \tag{14.21}$$

The working time weighted average of the first derivative of the wage function is nil on the whole interval. In our special case where the compensating wage is quadratic, $w'(h_t) = \alpha(h_t - \hat{h})$ and (14.21) becomes:

$$\frac{1}{T} \int_{t=0}^{T} h_t^2 (h_t - \hat{h}) dt = \frac{\theta}{\alpha} \qquad (14.22)$$

$\frac{\theta}{\alpha} \to 0 \Rightarrow h_t \to \hat{h}$ $\forall t$; in the absence of fixed cost or with no flexibility ($\alpha \to \infty$), optimum working time coincides with $\hat{h}$. This last equation expresses a constraint to the distribution of working time around the wage minimizing value $\hat{h}$. Defining moments centered around $\hat{h}$ by $\sigma_i = \frac{1}{T} \int_{t=0}^{T} (h_t - \hat{h})^i dt$, and since $\sigma_1 = \bar{h} - \hat{h}$, this constraint on working time distribution (14.22) may be written, using the identity $h_t^2 = \left[h_t - \hat{h} + \hat{h} \right]^2$:

$$\sigma_3 + 2\hat{h}\sigma_2 + \hat{h}^2(\bar{h} - \hat{h}) = \frac{\theta}{\alpha} \qquad (14.23)$$

In this last equation, σ_3 indicates the skewness of working time around $\hat{h}$. It must be noticed that this relation must hold whatever the output trajectory y_t and the value of γ.

14.7   Conclusion

In a deregulated context, pure market constraints or flexibility accords tend to replace the traditional legal system of overtime premium rules. Intended as a trade-off between workers' preferences and optimum utilization of collective equipment, such accords usually define sophisticated constraints and an implicit price structure on labor services. Whereas a legal premium scheme may be considered as predetermined, the terms of flexibility agreements in decentralized economies should be viewed as a form of market equilibrium. Explaining them requires first an understanding of their consequences on labor demand.

Our model being of a heuristic nature, it may only aim at giving first indications about the basic features of dynamic demand for workers and hours. It confirms the intuitive view according to which in the case of monotonously increasing participation costs, flexibility of working time tends to rule out labor hoarding of the demand constrained firm with point expectations. If there is a working time for which the worker participation cost is minimized, labor hoarding may be the natural choice of the cost minimizing firm during the upturn. In this case, increased rigidity increases slack workers and firms' costs.

Labor hoarding is usually considered as an unobservable variable, exposed only to indirect measurement, since it does not take the form of visible idle workers, countable in the productive sector, but manifests itself in reality by less active workers or by situations in which part of the workforce is assigned less productive activities. Theoretical approaches are therefore especially needed, introducing profit maximizing behavior and trading uncertainty (Wakita, 1997). More detailed indications should be derived from comparative dynamics in more closely descriptive models, whose development should be considered in particular for a better understanding of the consequences of recently adopted flexibility agreements.

14.8   Appendix: Participation constraint

The compensation of workers embodied by the function $c(h)$ is supposed to follow the same pattern whatever the length of their participation in production. It should be noticed that if we interpret the participation cost as a compensation for working time disutility transmitted by flexibility accords or directly expressed on a free labor market, the participation constraint could be inferred from consumption/leisure preferences. If we use a quasi-linear instantaneous utility function, the participation constraint on a given interval (t_0, t_1) could be of the form:

$$\int_{t=t_0}^{t_1} e^{-\psi t} \left[c_t - v(h_t) \right] dt \geq \int_{t=t_0}^{t_1} \bar{u} e^{-\psi t} dt \tag{14.24}$$

where ψ is a psychological discounting factor, $v(h)$ is a convex function and where $\bar{u}$ is the instantaneous utility flow derived from alternative conditions available out of the firm.

For a worker participating over the whole output period, the constraint on the compensation path c_t should therefore be written:

$$\int_{t=0}^{T} e^{-\psi t} c_t dt \geq \int_{t=0}^{T} e^{-\psi t} v(h_t) dt + (1 - e^{-\psi T}) \frac{\bar{u}}{\psi} \tag{14.25}$$

In order to justify a stationary instantaneous compensating function $c(h)$ as used in the problem (14.2), we have to think of a situation in which all workers must be treated equally, whatever the length of their participation. This can be relevant in some contexts, but is somewhat at odds with some particular situations in which firms are supposed to have a long run commitment to insiders (for instance, in Japan). If the workers and the firm have access to the same financial market or more generally, if $\rho = \psi$,

$$c(h_t) = v(h_t) + \bar{u} \tag{14.26}$$

makes it possible to interpret the problem (14.2) as exactly satisfying the participation constraint for intervals of any duration, eliminating any difference between internal and external labor markets.

References

[1] Åberg, Yngve. *The Impact of Working Hours and Other Factors on Production and Employment.* Aldershot, United Kingdom: Avebury, Hants, 1987.

[2] Akerlof, George A. "Labor Contracts as a Partial Gift Exchange," *Quarterly Journal of Economics,* *97*:543–569 (1982).

[3] Andersen, Torben M. "Short and Long-Run Consequences of Shorter Working Hours." *Unemployment Theory, Policy and Structure* edited by P. Pedersen and R. Lund, 147–165, De Gruyer, 1987.

[4] Anxo, Dominique. "Working-Time Policy in Sweden." *Proceedings of the Joint Conference of the European Trade Union Confederation and The European Trade-Union Institute* edited by R. Hoffman and J.A. Lapeyre, 1995.

[5] Becker, Garry. "A Theory of the Allocation of Time," *Economic Journal,* *55*(299):493–517 (1965).

[6] Bell, David N. and Robert A. Hart. "Working Time in Great Britain, 1975-1994: Evidence from the New Earnings Survey Panel Data," *Journal of the Royal Statistical Society,* *161*(3):327–348 (1998).

[7] Bell, Linda and Richard Friedman. "Why Do Americans and Germans Work Different Hours," *NBER Working Paper,* *4808* (1994).

[8] Bienefeld, Michael A. *Working Hours in British Industry: An Economic History.* London: Wiedenfeld and Nicholson, 1972.

[9] Binmore, Ken, et al. "The Nash Bargaining Solution in Economic Modeling," *Rand Journal of Economics*, *17*(2):176–188 (1986).

[10] Blaug, Mark. *Economic Theory in Retrospect*. Cambridge, United Kingdom: Cambridge University Press, 1985.

[11] Blundell, Richard. "Labour Supply and Taxation: A Survey," *Fiscal Studies*, *13*(3):15–40 (1993).

[12] Blyton, Paul and Rainer Trinczek. "Renewed Interest in Work-Sharing? Assessing Recent Developments in Germany," *Industrial Relations Journal*, *28*(1):3–13 (1997).

[13] Böhm-Bawerk, Eugene. *Capital and Interest* (1959 Edition), *2*. South Holland, Illinois: Libertarian Press, 1888.

[14] Boisard, Pierre and Jean-David Fermanian. "Les Rythmes de Travail Hors Norme," *Economie et Statistique*, *321-322*(1/2):111–131 (1999).

[15] Booth, Alison. *The Economics of the Trade Union*. Cambridge, United Kingdom: Cambridge University Press, 1995.

[16] Booth, Alison and Martin Ravallion. "Employment and the Lengh of the Working Week in a Unionized Economy in Which Hours of Work Influence Productivity," *Economic Record*, *69*(207):428–436 (1993).

[17] Booth, Alison and Fabio Schiantarelli. "The Employment Effect of a Shorter Working Week," *Economica*, *54*:237–248 (1987).

[18] Booth, Alison and Fabio Schiantarelli. "Reductions in Hours and Employment: What Do Union Models Tell Us." *Employment, Unemployment and Labor Utilization* edited by Robert A. Hart, 142–161, Boston: Unwin Hyman, 1988.

[19] Bosch, Gerhard. "Annual Working Hours, an International Comparison." *Working Time: New Issues, New Norm, New Measures* edited by Gerhard Bosch, et al., 14–35, Bruxelles: Dublea, 1997.

[20] Cahuc, Pierre and Pierre Granier. "The Consequences of a Shorter Working Time: Some Lessons from a General Equilibrium Analysis," *Recherches Economiques de Louvain*, *63*(1):13–29 (1997).

[21] Cahuc, Pierre and André Zylberberg. *Economie Du Travail*. Bruxelles: De Boeck, 1996.

[22] Cain, Glen G. "The Economic Analysis of Labor Market Analysis." *Handbook of Labor Economics* edited by Orley Ashenfelter and Richard Layard, chapter 13, 693–781, Amsterdam: North-Holland, 1986.

[23] Calmfors, Lars. "Work Sharing, Employment and Wages," *European Economic Review*, *29*:293–309 (1985).

[24] Calmfors, Lars and Michael Hoel. "Work Sharing, Employment and Shiftwork," *Oxford Economic Papers*, *41*:758–773 (1989).

[25] Chapman, S. J. "Hours of Labour," *Economic Journal*, *19*(75):353–373 (1909).

[26] Coleman, Mary T. and John Pencavel. "Changes in Work Hours of Male Employees, 1940-1988," *Industrial and Labor Relations Review*, *46*(2):262–283 (1993).

[27] Contensou, François and Radu Vranceanu. "A Model of Working Time under Utility Competition in the Labor Market," *Journal of Economics*, *67*(2):146–166 (1998).

[28] Corneo, Giacomo. "Distributional Implications of a Shorter Working Week: An Unpleasant Note," *Journal of Economics*, *62*(1):25–31 (1995).

[29] Costa, Dora L. "The Unequal Work Day: A Long Term View," *American Economic Review*, *88*(2):330–334 (1998).

[30] Craine, Roger. "On the Service Flow from Labour," *Review of Economic Studies*, *40*:39–46 (1973).

[31] Crépon, Bruno and Francis Kramartz. "Working 40 Hours or Not Working 39: Lessons from the 1981 Mandatory Reduction of Weekly Working Hours," *CEPR Discussion Paper Series*, *2158* (1999).

[32] Cross, Gary. *A Quest for Time in Britain and France, 1840-1940*. Berkeley: University of California Press, 1989.

[33] D'Autume, Antoine and Pierre Cahuc. "Réduction de la Durée de Travail: De la Contrainte Légale À la Négociation," *Revue Economique*, *48*(3):549–558 (1997).

[34] Diamond, Peter A. "A Model of Price Adjustments," *Journal of Economic Theory*, *3*:156–168 (1982).

[35] Douglas, Paul H. *The Theory of Wages* (1964 Edition). New York: A.M. Kelly, 1934.

[36] Drolet, Marie and René Morissette. "Working More? Less? What Do Workers Prefer?," *Statistics Canada. Catalogue 75-001-XPE*, *4*:32–38 (1997).

[37] Duchesne, Doreen. "Working Overtime in Today's Labour Market," *Statistics Canada. Catalogue 75-001-XPE*, *4*:9–24 (1997).

[38] Dunlop, John. *Wage Determination under Trade Unions*. London: Macmillan, 1944.

[39] Edgeworth, Francis Y. *Papers Related to Political Economy*. London: Macmillan, 1925.

[40] Ehrenberg, Ronald G. "Heterogenous Labor, the Internal Labor Market and the Dynamics of the Employment-Hours Decision," *Journal of Economic Theory*, *3*:84–105 (1971).

[41] Ehrenberg, Ronald G. and Robert S. Smith. *Modern Labor Economics*. New York: Harper Collins, 1994.

[42] Elmeskov, Jurgen. "High and Persistent Unemployment: Assesment of the Problem and Its Causes," *OECD Working Paper*, *132* (1993).

[43] EuropeanCommission. "Performances of the European Union Labour Market. Results of an Ad Hoc Labour Market Survey Covering Employers and Employees," *European Economy*, *3* (1995).

[44] Eurostat. *Labour Force Survey, Results 1997*. Luxembourg: Eurostat, the Statistical Office of the European Communities, 1998.

[45] Feldstein, Martin. "Specification of the Labour Input in the Aggregate Production Function," *Review of Economic Studies*, *34*:375–386 (1967).

[46] FitzRoy, Felix R. "On the Uniqueness of Competitive Equilibrium with an Intensive Margin," *Scottish Journal of Political Economy*, *40*(3):283–294 (1993).

[47] FitzRoy, Felix R., et al. "Working Time, Taxation and Unemployment," *University of St. Andrews Discussion Paper*, *9901* (1999).

[48] FitzRoy, Felix R. and Robert Hart. "Hours, Layoffs and Unemployment Insurance Funding: Theory and Practise in an International Perspective," *Economic Journal*, *95*:700–713 (1985).

[49] Freyssinet, Jacques. "La Loi Robien: Rupture Qualitative Ou Aubaine Éphémère," *Revue de l'IRES*, *23*:5–36 (1997).

[50] Fudemberg, Drew and Jean Tirole. *Game Theory*. Cambridge, Massachusetts: MIT Press, 1991.

[51] Gronau, Reuben. "Home Production - A Survey." *Handbook of Labor Economics* edited by Orley Ashenfelter and Richard Layard, chapter 4, 273–304, Amsterdam: North-Holland, 1986.

[52] Hamermesh, Daniel S. "The Demand for Labor in the Long Run." *Handbook of Labor Economics* edited by Orley Ashenfelter and Richard Layard, chapter 8, 429–468, Amsterdam: North-Holland, 1986.

[53] Hamermesh, Daniel S. "Labour Demand and the Source of Adjustment Costs," *Economic Journal*, *105*:620–634 (1995).

[54] Hamermesh, Daniel S. and Stephen S. Trejo. "The Demand for Hours of Labor: Direct Evidence from California," *Review of Economics and Statistics* (1999). Forthcoming.

[55] Hart, Robert A. *The Economics of Non-Wage Labour Costs*. London: Allen and Unwin, 1984.

[56] Hart, Robert A. *Working Time and Employment*. London: Allen and Unwin, 1987.

[57] Hart, Robert A., et al. "What Shapes are Overtime Premium Schedule? Some Evidence from Japan, the UK and the US," *Economics Letters*, *53*:97–102 (1996).

[58] Hart, Robert A. and Peter McGregor. "The Returns to Labor Services in West German Manufacturing Industry," *European Economic Review*, *32*:947–963 (1988).

[59] Hart, Robert A. and Robin J. Ruffell. "The Cost of Overtime Hours in British Production Industries," *Economica*, *60*:183–201 (1993).

[60] Hicks, John. *The Theory of Wages* (1966 Edition). London: Macmillan, 1932.

[61] Hoel, Michael. "Employment and Allocation Effects of Reducing the Lenght of the Workday," *Economica*, *53*:75–85 (1986).

[62] Hoel, Michael and Bent Vale. "Effects on Unemployment of Reduced Working Time in an Economy Where Firms Set Wages," *European Economic Review*, *30*:1097–1104 (1986).

[63] Hunt, Jennifer. "Hours Reductions as Work-Sharing," *Brookings Papers on Economic Activity*, *1*:339–381 (1998).

[64] Hunt, Jennifer. "Has Work-Sharing Worked in Germany?," *Quarterly Journal of Economics*, *114*(1):117–148 (1999).

[65] Idson, Todd L. and Philip K. Robins. "Determinants of Voluntary Overtime Decisions," *Economic Inquiry*, *29*:79–91 (1991).

[66] ILO. *World Labour Report 1997-1998. Industrial Relations, Democracy and Stability*. Geneva: International Labor Office, 1997.

[67] Jevons, Stanley. *The Theory of Political Economy* (1888 Edition). London: Macmillan, 1871.

[68] Kahn, Shulamit and Kevin Lang. "The Causes of Hours Constraints: Evidence from Canada," *Canadian Journal of Economics*, *28*:914–928 (1996a).

[69] Kahn, Shulamit and Kevin Lang. "Hours Constraint and the Wage/Hours Locus," *Canadian Journal of Economics*, *29*:S71–S75 (1996b).

[70] Killingsworth, Mark R. and James J. Heckman. "Female Labor Supply: A Survey." *Handbook of Labor Economics 1*, edited by Orley Ashenfelter and Richard Layard, chapter 2, 103–198, Amsterdam: North-Holland, 1986.

[71] Knight, Frank H. *Risk, Uncertainity and Profit*. Boston and New York: Houghton Mifflin Co, 1921.

[72] Kume, Ikuo. *Disparaged Success. Labor Politics in Postwar Japan*. Ithaca: Cornell University Press, 1998.

[73] Layard, Richard, et al. *Unemployment. Macroeconomic Performances and the Labour Market*. Oxford: Oxford University Press, 1991.

[74] Leslie, Derek and John Wise. "The Productivity of Hours in U.K. Manufacturing and Production Industries," *Economic Journal*, *90*:74–84 (1980).

[75] Maddison, Angus. *Monitoring the World Economy, 1820-1992*. Paris: OECD, 1995.

[76] Marimon, Ramon and Fabrizio Zilibotti. "Employment and Distributional Effects of Restricting Working Time," *CEPR Discussion Paper Series*, *2127* (1999).

[77] Marshall, Alfred. *Principles of Economics* (Eighth Edition). London: Macmillan, 1920.

[78] Marx, Karl. *Capital: A Critique of Political Economy* (1975 Edition), *1*. New York: International, 1867.

[79] Mas-Colell, Andreu, et al. *Microeconomic Theory*. Oxford: Oxford University Press, 1995.

[80] McCall, John J. "Economics of Information and Job Search," *Quarterly Journal of Economics*, *84*:113–126 (1970).

[81] McDonald, Ian and Robert M. Solow. "Wage Bargaining and Employment," *American Economic Review*, *69*:896–908 (1981).

[82] McGrattan, Ellen and Richard Rogerson. "Changes in the Hours Worked Since 1950," *Federal Reserve Bank of Minneapolis Quarterly Review*, *Winter*:2–19 (1998).

[83] Mortensen, Dale T. "Property Rights and Efficiency in Mating, Racing and Related Games," *American Economic Review*, *72*:968–979 (1982).

[84] Mortensen, Dale T. and Christopher A. Pissarides. "New Developments in Models of Search in the Labour Market," *CEPR Discussion Paper Series*, *2053* (1999).

[85] Moselle, Boaz. "Efficiency Wages and the Hours/Unemployment Trade-Off," *Northwestern University, Center for Mathematical Studies in Economics and Management Science Discussion Paper*, *1153* (1996).

[86] Nash, John F. "The Bargaining Problem," *Econometrica*, *18*(2):155–162 (1950).

[87] Nickell, Stephen J. "A Bargaining Model of the Phillips Curve." LSE Center for Labour Economics Discussion Paper, 1982.

[88] Nickell, Stephen J. "Dynamic Models of Labour Demand." *Handbook of Labour Economics* edited by Orley Ashenfelter and Richard Layard, chapter 9, 473–523, Amsterdam: North-Holland, 1986.

[89] OECD. *La Flexibilité de la Durée Du Travail*. Paris: OECD, 1995.

[90] OECD. *Employment Outlook*, chapter Collective Bargaining and Economic Performances. Paris: OECD, 1997.

[91] OECD. *Employment Outlook*, chapter Working Hours: Latest Trends and Policy Initiatives. Paris: OECD, 1998.

[92] OECD. *Economic Survey of France, 1999*. Paris: OECD, 1999.

[93] Oi, Walter. "Labor as a Quasi-Fixed Factor of Production," *Journal of Political Economy*, *70*:538–555 (1962).

[94] Pemberton, James. "A Managerial Model of the Trade Union," *Economic Journal*, *98*:755–771 (1988).

[95] Pencavel, John. "Labor Supply of Men: A Survey." *Handbook of Labour Economics* edited by Orley Ashenfelter and Richard Layard, chapter 1, 3–96, Amsterdam: North-Holland, 1986.

[96] Phelps, Edmund S. *Microeconomic Foundations of Employment and Inflation Theory.* New York: Norton, 1970.

[97] Pissarides, Christopher A. "Efficient Job Rejection," *Economic Journal*, *94S*:97–108 (1984).

[98] Pissarides, Christopher A. *Equilibrium Unemployment Theory.* Oxford: Basil Blackwell, 1990.

[99] Proudhon, Pierre Joseph, "Qu'est-Ce Que la Propriété." Académie des Sciences Morales, Besançon, France, 1840.

[100] Robbins, Lionel. "The Economic Effects of Variations of Hours of Labour," *Economic Journal*, *March*:25–40 (1929).

[101] Robbins, Lionel. "On the Elasticity of Demand for Money in Terms of Effort," *Economica*, *10*:123–129 (1930).

[102] Rocheteau, Guillaume. "Working Time Regulation in a Search Economy with Worker Moral Hazard." Mimeo, DEEP - HEC, University of Lausanne., 1999.

[103] Rones, Philip L., et al. "Trends in Hours of Work Since the Mid-1970s," *Monthly Labor Review*, *April*:3–14 (1997).

[104] Rosen, Shervin. "Short-Run Employment Variation on Class-I Railroads in the U.S., 1947-1963," *Econometrica*, *36*(3-4):511–529 (1968).

[105] Ross, Arthur M. *Trade Union Wage Policy.* Berkeley: University of California Press, 1948.

[106] Roth, Alvin E. *Axiomatic Models of Bargaining.* Berlin: Springer Verlag, 1979.

[107] Rubinstein, Ariel. "Perfect Equilibrium in a Bargaining Model," *Econometrica*, *50*(1):97–109 (1982).

[108] Sargent, Thomas. "Estimation of Dynamic Demand Schedules under Rational Expectations," *Journal of Political Economy*, *86*:100–144 (1978).

[109] Sasajima, Yoshio. "Japon, Le Cas de L'industrie Métallurgique." *La Flexibilité Du Travail* Paris: OECD, 1995.

[110] Schmidt-Sorensen, J. B. "An Efficiency-Wage-Hours Model and Shorter Working Hours," *Scottish Journal of Political Economy*, *38*(2):113–131 (1991).

[111] Schor, Juliet B. *The Overworked American: The Unexpected Decline of Leisure.* New York: Basic Books, 1991.

[112] Screpanti, Ernesto and Stefano Zamagni. *An Outline of the History of Economic Thought*. Oxford: Clarendon Press, 1993.

[113] Shapiro, Carl and Joseph E. Stiglitz. "Equilibrium Unemployment as a Worker Discipline Device," *American Economic Review*, *74*:433–444 (1984).

[114] Simiand, François. *Les Salaires Des Ouvriers Des Mines de Charbon En France; Contribution À la Théorie Économique Du Salaire*. Paris: Cornély et Cie, 1907.

[115] Solow, Robert M. "Another Possible Source of Wage Stickiness," *Journal of Macroeconomics*, *1*:79–82 (1979).

[116] Stewart, Mark B. and Joanna K. Swaffield. "Constraints on the Desired Hours of Work of British Men," *Economic Journal*, *107*:520–535 (1997).

[117] Stigler, George J. "The Economics of Information," *Journal of Political Economy*, *69*(3):213–215 (1961).

[118] Stigler, Georges J. *The Theory of Prices*. New York: Macmillan, 1966.

[119] Sugeno, Kazuo. *Japanese Labor Law*. Washington DC: University of Washington Press, 1992.

[120] Sutton, John. "Non-Cooperative Bargaining Theory: An Introduction," *Review of Economc Studies*, *53*(4):709–724 (1986).

[121] Takagi, Ikuro. "Japan." *Times are Changing: Work Time in 14 Industrialized Countries* edited by G. Bosch, et al., 213–228, Geneva: International Institute for Labour Studies, 1993.

[122] Vroey, Michel De. "Accounting for Involuntary Unemployment in Neoclasscal Theory: Some Lessons from Sixty Years of Uphill Struggle." *Economics and Methodology: Crossing Boundaries* edited by R. Backhouse, et al., chapter 4, 177–223, London: Macmillan, 1998.

[123] Wakita, Shigeru. "Chronic Labour Hoarding: Direct Evidence from Japan," *Japanese Economic Review*, *48*(3):307–323 (1997).

[124] West, Ewin G. "Marx Hypotheses on the Length of the Working Day," *Journal of Political Economy*, *83*(2):266–281 (1983).

Index

Printed and bound by CPI Group (UK) Ltd, Croydon, CR0 4YY

23/04/2025

14660988-0002